Aspects of Teaching Secondary Music

The Open University *Flexible*
Postgraduate Certificate of Education

The readers and the companion volumes in the *flexible* PGCE series are:

Aspects of Teaching and Learning in Secondary Schools: Perspectives on practice

Teaching, Learning and the Curriculum in Secondary Schools: A reader

Aspects of Teaching Secondary Mathematics: Perspectives on practice

Teaching Mathematics in Secondary Schools: A reader

Aspects of Teaching Secondary Science: Perspectives on practice

Teaching Science in Secondary Schools: A reader

Aspects of Teaching Secondary Modern Foreign Languages: Perspectives on practice

Teaching Modern Foreign Languages in Secondary Schools: A reader

Aspects of Teaching Secondary Geography: Perspectives on practice

Teaching Geography in Secondary Schools: A reader

Aspects of Teaching Secondary Design and Technology: Perspectives on practice

Teaching Design and Technology in Secondary Schools: A reader

Aspects of Teaching Secondary Music: Perspectives on practice

Teaching Music in Secondary Schools: A reader

All of these subjects are part of the Open University's initial teacher education course, the *flexible* PGCE, and constitute part of an integrated course designed to develop critical understanding. The set books, reflecting a wide range of perspectives, and discussing the complex issues that surround teaching and learning in the twenty-first century, will appeal to both beginning and experienced teachers, to mentors, tutors, advisers and other teacher educators.

If you would like to receive a *flexible* PGCE prospectus please write to the Course Reservations Centre at The Call Centre, The Open University, Milton Keynes MK7 6ZS. Other information about programmes of professional development in education is available from the same address.

Aspects of Teaching Secondary Music

Perspectives on practice

Edited by Gary Spruce

London and New York

First published 2002
by RoutledgeFalmer
11 New Fetter Lane, London EC4P 4EE

Simultaneously published in the USA and Canada
by RoutledgeFalmer
29 West 35th Street, New York, NY 10001

RoutledgeFalmer is an imprint of the Taylor & Francis Group

© 2002 Compilation, original and editorial matter,
The Open University

Typeset in Bembo by Bookcraft Ltd, Stroud, Gloucestershire
Printed and bound in Great Britain by Bell & Bain Ltd, Glasgow

British Library Cataloguing in Publication Data
A catalogue record for this book is available from the British Library

Library of Congress Cataloging in Publication Data
A catalog record has been requested

ISBN 0–415–26085–X

Contents

SECTION 3 Developing the Music curriculum

Illustrations

Figures

Tables

Abbreviations

ACCAC	Qualifications Curriculum and Assessment Authority for Wales
AQA	Assessment and Qualifications Alliance
AVCE	Advanced Vocational Certificate in Education
BTEC	Business and Technology Education Council
CGLI	City of Guilds of London Institute
CSE	Certificate of Secondary Education
DENI	Department of Education Northern Ireland
DfEE	Department for Education and Employment (now Department for Education and Skills)
GCE	General Certificate of Education
GCSE	General Certificate of Secondary Education
GNVQ	General National Vocational Qualification
HMI	Her Majesty's Inspectorate
ICT	Information and Communication Technology
IEP	Individualized Education Plan
LEA	Local Education Authority
NFAE	National Foundation for Arts and Education
NFER	National Foundation for Education Research
NCVQ	National Council for Vocational Qualifications
NVQ	National Vocational Qualification
OCR	Oxford, Cambridge and RSA Examinations
QCA	Qualifications and Curriculum Authority
RSA	Royal Society of Arts
VET	Vocational Education and Training

Sources

Where a chapter in this book is based on or is a reprint or revision of material previously published elsewhere, details are given below, with grateful acknowledgements to the original publishers. In some cases chapter titles have been changed from the original; in such cases the original chapter is given below.

Chapter 1 This is an edited version of a chapter originally published in *Teaching Music in Secondary Schools*, PGCE Music Document 1, The Open University, Milton Keynes (1995).

Chapter 4 This is an edited version of an article originally published in the *Music Educators Journal* 87(4), MENC, Ann Arbor (2001).

Chapter 5 This is an edited version of an article originally published in *Music Education Research* 1(2), Carfax Publishing, Taylor & Francis Ltd, Basingstoke (1999).

Chapter 6 This is an edited version of an article originally published in the *British Journal of Music Education* 16(1), Cambridge University Press, Cambridge (1999).

Chapter 8 This is an edited version of a chapter originally published in Spruce, G. (ed.) (1996) *Teaching Music*, Routledge, London. Original source: *British Journal of Music Education* 10, Cambridge University Press, Cambridge (1993).

Chapter 10 This is an edited version of an article originally published in the *British Journal of Music Education* 17(2), Cambridge University Press, Cambridge (2000).

Chapter 11 This is an edited version of an article originally published in *Music Education Research* 2(1), Carfax Publishing, Taylor & Francis Ltd, Basingstoke (2000).

Chapter 13 This is an edited version of a chapter originally published in Spruce, G. (ed.) (1996) *Teaching Music*, Routledge, London. Original source: *International Journal of Music Education* 21 (1993).

Chapter 14 This is an edited version of a chapter originally published in Spruce, G. (ed.) (1996) *Teaching Music*, Routledge, London. Original source: *International Journal of Music Education* 23 (1994).

Chapter 15 This is an edited version of a chapter originally published in *Teaching Music in Secondary Schools*, PGCE Music Document 17, The Open University, Milton Keynes (1995).

Foreword

The nature and form of initial teacher education and training are issues that lie at the heart of the teaching profession. They are inextricably linked to the standing and identity that society attributes to teachers and are seen as being one of the main planks in the push to raise standards in schools and to improve the quality of education in them. The initial teacher education curriculum therefore requires careful definition. How can it best contribute to the development of the range of skills, knowledge and understanding that makes up the complex, multi-faceted, multi-skilled and people-centred process of teaching?

There are, of course, external, government-defined requirements for initial teacher training courses. These specify, amongst other things, the length of time a student spends in school, the subject knowledge requirements beginning teachers are expected to demonstrate or the ICT skills that are needed. These requirements, however, do not in themselves constitute the initial training curriculum. They are only one of the many, if sometimes competing, components that make up the broad spectrum of a teacher's professional knowledge that underpin initial teacher education courses.

Certainly today's teachers need to be highly skilled in literacy, numeracy and ICT, in classroom methods and management. In addition, however, they also need to be well grounded in the critical dialogue of teaching. They need to be encouraged to be creative and innovative and to appreciate that teaching is a complex and problematic activity. This is a view of teaching that is shared with partner schools within the Open University Training Schools Network. As such it has informed the planning and development of the Open University's initial teacher training programme and the *flexible* PGCE.

All of the *flexible* PGCE courses have a series of connected and complementary readers. The *Teaching in Secondary Schools* series pulls together a range of new thinking about teaching and learning in particular subjects. Key debates and differing perspectives are presented, and evidence from research and practice is explored, inviting the reader to question the accepted orthodoxy, suggesting ways of enriching the present curriculum and offering new thoughts on classroom learning. These readers are accompanied by the series *Perspectives on practice*. Here, the focus is on the application of these developments to educational/subject policy and the classroom, and on the illustration of teaching skills, knowledge and understanding in a variety of school contexts. Both series include newly commissioned work.

This series from RoutledgeFalmer, in supporting the Open University's *flexible* PGCE, also includes two key texts that explore the wider educational background. These companion publications, *Teaching and Learning and the Curriculum in Secondary Schools: A reader* and *Aspects of Teaching and Learning in Secondary Schools: Perspectives on practice,* explore a contemporary view of developments in secondary education with the aim of providing analysis and insights for those participating in initial teacher training education courses.

Hilary Bourdillon – Director ITT Strategy
Steven Hutchinson – Director ITT Secondary
The Open University
September 2001

Introduction

In this book, a range of authors contribute their own particular perspectives to aspects of music education. The common feature of these contributions is that they address issues which music teachers meet on a regular basis in the music classroom. They do not attempt to provide solutions to problematic areas but rather to identify and analyse issues and contexts and to suggest possible strategies.

The volume is divided into three sections. In the first section, 'What is music learning and how do we identify it?', we look at the planning and organizational issues which impact on music learning and teaching. In the second section, 'Musical activities', we consider activities such as listening, composing and facets of performing. Finally, in Developing the Music curriculum', we look at ways in which teaching and learning might be enhanced through, for example, the use of ICT, by drawing on a range of musical styles and cultures and a knowledge of research methods.

In Chapter 1, Charles Plummeridge poses the fundamental question: 'What is music in the curriculum?'. Drawing on a wide range of sources, he explores five related issues: the place of music in education; rationales and practices; the National Curriculum; music, combined arts and the whole curriculum; and music beyond the timetabled curriculum – 'all of which are to some extent problematic and contro-versial and therefore subject to ongoing debate'.

Chapter 2 examines some of the issues teachers have to consider when planning for music teaching and learning. The chapter begins by considering the various levels of planning (schemes of work, modules and lesson plans, etc.), proceeding then to look at the curriculum models around which teachers might structure their planning for children's progression in music learning. Finally, specific issues of planning are looked at, such as identifying learning aims, providing for the range of needs within a class, the appropriate use of resources and classroom management.

In 1984, the Welsh Inspectorate wrote that 'whether a pupil achieves or under-achieves is largely dependent on the quality of planning, execution, and evaluation that takes place within individual departments' (Her Majesty's Inspectorate (HMI) Wales 1984). This is equally true now as it was then. Indeed, the importance of the discrete subject area, which had to a certain degree waned from the 1960s to the early 1980s in favour of cross-curricular initiatives, has increased since the introduction of the National Curriculum, with its model of core and foundation subjects. In Chapter 3, Gary Spruce considers the role of the music department. He looks at the function of the music department in the context of the whole school, investigates the role of the head of department and considers ways in which the department can articulate and promote the distinctive role of music learning in the curriculum.

One of the great challenges for music teachers is to develop strategies for the inclusion of children with special needs. In Chapter 4, Mary Adamek considers ways in which this might be achieved through tailoring learning strategies to each student's strengths and weaknesses. Although focusing on special needs, the principles of differentiation that she outlines are applicable to the teaching of all children.

In Chapter 5, Lucy Green looks at the relationship between 'gender identity, musical experience and schooling'. She begins by identifying 'two virtual aspects of music meaning': *inherent meaning,* which resides within the musical materials, and *delineated meaning,* which is articulated through contextualizing factors. She suggests that it is 'through the mutual interaction of the different aspects of music meaning, that we learn, amongst other things, our gendered relationships with music'. Green goes on to consider the gendered delineations of women singing, playing instruments and composing. She continues by demonstrating how, in the context of the school, 'music delineates gender in a variety of ways according to the gender of the performer and/or the composer', concluding that school 'perpetuates subtle definitions of femininity and masculinity as delineations of different musical practices'.

Christopher Murphy[1] in Chapter 6 suggests that traditional conceptions of musical ability, as advanced in psychometrics, tell us very little about the nature of musical behaviour and how it is to be developed. The psychometric tradition, with its view that musical ability is innate rather than learned, has exerted a powerful and potentially damaging influence on the practice of music education over the past fifty or so years. It is only relatively recently, mainly in the field of developmental psychology, that these ideas have been challenged. In contrasting theories advanced by different psychological schools, the chapter gives a broader perspective to the psychological debate on human intelligence/musical ability and shows the context in which music behaviour might be viewed as a distinct or even autonomous form of intelligence: 'a way of knowing'. It suggests that musical thinking should be considered as an 'intellectual' as well as aesthetic mode of thought and that musical ability, in the traditional sense, has little educational utility or relevance to music as a curriculum subject in schools.

Assessment is central to planning for music teaching and learning. Without appropriate assessment strategies and systems, we cannot hope to know how well the pupil is learning and by implication how effective our teaching is. In Chapter 7, David Bray considers assessment from a range of perspectives. He poses the question as to why teachers find some aspects of music assessment problematic (particularly the assessment of composing) and suggests that a possible way through these difficulties is to make a distinction between musical activity (and the learning that takes place through that activity) and the end-product. He goes on to look at the reasons why we need to assess, the differences between assessment, recording and reporting and between formative and summative assessment and the ways in which we can involve pupils in assessment.

An increasing emphasis on composing and performing in the music curriculum has sometimes resulted in the marginalization of listening activities. This is a pity, for, as Philip Priest argues in Chapter 8, developed aural skills are fundamental to musical experiences and understanding. He considers that the ability to have an aural vision of an intended musical outcome is essential to composing, performing and, in particular, improvising. He is particularly critical of those music teachers who, through an overemphasis on music literacy, fail to develop pupils' aural skills.

Another activity that has perhaps become marginalized within the music curriculum is the development of children's vocal skills. In Chapter 9, Nicholas Bannan, drawing on a range of research, outlines strategies that can lead not only to the development of vocal skills but can also provide 'a powerful underpinning to other aspects of music learning'. He looks at how voices work, how teachers might use their own voices as a teaching resource, resources available for voice-based teaching and ideas for developing teaching materials. He concludes by considering whole-school aspects of vocal development in order to create 'a singing culture'.

Composing is a requirement for all pupils at Key Stage 3 in the English and Welsh National Curriculums. Chapter 10 is based on a research programme undertaken by the authors George Odam and Anice Patterson into children's composing. Through field visits, seminars and questionnaires, they 'seek to identify a basis for effective classroom practice through direct observation of experienced teachers and their pupils in twenty-six state secondary schools across England'. Odam believes that composing is an essentially individual activity, concluding that a good deal of time spent in group work is time wasted and contributes to stress in both pupils and teachers. He argues that teachers often 'use methods inappropriate to the resources available to them' and that there are 'problems with progression and preservation of pupils' work' (Odam 2000). However, he makes the important point that when composing is taught well, pupils enjoy lessons and the composing activities that take place in them.

The importance of practice is self-evident to instrumental teachers and parents, who will put considerable energy into ensuring that pupils work between lessons to maintain progress on their instrument.[2] A longitudinal study at the University of New South Wales, Sydney, has been investigating the cognitive strategies used by young instrumentalists when they practise, relating this and other factors, such as environment, motivation and general ability, to the progress that is made in the first years of learning. In Chapter 11, case studies of three of the pupils involved in that study are used to demonstrate the range of practice strategies that children devise, and to analyse their efficiency in promoting musical development. The implications for teachers and parents are considered, and a definition of 'effective practice' is sought.

Music technology is a vital resource in contemporary music education. It has opened up new vistas of creativity for both pupils and teachers. Technology addresses issues of access, allowing those who do not have traditional literacy or instrumental skills to engage creatively with musical sound. However, for a teacher inexperienced in its use, technology can seem like one more variable in an already demanding context. Furthermore, technology is something with which students are sometimes more at ease than are teachers. Peter Desmond, in Chapter 12, looks at the role of technology in the music curriculum. He begins by outlining the common uses for technology, going on to describe how these resources might be used to 'enhance the teaching of music as a creative subject'. He then looks at aspects of planning and classroom management in relation to music technology, concluding with explanations of some basic music technology concepts and a checklist of ICT skills.

It is important that the music curriculum reflects music from a wide range of styles and cultures so that pupils can 'actively explore specific genres, styles and traditions from different times and cultures with increasing ability to discriminate' (Curriculum 2000: Music). In the next three chapters we look at types of music which are relatively newcomers to the music curriculum – popular musics, non-western musics and jazz. In Chapter 13, Peter Dunbar-Hall demonstrates two different ways of considering the nature of music and then applies these to the processes involved in designing a teaching model for popular music. In Chapter 14, Jonathan Stock argues that our commonly-accepted definitions of what music is are often unsatisfactory when considering music of non-western cultures. In a discussion that draws parallels between music and language, he shows that those musical characteristics that we associate with certain emotions are not universally held. Furthermore, he challenges the notion of valuing all music in terms of western ideas of development and complexity (i.e. the kind of view that describes folk music as primitive and considers all music in the context of a stage in music's development towards a pinnacle represented by western 'high art'). Returning to the relationship between music and language, he analyses those things that he sees as being common to most music cultures and which could provide a starting point for incorporating world music into the curriculum. Throughout the chapter, he provides examples of classroom activities that support the concepts under discussion. Bill Charleson, in Chapter 15, argues that 'jazz is a spontaneous expression of ... background, culture, emotions and experience ... is essentially a group experience ... a sharing of collective skills, knowledge and experience'. He demonstrates how working with jazz can develop a whole range of musical skills both within and outside the formal curriculum.

Paul Atkinson and Gary Spruce begin their chapter (Chapter 16) about GCSE Music with an overview of the development of post-14 music examinations over the last thirty years. They demonstrate how changes in examinations have been reflected in developing notions of what constitutes valuable music knowledge, understanding and learning. They go on to explore the new criteria for GCSE Music and look at effective strategies for teaching GCSE, emphasizing that, notwithstanding the importance of maximizing examination results, the GCSE curriculum needs to ensure that *all* pupils develop their skills and understanding of music through worthwhile and fulfilling musical experiences.

It should be axiomatic that developments in teaching and learning be supported by rigorous research findings. Unfortunately this is not always the case, and changes in education are often ideologically or politically driven. In the final chapter (Chapter 17), Alexandra Lamont looks at the potential role for research in music education. She identifies and offers a critique of a number of research types and then explores what they have to offer to music teaching and learning.

Notes

1   Taken from the abstract to the original article.
2   Taken from the abstract to the original article.

1 What is music learning and how do we identify it?

1 What is music in the curriculum?
Charles Plummeridge

Introduction

Music is a foundation subject in the National Curriculum, yet it is taken for granted that musical activity in the vast majority of schools encompasses far more than timetabled class lessons. Normally, teachers organize a range of optional musical pursuits that take place in lunch hours, after school, sometimes at weekends, and often at venues beyond the school. In some cases, a school's curriculum policy will be to group-related (or cognate) disciplines and in these circumstances music may be taught as part of a wider programme of arts education.

It soon becomes apparent that to ask the question, 'What is music in the curriculum?' leads to a consideration of several educational, musical, pedagogical and organizational matters that are of importance to professional teachers. The intention in this chapter is to explore five related issues, all of which are to some extent problematic and controversial, and therefore the subject of an ongoing debate amongst members of the teaching community. These are as follows:

- the place of music in education;
- rationales and practices;
- the National Curriculum;
- music, combined arts and the whole curriculum;
- music beyond the timetabled curriculum.

The place of music in education

In order better to appreciate the place of music within the curriculum, it is useful to reflect on its history as a component of a general education, since many ideals and attitudes of the past continue to have a bearing on contemporary discussions, policies and practices. In a wide-ranging historical survey, Bernarr Rainbow (1989) has shown that, from ancient times, arguments for the inclusion (or exclusion) of music in educational programmes have taken many forms. Some advocates have regarded it as necessary for religious reasons, whilst others have valued its aesthetic and civilizing qualities. There have also been those who have viewed music as little more than a frivolous pursuit and therefore largely a waste of time in the context of education. At certain periods, such as during the Middle Ages and the nineteenth century, musical education in schools has flourished. But there have also been periods of decline. Following the Reformation, for example, some church leaders and educators in England (unlike their counterparts in other areas of protestant Europe) saw musical instruction not only as unnecessary but also as positively harmful. However, even in the eighteenth century, when many renowned English educationists thought of the arts as elegant but never *serious* pastimes, there were lone voices that kept alive the principle of musical studies as a worthwhile dimension of a liberal education.

The origins of what we now refer to as a system of 'music education' are to be located in the social and educational reforms of the nineteenth century. Prominent churchmen encouraged singing in elementary schools in the hope of improving congregational participation in church services, and there was a related belief that, through choral activity, young people would acquire an accomplishment which would enable them to participate in wholesome recreational pursuits. Certain Victorian reformers also maintained that, through music, children would develop desirable character traits, good habits and even kindly dispositions. Imaginative and dedicated teachers like Sarah Glover, John Hullah and John Curwen (see Rainbow 1989) devised schemes of teaching for large groups and thereby established the principle of music as a class subject. In the growing number of independent (private, fee-paying) schools, for both boys and girls, music seldom featured as a curriculum subject, but choirs and orchestras were encouraged as worthy activities which added to the cultural and social life of an institution. Today, schools in both the independent and state sectors provide for regular class music lessons as well as those familiar extracurricular pursuits such as instrumental tuition schemes, choirs, orchestras, bands, recorder groups and other ensembles. One of the issues that has occupied the minds of music educators for many years is finding the appropriate relationship between curriculum and extracurricular activities. We shall return to this point in section six.

There is still a variety of opinion regarding the place of music in a general education. It is often assumed, as it was in the nineteenth century, that musical skills and techniques learned in school enable people to engage in music in adult life. The well-known and popular music educator, Atarah Ben-Tovim (1979), makes just this point when she talks about performing and appreciating music as a 'lifelong enrichment' of leisure time. This notion of music studies as part of an education that 'prepares' children for the life of work and leisure was the message conveyed in the famous and influential Newsom Report (Central Advisory Council for Education, 1963) and it remains embedded in much current thinking. In the 1970s, a group of forward-looking arts educators, inspired by progressive, child-centred ideals, began to question some of the assumptions underlying prevailing attitudes and practices. They argued the case for the arts disciplines in terms of the education of 'feeling'. A celebrated version of this thesis appears in the writings of Malcolm Ross (1975, 1978) and Robert Witkin (1974) who described education as an adaptive process consisting in the nurturing of both intellectual and affective capacities. According to Ross and Witkin, objective knowledge of the world 'out there' needs to be complemented by the individual's growing understanding of his or her inner feelings. The arts are expressive media for the development of 'self-knowledge' and creative self-expression through which pupils come to know and understand their 'inner world' of subjective reality. Although Ross and Witkin have often been severely criticized, their innovative theoretical framework has had a major impact on arts education over the past twenty-five years.

Some observers continue to justify the arts in terms of the education of feeling, but there is also a growing tendency to argue the case for music on the grounds of transfer of learning: music can enhance pupils' performance across the curriculum. This view (actually by no means new) is outlined with some considerable enthusiasm in a widely publicized paper from the Campaign for Music in the Curriculum (1998) entitled *The Fourth R*. However, opinion is sharply divided over the validity of some of the research methods, findings and conclusions reported in this publication. In fact, findings from recent studies carried out by John Harland and others (2000) seem to indicate that there is little to substantiate many of the transfer claims.

Current justifications for music in the curriculum are more likely to be determined by a conception of education central to which is the development of categories of thought through different modes of experience. Again, this is not a particularly new position. The philosophers Philip Phenix (1964) and Paul Hirst (1973) maintain that, because of their unique ability to create symbolic systems, human beings have developed a number of distinct rule-governed categories of understanding or realms of meaning. A truly liberal education, to which all children are entitled in a democratic society, is one that provides for experience within each realm. This line of argument has obviously had some influence on the popular idea of a 'broad and balanced' curriculum, much favoured by politicians. One of the most scholarly and properly-formulated statements of this educational position, and its curriculum implications, is by Professor Denis Lawton (1989) whose writings will be of interest and relevance to teachers of all subjects. The conception of the arts as constituting a 'way of knowing' is convincingly argued by Peter Abbs (1994); the various arts disciplines are to be seen not as 'cultural pastimes' or 'emotional expressions', but as powerful and vital forms of meaning and discourse.

Clearly, music teachers need to be able to justify their subject in the curriculum. This is not only because they are often obliged to explain their work to colleagues, parents, school governors and other audiences, but also because any particular justification will have a bearing on how the subject is conceived, presented and taught to pupils in schools. A review of the music education literature, research findings and curriculum materials reveals trends in music teaching that are informed, either implicitly or explicitly, by particular ideas regarding the value and aims of musical studies in education as a whole. There is always some link between justifications and proposed practices, although this is not to suggest that there are necessarily distinct styles of music teaching. In fact, within the classroom, teachers are likely to be fairly pragmatic. Practices are determined by a complex mixture of values, traditions and methodologies, as well as very important practical organizational factors which include accommodation, timetabling, staffing and resources.

Rationales and practices

During the 1950s and early 1960s, the main focus in class teaching tended to be on the promotion of choral and instrumental performance, the acquisition of conventional aural and literacy skills, and the appreciation of the works of those 'great' composers who represent the 'best' of the cultural heritage. In their lessons, pupils might have performed and listened to many types of music, but the materials chosen were largely from the post-Renaissance classical tradition, since operational competency within this system of tonality was a main aim of music education. The emphasis on aural and literacy skills stemmed from the notion of music as a kind of language, which children had to learn to 'speak', 'read' and 'write' in order to develop 'inner hearing' and thus gain musical insight and understanding. These ideals are associated with the pedagogical systems of influential figures including John Curwen, Thomas Henry Yorke Trotter, Arthur Somervell and Walford Davies. In modern times, the same principles have been endorsed by Zoltan Kodály and his followers. Interesting accounts of these music educators' teaching approaches are provided by Kenneth Simpson (1976), David Allsobrooke (1992) and Gordon Cox (1993). For those who incline towards this conception of music education, classroom activities are largely teacher-directed. The teacher is *the* authority whose task is to instruct and train pupils in recognized musical techniques, and thereby lead them towards an appreciation of the 'Great European tradition'. One of the best examples of curriculum materials reflecting such ideals would be the *Oxford School Music Books* (Dobbs and Fiske 1956). Although written over forty years ago, these beautifully designed books for teachers and pupils contain a wealth of music for singing, playing and listening activities, much of which could still be used in classrooms today. In some schools these materials may be hidden away in store cupboards. If located, it is well worth giving them more than a cursory glance.

The above approach to music teaching, often described as 'traditional', has never been entirely rejected, but progressive educators committed to child-centred principles and practices have concentrated more on pupils' discovery and manipulation of sound itself. Activities such as individual and group composition and improvisation, sometimes in a style which reflects avant-garde and experimental compositional techniques, allow for creative exploration of the medium. The teacher's role changes from 'instructor' to 'facilitator', the task being to set up an appropriate learning environment, stimulate pupils' imaginative powers and provide guidance and feedback. Less attention is given to conventional skill development and the so-called 'cultural heritage'. The focus is on the present rather than the past.

These sorts of practices became extremely popular during the 1970s. Materials produced by innovators including George Self (1967), Brian Dennis (1970), and John Paynter and Peter Aston (1970) were welcomed by teachers, and the ideas are still used in many schools. An especially important recent publication, which extends many of the teaching techniques introduced during this period, is John Paynter's (1992) *Sound and Structure*. This splendid book contains a number of very imaginative projects for use in the classroom and is an extremely valuable resource for teachers and pupils.

Over the past twenty years, we have witnessed moves to further broaden children's musical education. A document prepared by HMI entitled *Music from 5 to 16* (DES 1985a) sets out many suggestions for musical activities that reconcile traditional and progressive styles of teaching. This eclecticism underpins the work of Keith Swanwick (1979, 1999) who has developed a well-known theory of musical knowledge and understanding, rooted in aesthetics, epistemology and developmental psychology. The framework provides a basis for a curriculum in which children experience music directly through three interrelated modes of:

- performing;
- composing;
- audition (that is, listening in audience).

For Swanwick, the development of literacy, technical skills and knowledge 'about' music is useful, but only in so far as competence in these domains enables learners to participate more effectively, and with growing confidence, in the three main forms of musical activity. Swanwick's *A Basis for Music Education* (1979) should be read carefully (and critically) since his ideas and principles have become the source for much current thinking on curriculum design and classroom practice.

This style of music teaching is further extended by the view that the European post-Renaissance classical tradition is only part, albeit an important one, of that 'form of life' which we call music. Changing conceptions of music arise from different types of inquiry. For example, Lucy Green (1988), adopting a sociological perspective, argues that what 'counts' as music in education has often been based on unchallenged assumptions about the superiority of classical forms. Ethnomusicologists and curriculum developers draw attention to the fact that, in a pluralist society, there are many 'musics' that are practised and valued by different groups; this factor needs to be taken into account in the selection and preparation of curriculum materials and in the organization of practical work. Such practice is not to be taken, however, as a tokenistic gesture. If musical understanding is to be effectively developed, then it will be important for pupils to experience the breadth and diversity of the musical realm of meaning. How this might be achieved is well illustrated in the writings of Gerry Farrell (1990), Trevor Wiggins (1993), Jonathan Stock (1996) and Robert Kwami (1998).

These various principles have been widely accepted during the past two decades. The General Certificate of Secondary Education (GCSE) in music is based on the performing, composing and listening paradigm, together with a broad view of music. According to the national criteria developed for GCSE (DES 1985b), all courses must provide opportunities for pupils to:

- engage in music through the three experiential modes;
- develop aural perception and skills;
- be able to respond to music from different cultures and contexts.

For those teachers not familiar with the GCSE, the national criteria provide a good introduction to the examination and should be read before studying the syllabuses of the different examination boards.

In an important sense, the GCSE confirmed the performing, composing, listening ideal as the current orthodoxy in school music teaching. Music lessons are now regarded as the means of 'initiating' children into the discipline or 'world' of music as part of a liberal education directed towards the opening and development of minds. The arts are a unique form of knowing and thinking, intrinsically worthwhile, and of equal importance to other forms of human knowledge and understanding. It must be stressed, however, that educators subscribing to the idea of music as a way of knowing are always at pains to point out that this is *experiential* or *acquaintance* knowledge, to be acquired through direct contact with music and not by merely learning about it. There have been occasions when some teachers adopted a quasi-academic style of class music teaching, with a focus on topics such as musical forms, historical studies and the rudiments of musical theory. It may be that this practice sometimes arose from the belief that, if music could be seen as 'academically respectable', then its status as a curriculum subject would be greatly strengthened. Of course, writing about the life of Beethoven or drawing an oboe (an extremely difficult assignment) might keep pupils quietly occupied. But learning 'about' music is a poor substitute for direct involvement in music; children want to be active in their music lessons and not engaged in musicological study. This issue has been highlighted in numerous reports and most recently by John Harland (2000) and his co-workers who have carried out extensive research into the effectiveness of arts education in secondary schools.

The most significant (some would say dramatic) contemporary development in school music teaching is the rapid growth and impact of ICT. With the ready availability of technological equipment, new possibilities emerge for every area of musical experience. Sophisticated classroom instruments, computer software for sequencing, sound processing and recording, and ready access to the internet, are all factors that contribute to what is a transformation of music in the classroom. Innovation also makes new demands on teachers, who are constantly having to upgrade their technology skills in order to keep abreast of developments. The numerous issues surrounding music technology and the curriculum are thoughtfully discussed by Richard Hodges (2001), one of the leading authorities in this ever-expanding field.

The National Curriculum

The decision to include music as a foundation subject in the National Curriculum, introduced in 1988 as part of the Educational Reform Act, was welcomed as an 'official' (although long overdue) acknowledgement of its educational value. Most people would agree that this represents an important event in the evolution of musical studies as part of a general education. At the present time, music is a compulsory subject until the end of Key Stage 3 (14 year-olds). Thereafter, pupils can normally exercise the option to follow courses leading to the GCSE. In some schools, music might form part of a general arts programme available to all pupils at Key Stage 4 (14–16 year-olds).

The Subject Working Group, appointed to advise the Secretary of State on the content of the music curriculum, received over 700 responses to its interim report (DES 1990). Inevitably, there were some dissenting voices but there appeared to be a nation-wide support for music in schools. In its final report (DES 1991) the Working Group made reference to the fact that music is 'a powerful focus of creative energy' and that the aim of music education is to 'develop aesthetic sensitivity and creative ability in all pupils'. These views, together with the recommended content and activities, were in keeping with what had become a fairly secure professional consensus regarding aims, values and good practices in music education. Children would be expected to participate in music through the three experiential modes (performing, composing and listening); they would be required to develop motor, vocal and aural skills and become aware of 'traditions, idioms, and musical styles from a variety of cultures, times and places' (DES 1991, par. 4.4).

The present Statutory Order (DfEE, QCA 1999) sets out *Programmes of Study* which indicate 'what pupils should be taught in music at Key Stages 1, 2 and 3'. An *Attainment Target,* consisting of eight *levels,* is designed to show what 'knowledge, skills and understanding' pupils could be expected to achieve by the end of each Key Stage. These levels thus provide the basis for assessment and reporting. The document also deals with how music can contribute to learning across the curriculum and help promote key, or transferable, skills. In addition to the music requirements, there are sections dealing with pupil inclusion, the use of language and the application of information and communication technology. Obviously, all teachers need to be fully acquainted with the Order, but there are also many useful ideas in the Subject Working Group's reports (DES 1990, 1991) and earlier versions of the Statutory Order (DES 1992, DfE 1995). These documents tend to be forgotten now, but they are certainly still worth reading, since they contain helpful references to materials and good practical advice for teachers.

Prior to the 1988 Education Act, individual music teachers were responsible for the design of the curriculum in their own schools and could adopt policies and programmes that were in accord with their own convictions. In consequence, the characteristic feature of music education in Britain, over a long period, has been its diversity. Now that the National Curriculum is in place, all teachers have to take notice of the prescribed framework. Not surprisingly, a certain amount of disagreement has arisen over the detail of the curriculum, but there is also a growing feeling amongst teachers that the previous lack of direction could have limiting effects. It sometimes led to situations in which children experienced a narrow form of musical education arising from a teacher's personal 'theories' and preferences. The principles of all pupils engaging in performing, composing and listening, acquiring some necessary skills and becoming acquainted with different styles and genres have now gained wide acceptance.

Of course, not everybody likes the idea of central control but most teachers, in the best tradition of English professionalism, are prepared to work to the curriculum. However, it always has to be recognized that no matter how well frameworks or curriculum specifications are designed and presented, they are nothing until translated into effective action in the classroom. The essential task and challenge for the teacher is to transform the written statements into qualitative musical encounters in which pupils follow musical procedures, work with a sense of purpose and interest, come to feel that they are acquiring some competence and mastery, and experience the true joy of music. For it is in these ways those pupils internalize the essentials of the discipline and achieve a deeper appreciation of the value of music in their lives.

Music, combined arts and the whole curriculum

Music teachers sometimes work closely with colleagues who teach visual art, drama, dance and literature, the disciplines usually referred to collectively as the 'expressive' or 'creative' arts. Many educationists see the arts as forms of experience characterized and united by a distinct mode of aesthetic meaning and understanding. This view was clearly stated in a much-quoted report published by the Calouste Gulbenkian Foundation (1982):

there are the 'languages' in which we express a special and quite distinct form of awareness and judgement. These are 'languages' in which our ideas of beauty, grace, harmony, balance, harshness, stridency and ugliness are conceived, formulated and expressed. We call this our aesthetic awareness and mode of discourse.

(Calouste Gulbenkian Foundation 1982, p. 18)

A similar conception of the arts underpins a major national arts curriculum development project, *The Arts 5–16* (National Curriculum Council (NCC) 1990), set up in 1985 to provide support for arts provision and teaching in primary and secondary schools:

the different arts disciplines have a number of common characteristics and should be planned for together as a generic part of the school curriculum.

(NCC 1990: 2)

Linking the arts subjects for the purpose of teaching does not receive universal approval, and combined arts programmes are likely to be objected to on philosophical, pedagogical and professional grounds. In actuality, educationists who draw attention to the connections between the separate disciplines are usually careful to explain that they are not suggesting that all the arts are somehow identical; there are obvious and considerable differences in their substances, procedures and methods. Furthermore, to identify common features and similarities is *not* to imply that the arts subjects should necessarily be taught together; indeed, most arts educators would probably argue that children should have an in-depth experience of each of the disciplines. Nevertheless, there are times when collaborative planning and practice can be beneficial in a number of ways. Programmes of combined arts vary widely in their content and organization, and the main approaches are well described in *The Arts 5–16* (NCC 1990: 41). One of the favoured strategies is for teachers of different disciplines to base their courses, or more usually part of a course, on an agreed theme that provides a focal point for pupils; this enables them to see connections across the arts and so extend and amplify their learning experiences. Such work may include some team teaching or other kind of collaborative pedagogy which can often be more easily facilitated when the arts subjects are grouped together in a single department or faculty structure. Arts departments have been established in a number of schools as a means of providing for greater professional exchange and Cupertino, coherent arts curriculum planning, flexible timetabling and efficient use of staff and material resources.

Of course, no school subject, or group of subjects, can be viewed in isolation; all are parts of a whole curriculum which, according to the 1988 Education Act, is designed to promote children's spiritual, moral, cultural, mental and physical development. The Subject Working Group for Music maintained in its final report (DES 1991) that the study of music contributes to the whole curriculum by developing pupils' skills and attitudes, which include self-motivation, delight in individual and group achievement, imagination and inventiveness, co-operation, tolerance and self-confidence. In the same document, attention is drawn to the many possible cross-curricular links between music and other subjects (DES 1991: 55–6). There is an important message here for teachers. In the planning of programmes, it will be necessary for the specialist to be aware not only of the scope of learning in music and the related arts; he or she will also need to bear in mind what pupils are experiencing in other curriculum areas and the numerous connections between subject matters.

Beyond the timetabled curriculum

One of the features of the English educational system, over a long period, is that schools, with the encouragement and backing of local education authorities (LEAs), have provided opportunities for children to learn to play musical instruments. Instrumental services were greatly extended during the 1960s and 1970s; this policy led to the further growth of orchestral and ensemble work in schools, as well as the formation of LEA youth orchestras and bands, many of which perform to a very high standard. Tuition is described as 'extracurricular' in so far as it is not compulsory; pupils have never been *obliged* to learn the piano, guitar or an orchestral instrument, and there is no such requirement in the National Curriculum. Even so, large numbers of pupils benefit from instrumental tuition provided by visiting teachers employed by the school or the LEA. As a result of changes in funding for education, and new forms of management, instrumental services have been re-organized in a variety of ways over the past ten years. Concern has been expressed by musicians and educationists that these changes have led to a marked decline in school instrumental tuition. The exact extent of the decline is unclear, but the government has allocated extra financial resources for music services to be administered by the newly-formed National Foundation for Youth Music. Nevertheless, it appears that provision remains variable. According to the findings of a survey carried out by the *Times Educational Supplement*, and reported by Jon Slater (2000), instrumental teaching services are still very limited in some parts of the country.

Choirs, orchestras, jazz bands, pop groups and other ensembles remain 'optional extras', but have become an integral part of music education in schools. However, it has often been argued that these activities do not cater for all pupils and that, in some schools, the numbers participating constitute only a small minority. Furthermore, it can sometimes happen that so much attention is given to extracurricular work that music within the regular curriculum is neglected. This is rarely intentional, although it is sometimes suggested that 'presentations' of arts activities can assume too much importance because such events contribute to the public image of the school. Whatever the rights and wrongs of this perspective, the relationship between class music and the extracurricular is not always entirely satisfactory. Since the introduction of the National Curriculum, teachers have been required to ensure in their planning and development strategies that there is a proper balance between these two aspects of music education.

Teachers, pupils, parents and school governors recognize that musical and other artistic pursuits make a special contribution to the general character and ethos of the school; the arts frequently permeate the life of the institution and add to its corporate identity. Concerts, productions and other 'public' presentations help pupils to sharpen up their musical awareness and to appreciate music as a social activity; these things are clearly important aspects of musical experience. It is frequently said that concerts and musical events are also valuable in that they are opportunities for pupils of different ages and abilities to work together in a co-operative venture. Corporate activities in music and the performing arts have been strongly supported by David Hargreaves (1982), who suggests that much conventional schooling places emphasis on competition and individual success, whereas, in arts projects, children commonly work as members of teams: achievements become a collective responsibility. For many pupils, taking part in such projects helps develop a sense of solidarity and self-esteem. Consequently, extracurricular activities in music and the arts may be seen as providing for some (but not all) pupils' personal and social education. Traditionally, musical, sporting and other cultural pursuits have constituted a broader educational programme beyond the timetabled curriculum. According to Michael Barber (1997) and others, such programmes, when properly organized, are characteristic of the effective school.

Another notable aspect of music, additional to the timetabled curriculum, is the increasing contact that pupils and teachers now have with practising musicians. There is a long history of professional concerts for children, but nowadays, orchestras, opera companies and other bodies appoint education officers to organize programmes that enable performers to work with children on musical projects in schools and in the concert hall. A useful and informative account of current initiatives and organizations offering educational services is provided by John Stephens, Jillian Moore and Julian Smith (1995). On the whole, these partnerships work successfully and add a further dimension to musical education in schools.

Conclusions

During the past fifty years there have been many changes in music teaching and a huge expansion of opportunities for children and young people to participate in various forms of music making. Attitudes towards musical studies in schools have also changed. At one time, music was thought of as a desirable cultural pursuit, but of only marginal significance in a system of general education. It now enjoys a more secure place in the curriculum, especially as it is a compulsory subject for all pupils of ages 5–14. Nevertheless, support for the arts subjects is still very dependent on the educational outlook which informs policy in individual schools. It would be a mistake to think that, as a result of government directives, there is now complete conformity in educational thinking and practice.

Music education may be described as a 'family' of activities consisting of class music lessons and a range of extended or extracurricular pursuits. Present approaches to class music teaching are informed by a view of the arts as a realm of meaning or form of knowing, into which all children should be introduced as part of a liberal education in and for a pluralist society. Curriculum programmes are designed to ensure that pupils gain direct experience of music through performing, composing and listening, with the intention of promoting a broad understanding of the discipline. However, music in and beyond the curriculum can never be adequately portrayed in documents, since education is a practical enterprise in which pupils and teachers interact with each other in a multitude of ways. As with any area of the curriculum, the effective operation of music education is dependent on teachers who, as well as being classroom practitioners, assume several additional roles. They are frequently conductors, composers, arrangers, accompanists, concert organizers and administrators. The present-day music teacher has to be a versatile and energetic all-rounder who is expected to take responsibility for the formal music curriculum and the various activities that constitute the 'musical life' of the institution.

Teaching music in schools is (and always has been) a challenging occupation and one that requires a great amount of determination and commitment. There is much talk, on the part of decision-makers, about the need for strategic planning, efficient organization and the importance of the drive to raise standards. Of course, these factors are central to effective teaching. But successful practice is also dependent on teachers' sense of vision and optimism, for these are the very things that bring meaning and excitement to the complex process of teaching and learning; they are vital not only to classroom transactions but also to the wider educational enterprise.

References

Abbs, P. (1994) *The Educational Imperative*, London: Falmer Press.

Allsobrooke, D. (1992) *Music for Wales,* Cardiff: University of Wales Press.

Barber, M. *et al*. (1997) *School Performance and Extra-curricular Provision,* London: DfEE.

Ben-Tovim, A. (1979) *Children and Music*, London: A. C. Black.

Calouste Gulbenkian Foundation (1982) *The Arts in Schools*, London: Gulbenkian Foundation.

Central Advisory Council For Education (1963) *Half Our Future* (The Newsom Report), London: HMSO.

Cox, G. (1993) *A History of Music in England, 1872–1928,* Aldershot: Scolar Press.

Dennis, B. (1970) *Experimental Music in Schools*, Oxford: Oxford University Press.

DES (Department of Education and Science) (1985a) *Music from 5 to 16*, London: DES.

—— (1985b) *General Certificate of Secondary Education: The National Criteria: Music,* London: DES.

—— (1990) *National Curriculum: Music Working Group Interim Report*, London: DES.

—— (1991) *Music for Ages 5 to 14*, London: DES.

DfE (Department for Education) (1995) *Music in the National Curriculum*, London: DfE.

DfEE (Department for Education and Employment) QCA (Qualifications and Curriculum Authority) (1999) *The National Curriculum for England: Music,* London: DfEE, QCA.

Dobbs, J. and Fiske, R. (1956) *The Oxford School Music Books. Teachers' Manuals*, London: Oxford University Press.

Farrell, G. (1990) *Indian Music in Education*, Cambridge: Cambridge University Press.

Green, L. (1988) *Music on Deaf Ears,* Manchester: Manchester University Press.

Hargreaves, D.H. (1982) *The Challenge for the Comprehensive School*, London: Routledge.

Harland, J. *et al*. (2000) *Arts Education in Secondary Schools: Effects and Effectiveness,* Slough: NFER.

Hirst, P. (1974) 'Liberal education and the nature of knowledge' in P. Hirst *Knowledge and the Curriculum*, London: Routledge.

Hodges (2001) 'Using ICT in music teaching' in C. Philpott and C. Plummeridge (eds) *Issues in Music Teaching,* London: RoutledgeFalmer.

Kwami, R. (1998) *African Songs for School and Community: a Selection from Ghana,* Mainz: Schott.

Lawton, D. (1989) *Education, Culture and the National Curriculum*, London: Hodder & Stoughton.

NCC (National Curriculum Council) (1990) *The Arts 5–16: a Curriculum Framework*, Harlow: Oliver & Boyd.

Paynter, J. (1992) *Sound and Structure,* Cambridge: Cambridge University Press.

Paynter, J. and Aston, P. (1970) *Sound and Silence*, Cambridge: Cambridge University Press.

Phenix, P. (1964) *Realms of Meaning,* New York: McGraw-Hill.

Rainbow, B. (1989) *Music in Educational Thought and Practice*, Aberystwyth: Boethius Press.

Ross, M. (1975) *Arts and the Adolescent* (Schools Council Working Paper, no. 54), London: Evans.

Ross, M. (1978) *The Creative Arts*, London: Heinemann.

Self, G. (1967) *New Sounds in Class*, London: Universal.

Simpson, K. (1976) *Some Great Music Educators*, London: Novello.

Slater, J. (2000) 'Decline arrested – but not enough', *Times Educational Supplement,* 17 November, p. 22.

Stephens, J., Moore, J. and Smith, J. (1995) 'Support for the music curriculum' in G. Pratt and J. Stephens *Teaching Music in the National Curriculum,* London: Heinemann.

Swanwick, K. (1979) *A Basis for Music Education*, Slough: NFER.

Swanwick, K. (1999) *Teaching Music Musically,* London: Routledge.

Wiggins, T. (1993) *Music of West Africa,* London: Heinemann/WOMAD.

Witkin, R. (1974) *The Intelligence of Feeling*, London: Heinemann.

2 Planning for music teaching and learning
Gary Spruce

Introduction

The purpose of this chapter is to identify and explore some of the issues to be taken into account when planning for teaching and learning in the music classroom. Although not overtly articulating a rationale for music education, the chapter assumes a shared understanding of the nature and purpose of music education as being, in Plummeridge's words, 'a way of knowing or realm of meaning ... in which students come to understand the "workings" of the discipline through direct partici-pation in musical activities' (Plummeridge in Philpott 2001: 17).

My suggestion is that the most effective music teaching occurs when:

- a music curriculum that addresses the needs and aspirations of all children and reflects the requirements of the National Curriculum is taught by ...
- a teacher who has a vision of the unique role that music can play in the edu-cation of all children, also possesses the teaching, management and musical skills needed to realize it.

Later in the chapter we will consider specific issues in planning, such as identifying learning aims, providing for the range of needs in a class, managing resources and classroom management. In this first section, however, we look at the main levels of planning that a teacher undertakes and some of the broad issues that need to be addressed. Planning generally takes place at the levels of:

- schemes of work;
- modules/units of work;
- individual lessons.

Levels of planning

Schemes of work

A coherent and appropriate scheme of work is fundamental to a department's effec-tiveness. It provides a map for teachers' teaching and for children's music learning. All effective schemes of work will:

- reflect the requirements of the National Curriculum;

- reflect the particular needs, aspirations, social and cultural backgrounds of the children within the school;
- identify clear overall learning aims – what pupils should have achieved and the understanding and skills they will demonstrate at the end of a year, Key Stage or examination syllabus;
- provide for progression and differentiation;
- identify appropriate teaching strategies and resources;
- contribute to whole-school aims and ethos;
- involve children in enjoyable, stimulating and challenging musical experiences that lead them on to new areas of musical experience;
- be linked into effective assessment strategies, the information from which will feed back into planning;[1]
- display an awareness of issues of equal opportunities, special needs and inclusivity.

In addition, schemes of work should be subject to constant re-evaluation: 'Where are we coming from? Where are we now? How do we progress from here?'

Units/modules of work

Units of work occupy a middle level between schemes of work and individual lesson plans. They usually describe a plan for learning across a number of lessons. The unit will identify in detail the learning aims for the sequence of lessons and will map out progression through the module by describing in broad terms the anticipated learning in each lesson. Units/modules tend to focus on one particular aspect or style of music. These aspects might include:

- a musical style such as reggae;
- a musical technique such as variations;
- music from a specific country or culture;
- music in a particular context such as film or dance.

Whatever the focus of the module, the learning aims will be rooted in musical learning and related to the National Curriculum Programmes of Study. Pupils will have the opportunity to perform, compose and appraise music through activities which integrate all three skills.

It is at the level of the unit or module that progression is often most evident as pupils work through a particular aspect of music. However, as we shall see later, focusing on progression solely at the level of the module has dangers for progression overall.

Individual lessons

The final level of formal planning is the individual lesson. The learning aims of individual lessons within a module may be included in the module planning. However, with the exception of the first lesson of a module, which may be common to all classes, teachers will adapt learning aims for subsequent lessons according to the needs and progress of each particular group.

Planning for lessons takes into account not only learning aims but also the way in which the teacher plans to assess whether the aims have been achieved. Planning will consider the allocation of resources and any anticipated classroom management issues. The following may be a useful checklist when planning lessons:

1 Musical activities are 'authentic': i.e. what children are asked to do would be recognizable as a musical activity outside of the classroom;
2 Learning aims are clearly identified and articulated and reflect the National Curriculum Programmes of Study in music;
3 Learning aims provide for continuity and progression from previous lessons;
4 Planning takes account of individual needs (differentiation);
5 Pupils are aware of the learning aims and how these are to be assessed;
6 Lesson objectives are clearly related to learning aims and pupil activities and the teaching strategies are clearly focused towards the successful achievement of the objectives;
7 Musical learning is developed through 'the interrelated skills of performing, composing and appraising' (Curriculum 2000);
8 Planning demonstrates high teacher expectations;
9 There is appropriate use of resources including music technology;[2]
10 Repertoire and stimuli are chosen which inspire children and broaden their musical horizons;
11 Teachers plan, where possible, to use music rather than talk to illustrate musical points and lesson aims. They draw particularly upon their own musical skills and those of the children to exemplify musical issues.

Planning for progression in music learning

The principle aim of music teaching is to ensure that children progress in their music learning and fulfil their musical potential. However, what seems like a straightforward proposition is in fact one of the most problematical areas for music teachers.

Writing in 1982, Paynter points out how one of the central concerns of music teachers is the problem of devising schemes of work which ensure that progression takes place. Teachers interviewed as part of the Schools Council Project, *Music in the Secondary School Curriculum* (1977), said the following:

> One of the biggest let-downs for children has been, too frequently, a lack of **progression**.
> Clear and progressive aims [are essential].
> Many teachers still find great difficulty in planning their courses over three years.
> [We need] … schemes of work showing development over a year or more.
> (Paynter 1982: 57)

Ten years on, Keith Swanwick wrote that the relative unpopularity of music as a curriculum subject in later years of schooling proceeds from a perception that classroom music lessons 'rarely seem to lead students on with any strong feeling of purpose' (Swanwick 1988: p. 144).

One of the problems in ensuring that progression takes place is establishing a definition of what progression in music actually is – in other words, deciding how it can be recognized and how it can be measured. It is tempting to consider musical progression purely in terms of increased technical facility – a view of progression once most obviously reflected in the graded instrumental and vocal exams of the Associated Board, Trinity College and Guildhall. Indeed, some readers will recognize this as being the model of their own musical education: an underdeveloped music curriculum in school, an active extracurricular life, and steady progression through instrumental/vocal grades. However, this is a deficient model of music education and musical progression. It bases the measurement of musical progress upon what Plummeridge describes as 'the notion of the virtuoso performer as the paradigm of musical achievement' (Plummeridge 1991: 82). A whole range of ways in which musical achievement might be demonstrated is ignored. It therefore fails to provide for the needs of all children. It fails to address sufficiently aspects of creativity, breadth of repertoire, listening skills, critical and appraising achievements, and most of all, it fails to provide for any increased understanding of the nature of music.

It can be argued that the introduction of the music National Curriculum in 1992 provided teachers with a template for progression through the Programmes of Study and the *Criteria for Success*, superseded in the 1995 revision by *Level Descriptors*. The criteria and level descriptors indicated what children were expected to be able to achieve at the end of a particular Key Stage. These level descriptors were further refined in the Exemplification of Standards published by the Schools Curriculum and Assessment Authority (SCAA) in 1996 through terms such as 'working towards' and 'working beyond' expectations.

However, the language used in these exemplifications was, as Keith Swanwick has pointed out, 'too imprecise or spuriously quantitative' (Swanwick 1999: 77) to be useful. Many of the criteria are either nebulous: 'pupils perform with expression … they demonstrate different moods/effects' (SCAA 1996), or imply an axiomatic link between musical complexity and musical quality and learning.

This second issue is particularly important in that a distinction needs to be drawn between the difficulty of task and its individual quality and/or the status of its contribution to the 'artistic whole'. It is a mistake necessarily to equate a composition's complexity or the technical demands it makes to realize it with inherent musical quality. Simply because something is easier to achieve technically does not in itself mean that it is musically less important or requires less musicianship than something more complex. Few would argue that the technical facility required to compose or perform one of the test pieces written for the Paris Conservatoire is greater than that required for a simple folk song, yet the expressive affect of the latter may well be infinitely greater. Also, as I have pointed out elsewhere (Spruce 2001), a tension is often created when western art-music-based criteria, which reify analytical skills, accurate realization of notation, and complex musical structure, are applied to music of styles and cultures which emphasize other attributes.

The point is, of course, that musical achievement is much more easily and objectively measurable if assessment remains on a technical level – correct notes and rhythms, observation of tempo and dynamic markings, analysis of the way in which the 'bits' of music fit together. Therefore there has been a tendency to emphasize this facet of musical achievement more than the more creative aspects of the subject.

This is perhaps why examinations have traditionally focused on practical skills or written and aural analysis of music and shied away from composing anything other than pastiche.

However, the consequence of concentrating upon technical facility is that many children fail to perceive music as being a creative subject. Research carried out by the National Foundation for Education Research, *Arts in their View: a study of youth participation in the arts* (1995), showed that only 5 per cent of children considered that music involved creativity and imagination. Even amongst those who had opted for it in Years 10 and 11, less than half considered that it possessed a creative element.

Equally, however, it is important that the notion of 'creativity' is not used as a reason for a lack of clarity in articulating clear learning aims and achievable goals. As the writers of *The Arts from 5 to 15: a curriculum framework* (1990) put it:

> These principles of progression are of central importance in raising expectations of attainment in the arts. Too often pupils' work in the arts in schools is well beneath their practical and conceptual capabilities. Primary pupils in Years 5 or 6 for example are often given unexacting tasks in the arts of which they were capable in Years 2 or 3. However, they may not have progressed appreciably in skills or understanding during these years, either through low expectations or a lack of clear objectives. One reason is that the arts are still sometimes seen as general expressive activities which have a value in balancing the more taxing, instruction-based work of other areas of the curriculum. In this view, the very idea of learning objectives would seem out of place. The framework we have offered here is at odds with this view. The arts are exacting forms of thinking and expression, which only confer genuine rewards on young people after they have understood and gained control over the disciplines involved.
>
> (NCC 1990: par. 176, pp. 67–8)

It is important that children should feel that they are involved in a creative activity that has a sense of direction, is worthwhile and is providing them with experiences that other subjects do not. Classroom music needs to be full of activities that challenge children's creativity, that develop the skills and knowledge they need to progress musically and that require them to express and justify opinions about their own work and that of others.

Devising a curriculum model for music

How then can musical progression be planned for and what curriculum model is likely to be most effective in promoting it? First, any curriculum must provide pupils with a balance of musical activities which focus on children's creative and critical development rather than on a simply technical instrumental facility for its own sake. As Ofsted reported in 1995:

> Lessons in which the teaching is good or very good usually have composing and appraising as their dominant activities, and employ performing as a supporting skill.
>
> (Ofsted 1995, par. 25, p. 12)

A purely linear approach to music education, which is implied by some performance-based models, is likely to be inadequate for most children's musical needs. The linear model presumes predictable and common stages of development and ignores children's social and cultural backgrounds which so affect their perception of what music is and *means* to them. Conversely, a curriculum model such as that provided by some modular schemes, in which there is no element of linear progression, is equally flawed. Ofsted writes that: 'Progression is addressed least effectively in courses organized as modules which may be delivered an any order' (Ofsted 1995, par. 41, p. 17).

Focusing on musical concepts or elements (pitch, rhythm, timbre, etc.) is one of two ways in which Paynter (1982) suggests schemes of work might be organized. However, Swanwick (1988) warns of the danger in extrapolating musical elements from the musical whole. He argues that, in focusing on the building bricks of music, we (and the children) lose sense of a musical encounter, destroying what Langer (1953) describes as 'the inviolable whole':

> [we] only pick up fragments of the whole experience: we [lose] the sense of the whole … [also] we tend to work from them and to them, looking for music which exemplifies their characteristics.
>
> (Swanwick 1988: 147)

Swanwick does not suggest that musical elements should not feature as such in a music curriculum, but rather argues strongly for a 'top-down' process, beginning with the whole musical experience and extrapolating from that the musical elements. For if musical elements are regarded purely as abstractions, then 'we are likely to forget their origins as expressive features encountered in "real" music. Their expressiveness must not be lost in the interests of curriculum tidiness' (Swanwick 1988: 148).

The curriculum should have at its foundation children's musical experience and, to begin with, children's previous knowledge of music: the music they have experienced in primary school, the music they hear at home and the music that is important to them. It will recognise the importance of children's cultural and social backgrounds in defining the role that music plays in their lives. If teachers do this, they will have, almost by definition, involved the children in devising the music curriculum. Using children's previous learning as a starting point, teachers can proceed to develop new musical skills, encourage children's creativity and introduce them to new and exciting music all within the context of real, authentic musical experience.

A curriculum based on authentic musical experience provides opportunities for similar musical concepts to be revisited in diverse musical contexts. Charles Plummeridge (1991) and the NCC Arts in Schools Project (1990) both look to Bruner's concept of the spiral curriculum as the means by which this might be achieved. Bruner's proposition is based upon the notion of revisiting basic concepts with ever-increasing understanding and interpretative insights:

> [The] basic themes that give form to life and literature are as simple as they are powerful. To be in command of these basic ideas, to use them effectively,

requires a continual deepening of one's understanding of them that comes from learning to use them in progressively more complex forms.

(Bruner 1966; quoted in NCC 1990, par. 172, p. 67)

This brings us close to Paynter's second curriculum model which takes as its starting point musical structures and techniques from a range of musical styles and cultures. Developing children's understanding of the many ways in which musical materials are used and how music makes its meaning in different contexts will go a long way to aiding progression, so that pupils are able to:

make the all-important evaluations of their work so that they are aware of the successes and the miscalculations. Obviously we should expect them to learn new techniques and acquire points of information that will assist them in further work, but the real progress will be measured by the extent to which they are able to use an increasing diversity of musical ideas with confidence.

(Paynter 1982: 60)

Planning for differentiation

Progression, which we have already identified as one of the most important consequences of good teaching, relies a great deal upon the ability of a teacher to recognize the range of abilities, attainments and backgrounds within a class or group, and then to provide learning opportunities appropriate to their needs. This, fundamentally, is what differentiation is about.

Differentiation – otherwise described as providing for individual needs or educational inclusion – is becoming of increasing importance. The National Curriculum has, for all subjects, a section devoted to 'Inclusion: providing effective learning opportunities for all pupils; and from 2001, the effectiveness of schools', and departments' provision for educational inclusion will be an important focus of Ofsted inspections. However, statutory requirements apart, all teachers committed to music as a subject to which all pupils have an entitlement will want to develop a curriculum which meets the needs of all pupils.

The National Curriculum proposes three principles for inclusion:

1   Setting suitable learning challenges;
2   Responding to pupils' diverse learning needs;
3   Overcoming potential barriers to learning and assessment for individuals and groups of pupils.

(DFE/QCA 2000: 24–6)

In this chapter, I want to focus specifically on the issues associated with planning suitable learning challenges.

Setting suitable learning challenges

The most significant word here is 'challenges', for, when planning for individual needs, our anxiety to ensure that every child can accomplish the task should not lead to a lowering of expectations or a setting of objectives which lack challenge. It is important that when planning for differentiation, we do not forget that the main aim of teaching is pupils' learning. Consequently we plan differentiated tasks which are at the edge of each pupil's knowledge in order to enable them to progress.

Traditionally, differentiation has been seen to be achievable in two ways: by *task* or by *outcome*. Differentiation by outcome is, broadly speaking, observing different levels of achievement from the setting of a common task, whilst differentiation by task involves setting varied learning activities designed to meet the range of needs within a particular group.

However, such 'ideal types' and the clear-cut distinctions which they imply are rarely helpful or particularly apposite when applied to music teaching; for example, there is a sense in which pupils themselves self-differentiate by, as Philpott says, engaging with 'areas of problem solving such as composing and listening … at their own particular level of musical development' (Philpott 2001: 124), irrespective of the tasks set by the teacher.

From the perspective of teachers' planning, differentiation both by task and by outcome is problematic. Where the teacher devises a single-level task that can be accomplished by all pupils, a situation can occur where the most capable pupils are insufficiently stretched. Sometimes, this issue is addressed in performing activities using keyboards by 'grading' tunes according to increasing technical difficulty. The problem with this approach is that repertoire is selected solely in terms of its technical demands rather than any other features it may demonstrate. Consequently, there is a danger that technical demands and musical quality (and logically following from this, technical skills and musical understanding) are perceived by pupils as being synonymous. Musical success *in the curriculum* is perceived as only capable of being demonstrated by those with developed instrumental skills.

When planning for differentiation, it is important to ensure that, while we demonstrate the opportunities that increased technical skills can provide, we do not lose sight of the distinction between technical facility and musical effectiveness: one does not necessarily result in the other. So that children's musical opportunities or status within a group are not wholly governed by their technical skills – that they, too, do not necessarily equate complexity with quality, but learn to value the creativity and feeling which everyone can bring to their music; for example, discovering how the simplest effect – a roll on a suspended cymbal, or an accompanying ostinato rhythm – can enhance a composition that they had hitherto thought of as complete. Technique should be at the *service* of creativity, and this applies equally to the Year 7 pupil and to the experienced composer, performer or listener.

One way of addressing this issue is for the teacher to provide differentiated tasks within a *common, shared musical experience* to which all children can contribute something of musical value. This approach is most often seen where teachers arrange music for school ensembles rather than purchasing arrangements 'off the peg'. Each part is written to best reflect the strengths of individual players whilst presenting a challenge within their capabilities. This results in music which motivates pupils and almost invariably leads to a more satisfying musical experience for the audience.

In the context of the classroom, the teacher might arrange or compose music that requires a range of skills, from the repetition of an ostinato rhythm through to the performance of a complex melodic line. The former might require the ability to maintain a complex rhythm within a steady pulse while the latter might demand manual dexterity. It might well be that the rhythmic element is simpler than the melodic line but this is not necessarily a given. Each will be musically satisfying, have its own criteria for success and contribute to a common musical goal. In composing or arranging music specifically for the range of skills and resources at his/her disposal, the teacher acts very much as a composer would in the 'real world' and consequently provides a model for pupils' own composing and arranging. Such a model has differentiation built into it rather than it being imposed *post facto*; for example, when composing in groups, pupils could be encouraged to compose specifically for the resources within their group. Further differentiation can be achieved through requirements of length, structure, instrumentation, style and genre. The stimuli used to initiate the creative process are also a way in which composing tasks can be differentiated. These stimuli can be specifically musical (for example, adding a simple ostinato figure to an existing composition) or non-musical (such as a picture, film or poem).

In listening to and appraising music, differentiation is typically achieved through the complexity and sophistication of style and structure of the music involved. Analysing music in terms of its constituent parts – pitch, rhythm, timbre – and the way in which these are structured has always formed an important part of the music curriculum and its assessment systems. Until relatively recently, this might have occurred by reference to a score only, rather than through making connections between what is heard and its notated form. Fortunately this kind of abstracted music learning is becoming less common.

However, listening and analysing music in terms of its musical 'building bricks' is only one way of perceiving music; and a way which is predicated upon the values and procedures of western art music. These values and procedures have, through their association with the high status music of the western art tradition, become perceived as self-evidently the values against which all music should be evaluated – thus perpetuating the musical hierarchical *status quo*.

When planning for the development of pupils' listening and appraising skills, teachers need to have cognizance of the varied ways in which music is understood and experienced according to its style, genre and social context and to differentiate the tasks accordingly; for example, structure may be of less importance in music that does not lay claim to autonomy but interacts with its social context, e.g. jazz. However, that does not mean that in an educational context we do not attempt to impose a structure and autonomy upon it in order to make it reflect high status values and musical procedures!

The problem of course is that music which does not conform to these values and procedures, or cannot be described in terms of the technical language through which these values and procedures are typically expressed, is viewed as an aberration or intrinsically of lesser value; for if music cannot be adequately described through the terminology of the western art music aesthetic, this is taken as an indicator of the inferior quality of the music rather than an indicator of the inadequacy of the terminology being used.

Furthermore, as Nicholas Cook points out, the requirement to verbally represent music – and its enactment – can restrict response:

if listeners responses are mediated … by verbal … representations of what they hear, then they will hear or at least respond to less than would otherwise be the case – especially if they are listening to music that is unfamiliar to them … words and symbols and images inevitably become sedimented. As a result the critic, whose listening naturally tends towards verbal representations, can easily find his musical responses becoming rigid and inflexible through being framed in what are literally musicological terms.

(Cook 1990: 176)

In school music, the experience of listening can become circumscribed by the terminology through which it is considered appropriate to express that experience. Pupils are required to describe in terminology specifically reflective of western art music processes, music of other cultures and styles. It may well be, as David Bray says, that one of the ways in which progression in music learning can be identified is through 'Development of attitudes … over a period of time students begin to listen to a wider range of music, they develop an open outlook and are prepared to try new ideas, they become adaptable and enquiring' (Bray 2000: 67). However, planning for differentiation needs to demonstrate an awareness that musical genres and cultures are defined to a great extent by the differing importance attached to musical concepts and the inter-relationships of composer–performer– listener. The musical diversity required by the National Curriculum provides opportunities for music teachers to develop a range of musical skills within specific musical contexts and an understanding that this musical context is fundamental to an understanding of the way in which musical concepts and techniques are used. The alternative is that we continue to articulate a hierarchy of musical styles in which much of the music to which children listen (popular and world) is considered as inherently inferior.

Planning resources[3]

Planning issues

Planning for the appropriate use of a wide variety of resources is as important as preparing activities and planning learning aims; for example, too many materials, or inappropriate repertoire, can stifle the expressive and practical nature of music-making. When considering resources, it is important to bear in mind the following points:

1   The knowledge, skills and understanding that young people bring with them to your lessons are vital resources.
2   Do not overload or confuse your lesson or project with too many resources. When looking at resources in isolation, there is a danger of losing sight of the intended learning. All of us find delight in discovering new things. Allow the pupils that excitement, but do not find yourself so involved in your own discovery of a new resource that the pupils miss the opportunity to learn to make music.

Evaluating the use of resources

The National Curriculum for music (DfEE/QCA 2000) outlines the Programmes of Study to be covered across the Key Stages. Teachers, however, *evaluate* the appropriateness and effectiveness of resources in supporting music teaching and learning. In selecting resources, teachers will involve all members of the department, including support teachers, instrumental/vocal teachers, resident musicians and the librarian, so drawing on a range of perspectives and expertise.

Increasingly, work schemes for music are being published (including one by the Qualifications and Curriculum Authority (2000)) that purport to take pupils right through a Key Stage: a package typically comprises textbooks, CDs, flash cards and posters and CD-ROMs. It is tempting to structure a music course around resources that are usually attractive and well-designed. However, there are dangers in doing this, not least because no published course is likely to provide for the range of needs in a particular school or can anticipate a pupil's rate of progress. It is much better to draw upon these resources as appropriate, adapting them for the specific needs of the department and creating your own resources for other occasions.

Below is a range of criteria that could be used to evaluate a department's existing resources, as well as helping to decide upon new resources.

The scheme of work	Is this up-to-date? Does it reflect contemporary curriculum issues and practice?
Values and attitudes	Materials, equipment and repertoire are not value-free. Resources raise important questions about whether music reflects society. As part of your planning, you should determine whether the resources reinforce entrenched attitudes or whether they enable pupils to make their own independent choices.
Pedagogic style	Do the resources stimulate critical thinking, or do they simply transmit knowledge? What teaching styles and learning outcomes will the resources support? Will they support the pupils' learning needs? Will they maintain pupils' interest? What is the value of the task in which the resources will be used?
The mix of resources	What is the balance between written resources, aural examples and demonstrations, recorded music, videos, photographs, specialist instrumental/vocal teacher support, music technology, etc.?
Checking accuracy	The information contained in resources and displays needs to be checked for accuracy and, particularly, for the way the resources handle fundamental concepts and principles.

Pupils' perceptions	Think about various kinds of stereotyping (ethnicity/gender/class/cultural diversity).
	■ Do the materials avoid racist, sexist, discriminatory attitudes?
	■ Do they enable pupils to raise issues of ethnicity, gender and class as dynamics of listening to and appraising music?
	■ Does the provision of any instrumental and vocal tuition or use of musical technology reinforce or challenge gender, racial or ethnic stereotypes?
Instruments and equipment	Is there a wide range of good quality instruments available to pupils, including chromatic, bass and electronic instruments, and instruments from around the world?
Language	Are the resources written in a language that is easily understood by the pupils? What is the style of writing – narrative/story/analysis? Does it increase pupils' knowledge of the specialist language of music?

Finally, there is the critical issue of efficiency. With limited finance, departments need to ask themselves the following questions:

- How much do the resources cost and will the pupils get value for money in terms of quality, content and fitness of purpose?
- How is the department developing its resources, availability and use to promote the quality of learning?
- How does the department evaluate the effectiveness of resources?
- How does the department review and develop the use of the accommodation?

Classroom management

Music teaching makes particularly challenging demands on teachers' skills of classroom management. The three quotes below summarize the main perspectives or 'takes' on classroom management. The first emphasizes the role of the teacher in the classroom and is predicated upon the belief that good classroom management emerges from the well-planned lesson:

> giving clear instructions and checking they had been understood; achieving an appropriate balance between instruction and classwork … striking a balance between whole-class teaching and attending to individual pupils; skilful use of questioning for purposes of recapitulation, to check that instructions have been understood, for exposition and to maintain order; and the application of immediate feedback – not only prompt marking, but also 'public praise and private criticism'.
>
> (Taylor in Moon and Shelton Mayes 1994: 163)

The second argues that even the best planning can be of little use if the pupils are insufficiently motivated:

> [disregard] the current 'Inspector speak' which says that pupils behave badly when the quality of teaching is insufficiently stimulating. They often behave badly when lessons are brilliantly planned because they stop the teacher from starting properly; they often behave badly because they have poor skills in the subject area they are being asked to study … but, most importantly, they behave badly because they have a very thin layer of motivation and a low level of concentration.
>
> (Blum 1998: 2)

In this third quote, John Paynter, drawing on comments made by teachers involved in the Schools Council Project, *Music in the Secondary School Curriculum* ('The evaluation of classroom activities'), emphasizes the importance of good teacher–pupil relationships:

> Teachers should be able to relate to pupils in a general way (i.e. 'pastorally' as well as musically). There must be a working relationship between the teacher and each individual; there must be interaction between teacher and class. An easy relationship with pupils is essential; nothing will work if there is difficulty in 'getting on' with pupils. [But] strict standards of conduct must be maintained – not in an authoritarian way but arising out of respect for what is being done…. Disciplined freedom: [it should be clear that the teacher is] in command [though] 'teacher-directed' [does not have to mean] 'teacher-dictated'. [Pupils need guidance; a lesson must not become chaotic] – Freedom can only arrive through discipline.
>
> (Paynter 1977: 10)

There is of course nothing mutually exclusive about any of the above. They are inter-linked, impact upon each other, and cannot in any meaningful way be considered discretely. This is particularly true of pupils' attitudes which, although resulting from a number of factors, some of which are external to the school, are nevertheless inevitably influenced by their prior experience of a subject and the person teaching it. The attitudes pupils demonstrate towards a subject will be based to a great extent upon the degree to which they feel the subject offers something that is worthwhile. In many schools considered 'difficult' to teach in, it is departments such as music and PE which are most effective in that they have the flexibility and resources to tailor their curriculum to meet the specific needs and interests of their pupils and to reflect their social and cultural backgrounds.

To a great extent, effective classroom management emerges from a strong philosophy about the purpose and nature of music and music education articulated through appropriate curriculum and pedagogy. Pupil motivation, positive teacher–pupil relationships and effective planning all result from this. Therefore, there is a sense in which all of this chapter (and indeed this book) is about creating a positive classroom context for pupil learning. However, there is one aspect of the management of music classrooms which might benefit from discrete discussion – the management of group work.

Managing group work

Group work is an important part of most music departments' pedagogical strategies. The appropriate use of group work is invaluable in delivering the music curriculum and has both musical and extra-musical benefits. However, it presents specific issues of classroom management which need to be addressed if it is to be used effectively.

Four issues need to be considered when planning for group work:

1   the membership of the group;
2   managing the transition between class and group work;
3   ensuring that pupils remain focused on their work while not being directly supervised by a teacher;
4   the dynamics that operate between the members of the group and how this impacts upon achievement.

Group membership

Membership of the group can be decided by the teacher or by the pupils themselves. The latter is most frequently observed in music lessons and will usually result in friendship groupings. There are occasions, however, when a pupil cannot find a group willing to accept them. Teachers will usually deal with this situation tactfully, perhaps by placing them in a group where their skills will be of particular value.

When the teacher considers it appropriate for her to decide on pupil groupings, the criteria she uses might be based on some of the following:

- attainment – the desire to have pupils of like- or mixed-attainment within a group;
- the need to have a particular 'spread' of instruments and/or skills within each group;
- the personalities of those in a group – ensuring that one member doesn't dominate or that another doesn't feel unable to contribute;
- a teacher's knowledge of how well pupils work together;
- a desire to have purely arbitrary groups.

Membership of groups can provide opportunities for differentiation. Groups can be either of varying levels of attainment with the tasks differentiated but nevertheless all contributing to a successful whole, or of similar attainment, concentrating upon one particular task and differentiated by outcome.

The transition from class to group work

Most lessons begin with the identification of new learning aims or, at the very least, a reprise of where the previous lesson ended. Therefore there will come a point in most music lessons where pupils move from whole-class to group activities. For groups based on other than arbitrary membership, many teachers select the groups before the lesson begins.

Organizing pupil-defined groups is often best achieved by making an explicit decision about how many are to be allowed in each group and sticking to it. The size of the groups will be related to the number of children in the class, the availability of resources and the nature of the task. Teachers allow a limited time (perhaps one minute) for pupils to discuss with each other the groupings in which they wish to work. If they are engaged in an on-going project, the same groups will be maintained from lesson to lesson with a record kept of these. Sometimes pupils are absent, distorting the groups. There are strategies for this, including amalgamating groups, adapting group membership and amending the nature of the task.

Working in groups

Experienced teachers are wary of expecting children to maintain their concentration over too long a period. Group work is therefore carefully planned, used for limited periods and employed as one of a number of classroom organizational models. The problem of ensuring that children remain focused on their work is fundamental to the successful management of group work. Critical factors are:

- the composition of the groups;
- the location of the groups;
- ensuring that the targets for group work are understood and achievable;
- ensuring that the teacher's expectations of standards of behaviour are understood and agreed.

Clearly defined targets for group work are important. It may be necessary to reinforce verbal guidance with written instructions or worksheets. Some children can retain verbal instructions for only a limited period; they may also have different perceptions of what you have said and spend much of their time arguing about this. *Simple* and explicit written instructions can overcome some of these problems.

Groups who have difficulty in remaining on-task are ideally located in or near the main classroom and visited regularly. The strengths and weaknesses of each group are identified and used as a means of setting interim targets. Teachers reinforce good behaviour and challenge that which is unacceptable. When the children return to whole-class working, they do so in an orderly manner. The connection between good behaviour, enjoyment of the lesson and successful completion of the activity is always emphasised.

Children who have worked hard and are pleased with their achievements are encouraged to demonstrate to other members of the class the progress that they have made with their performances or compositions. However, the imperative of a classroom performance is also used as a means of encouraging wayward groups to focus on their work. The knowledge that they have to perform to their peers concentrates the minds of some pupils wonderfully! Effective teachers insist that the class listen attentively, positively and actively, involving the class in deciding what criteria are being used to evaluate success and making this the basis of the listening. They emphasise the connection between a successful 'product' and the quality of the work invested, and use successful work as a model for other groups.

Conclusion

Careful and detailed planning is critical in ensuring that children receive a worthwhile experience in music lessons. Department handbooks, schemes of work and lesson plans are an extremely important part of this process. However, it is important that documentation is not seen as the *primary outcome* of planning or that planning be so prescriptive that it discourages effective individual teaching styles or fails to allow teachers to: 'capitalise on the unexpected and to turn it into learning which is creative and enjoyable' (DES 1985c: 9). Neither, however, should an unwillingness to be overly prescriptive be used as a rationale for ill-focused learning aims or lack of well-thought-out planning. In fact the reverse is true. As HMI have pointed out, it is only within the 'carefully planned syllabus or individual lesson, [that] the confident and competent teacher will … recognise the need for a spontaneous response either to an external event or to a surge of interest and excitement from the pupils themselves' (DES 1985c: 8–9).

This is the crux of the matter, for what effective teaching and learning are dependent upon are the skills of the individual teacher *supported* by effective planning. As Charles Plummeridge says:

> we can write or talk about quality and even emphasise it in curriculum documents: achieving it in practice is another matter. However well planned and documented curriculum specifications might be, their effective implementation is entirely dependent on the actions of teachers.
>
> (Plummeridge 1991: 64)

Notes

1 See Chapter 7 for a detailed discussion of the issues involved in planning for assessment.
2 See Chapter 12 for a detailed discussion of the role of ICT in music teaching.
3 The section draws on material written by Mark Wyatt for the Open University PGCE course in 1996.

References

Blum, P. (1998) *Surviving and Succeeding in Difficult Classrooms,* London: Routledge Falmer.

Bray, D. (2000) *Teaching Music in the Secondary School*, Oxford: Heinemann.

Bruner, J. (1966) *Toward a Theory of Instruction*, Cambridge MA: Harvard University Press.

Cook, N. (1990) *Music, Imagination and Culture*, Oxford: Clarendon Press.

DES (1985c) *Education Observed: Good Teachers,* London: HMSO.

DfEE/QCA *The National Curriculum (Music)*, London: HMSO.

Harland, J., Kinder, K. and Hartley, K. (1995) *Arts in Their View: a Study of Youth Participation in the Arts,* Slough: National Foundation for Educational Research.

Langer, S. (1953) *Feeling and Form: a Theory of Art Developed from Philosophy in a New Key,* London: Routledge & Kegan Paul.

Moon, B. and Shelton Mayes, A. (1994 edn) *Teaching and Learning in the Secondary School*, London: Routledge.

National Curriculum Council Arts in Schools Project (1990) *The Arts 5–16. A Curriculum Framework*, Harlow: Oliver & Boyd.

Ofsted (1995) *Music: a Review of Inspection Findings 1993/4*, London: HMSO.

Paynter, J. (1977) 'The evaluation of classroom music activities', Working Paper 4 of *Schools Council Project: Music in the Secondary School*.

—— (1982) *Music in the Secondary School Curriculum*, Cambridge: Cambridge University Press.

Philpott, C. (ed.) (2001) *Learning to Teach Music in the Secondary School*, London: RoutledgeFalmer.

Plummeridge, C. (1991) *Music Education in Theory and Practice*, London: Falmer Press.

—— (2001) 'The place of music in the school curriculum' in C. Philpott (ed.) (2001) *Learning to Teach Music in the Secondary School*, London: RoutledgeFalmer.

Qualifications and Curriculum Authority (2000) *Music: a Scheme of Work for Key Stage 3*, London: QCA.

Schools Curriculum and Assessment Authority (1996) *Consistency in Teacher Assessment. Exemplification of Standards (Key Stage 3 Music)*, London: HMSO.

Spruce, G. (2001) 'Music assessment and the hegemony of musical heritage' in C. Plummeridge and C. Philpott (eds) *Issues in Music Education*, London: Routledge.

Swanwick, K. (1988) *Music, Mind, and Education*, London: Routledge.

—— (1999) *Teaching Music Musically*, London: Routledge.

Taylor, W. (1994) 'Classroom variables' in B. Moon and A. Shelton Mayes (eds) *Teaching and Learning in the Secondary School*, London: Routledge.

Wyatt, M. (1996) *Resources for Music Education*, Milton Keynes: Open University.

3 The Music department
Gary Spruce

Introduction

- What are the characteristics of an effective department?
- What is the role of individual departments within schools?
- What is the relationship between departments and the management of the school?

The observant reader will notice that, in posing these questions, I have not referred specifically to 'the *music* department'. This is not a sin of omission, but rather a way of pointing out that many of the issues and attitudes that impact upon a music department are those that affect *all* departments irrespective of subject. Common issues simply acquire specific subject focus.

This view is supported in the HMI (1985) document *Music from 5–16*. Published as an appendix to that document is a checklist of responsibilities for heads of music departments (see opposite page).

Of the seven points in this checklist, four are wholly generic (applicable to all subject areas), and two are substantially generic, while only one – liaising with visiting instrumental staff and music centres – is music-specific. It can therefore be seen that, at least in the view of the HMI of the time, qualities that characterize a good head of department (and which, in a subject area with as large a proportion of one-person departments as music, by implication characterize the department itself) are essentially common to all subject areas.

The danger of professional isolation

The final item on HMI's list – the music-specific one – places an obligation on heads of music to: 'keep musically alert and alive; avoid a closed mind and *professional isolation*' (my italics). This acknowledges the feelings of professional isolation that many music departments and music teachers experience due to the prevalence of one-person music departments. It is an issue that is recognized again in HMI's report on the first year of the music National Curriculum: *Music at Key Stages 1, 2 and 3* (HMI 1994, par. 3). Indeed, the sense of isolation experienced by some music teachers working in such departments is, in Ribbins' view, axiomatic. For he believes that there can be no 'department' in any meaningful sense unless there are in the school at least two people teaching a particular subject:

Checklist of responsibilities of the head of department (secondary)

1   After consultation with colleagues, the preparation of a scheme of work in relation to the staff, time and resources available.
2   Such a scheme should set out:
    - aims;
    - objectives;
    - knowledge, understanding, attitudes and skills to be achieved by specified ages and stages;
    - the areas of study and styles of teaching (including class management) through which these goals are to be achieved.
3   Support pupils by diagnosing their strengths and weaknesses, providing remedial help/extra tuition for particular pupils, analysing and attending to special needs or interests.
4   Maintain a continuing debate within the department by holding regular, minuted staff meetings to consider the above, test new approaches and materials as required and to revise and re-evaluate schemes of work in response to changing circumstances.
5   Arrange close liaison with the music adviser, visiting instrumental staff, contributory/receiver schools, music centre(s) and other centralized activities.
6   Work closely with departmental and senior management colleagues over such issues as:
    - time allocation including duration and frequency of periods;
    - timetabling – size of teaching groups, blocking setting, team teaching;
    - accommodation for music – its adequacy, deployment, preservation, development;
    - purchase, allocation and security of all forms of musical equipment used in the department;
    - relationship and possible co-operation with other departments/disciplines;
    - extracurricular activities including likely target groups, timing/siting, liaising with other staff members likely to attract a similar clientele;
    - support for other staff (including helping probationers to develop strengths and overcome weaknesses) to provide in-service training and maintain productive contact with visiting staff.
7   Keep musically alert and alive; avoid a closed mind and professional isolation.

(HMI (1985) Music from 5–16, Appendix 3, HMSO)

'Departments, then, may be said to exist only where deliberate collaboration takes place, enabling an exchange of ideas and knowledge and facilitating some specialisation of task through various divisions of labour' (Ribbins 1985: 358).

In order to address the issue of singleton departments, schools whose size cannot support a second full-time music teacher sometimes employ a teacher of music who can also teach another subject. Other schools cluster subjects into faculties, which alleviates the one-teacher department problem to some degree, and provides 'a forum for like minds' (NFAE 1994: 63). However, the National Foundation for Arts Education (NFAE) also points out that there are disadvantages as well as advantages associated with such a model, not least being that 'The formation of an arts faculty may result in reduced time, staffing, finance and resources' (NFAE 1994: 64). However, there are dangers that in creating, for example, an expressive or performance arts faculty, the opportunity is taken to reduce the overall time allocated to 'the arts'. Furthermore, as we shall see later, although there are areas of commonality between arts domains, each has its own unique character and contribution to make to a child's intellectual development. Indee‚d this can be the only rationale for its place on the curriculum.

The professional isolation with which HMI is concerned is isolation from other practising music teachers. But there is another kind of isolation which is of equal concern: that of music teachers and music departments from the decision-making process of the school in which they teach. This isolation can be said to be caused by three interrelated factors:

1   by music departments failing to develop an awareness of the whole-school and wider educational issues that impact upon *all* subject areas;
2   by the balance between curricular music and extracurricular music becoming distorted;
3   by music departments failing to articulate a rationale for the place of music in the curriculum.

In this chapter we will look at those issues that impact upon all subject areas and which form common links between departments, considering how these issues specfically impact on the music department. For if music departments are to contribute to, and influence, whole-school policies, they need to be aware of, and act upon, these issues. It is only by engaging with issues which are common to all subjects, and contributing to the overall aims and ethos of the school, that the music department can avoid professional isolation. We will then turn to the way in which a balance and relationship between curricular and extracurricular activities can be created and maintained. Finally we will look at the important role the department has in articulating a rationale for the place of music in the curriculum.

Are subject departments a 'good thing'?

In 1984, the Welsh Inspectorate wrote that 'Whether a pupil achieves or underachieves is largely dependent on the quality of planning, execution, and evaluation that takes place within individual departments' (HMI Wales 1984). The is just as true now as it was then. Indeed, the importance of the discrete subject area, which had to a certain degree waned from the 1960s to the early 1980s in favour of cross-curricular initiatives, has increased since the introduction of the National Curriculum with its model of core and foundation subjects. Ofsted, which adopts a similar subject-based approach in its inspections, has further reinforced this model of the school curriculum.

Although a study of school effectiveness at A level, researched by Carol Fitz-Gibbon (1992), confirms that the quality of the education a school provides is directly related to the accomplishments of its individual departments (both pastoral and academic): 'The school department is the desirable unit on which to focus as a first level of aggregation in school effects studies' (Fitz-Gibbon 1992: 117). There-fore, efforts to improve education are more likely to be effective if they are 'made *within schools*, department by department rather than by setting schools in competi-tion' (Fitz-Gibbon 1992: 102).

There are, however, potentially negative consequences of a developed, discrete departmental structure, such as the decline in the cohesion afforded by some cross-curricular work. As Falk (1980) points out:

> some say that 'departmentalism erodes the unity of knowledge' and that, in ad-dition, departments actually prevent the growth of new areas of endeavour be-cause [of] 'established' faculty fear that new ideas could threaten their control over funds and students'.
>
> (Falk 1980: 79; quoted in Hughes, Ribbons and Thomas (eds) 1995)

Another potentially negative consequence is that, whilst the notion of the depart-ment being a microcosm of the school has positive consequences in developing a potentially creative autonomy in the context of common aims, it can also give rise to a separate group with its own agenda. The department can become inward-looking, setting an agenda based upon self-interest rather than one possessed of a whole-school perspective.

> In the secondary school … the department … provides the basis for political ac-tion and as such demands allegiance from its members. The rewards of cohe-sion are tangible and immediate in such fields as the timetable, teaching of desirable and undesirable pupils, accommodation, … and secure academic sta-tus. Cohesion, therefore, demands strategic compliance from actors on a whole range of issues that contain within them differences of importance when viewed from the perspective of the subject discipline. In other words, differen-tiation of the epistemic community is normally suppressed in favour of organi-sation and status gains.
>
> (Ball and Lacey 1980: 350–1)

A department which, for whatever reason, feels marginalized is more likely to look inward and set its own agenda than one that feels involved in the decision-making process. It is therefore important that the school has strongly defined aims and an ethos to which all departments have an opportunity to contribute.

> The contribution and attitude of the 'ordinary' member of staff need to be re-cognised, especially in a professional organisation. The teacher in the classroom is the embodiment of the school. A wise head therefore values and creates space for 'hearing the voice' of ordinary members of staff.
>
> (Handy and Aitken 1994: 312)

However, it is equally the responsibility of individuals and departments actively to pursue such opportunities. The essential aim of both management and individual teacher is to change:

> the focus of control from outside the individual to within; the objective being to make everybody accountable for their own performance, and to get them committed to attaining quality in a highly motivated fashion. The assumptions a manager must make in order to move in this direction are simply that people do not need to be coerced to perform well, [they] want to achieve, accomplish, influence activity, and challenge their abilities.
>
> (DTI 1992; quoted in Ribbins and Burridge 1992: 199)

Working towards departmental effectiveness

The most important characteristic of an effective department is that its effectiveness should be apparent. As Scheerens (1992: 79) says, 'effectiveness … cannot be inferred from intrinsic characteristics of processes'. In other words, a department's effective-ness cannot be presumed simply by the existence of particular structures, documenta-tion or teaching models, but only from clear evidence of effective teaching and learning. The presence of the former will make the achievement of the latter more likely, but it is wrong to assume that one *inevitably* proceeds from the other.

Departmental effectiveness can best be assured by the department constantly engaging in reflection and self-evaluation. A model for such self-evaluation is provided by Ribbins and Burridge (1992). They propose a six-stage model based on the four-stage development sequence suggested by School Development Plans project (DES 1989, 1991). The four original stages were:

1　audit (strengths and weaknesses are revised);
2　construction (development priorities are selected and turned into specific targets);
3　implementation (of the planned priorities and targets);
4　evaluation (the success of implementation is checked).

The following six-stage model then proceeds from this:

1　Audit, stock-taking – 'Where are we now?'
2　Objective setting – 'Where do we want to get to?'
3　Establishing priorities, target setting – 'What do we need to focus on?'
4　Identifying tasks, roles, responsibilities, milestones – 'How do we get there?'
5　Progress review, formative evaluation – 'How are we doing?'
6　Success checks, final review, summative evaluation – 'How have we done?'

However, as I suggested earlier, although the presence of such mechanisms may be a useful tool in raising standards, its existence will not in itself realize success. Such a system of departmental evaluation needs to be part of a whole-school strategy for effectiveness. Furthermore, in order to avoid perceptions of departmental isolation, all subject and pastoral areas need to be involved in the formulation of such strategies. As Mike Ash (1992) says:

> the key element in improving the quality of educational provision in schools is linking the review process itself with the improvement of the effectiveness of practice. This must place the teacher and the learner, the school and its community, at the centre of the process. Quality assurance must be owned by those involved in managing the school. The government, be it national or local, must ensure that there is true accountability and consequently avoid the risk of 'professional collusion'. This can only be done … by the establishment of a rigorous framework for review.
>
> (Ash 1992: 197)

The role of the head of department

As long ago as 1971, Michael Marland (Headmaster of North Westminster Community School) wrote that the success of a school depended to a great degree on the effectiveness of heads of departments.

The role of the head of department in the 1960s is described by Bailey (1973: 53) as that of proselytizer for their subject specialism within the school. Their main responsibilities include:

- keeping abreast of all developments in the subject and defining the contribution that their subject makes to the education of the child;
- representing the subject in various forums;
- planning teaching and resourcing the subject;
- evaluating pupils' progress and their own performance 'partly in an intuitive way but also by reference to pupils' examination results'.

Bailey goes on to describe four further functions of the head of department in the large comprehensive school which, by the early 1970s, had added a management perspective to the role which had not previously applied:

1   Staff control – [to] deploy and manage assistant staff, evaluate their performance and take steps to improve their professional competence … to participate in the recruitment of new assistants;
2   Pupil control – to take some part … in decisions about the deployment and management of … pupils;
3   Resources control – to ensure that all … courses are properly resourced … and also that resources … are used efficiently;

4   Communications – in order to do these things, [to] set up an adequate communications procedure within [the] department, and between [the] department and the rest of the school.

(Bailey 1973: 53)

These functions, described by Bailey in 1973, although reinterpreted and made more explicit by the requirements of the National Curriculum and Ofsted, have essentially held true. The increased managerial perspective has, by definition, resulted in an increased workload for heads of departments but has brought with it greater opportunities for influencing events. The head of department is no longer simply an extension of the head in the classroom (Richardson 1973) but is to a great degree an autonomous professional, charged with making decisions that affect the education of large numbers of children and the professional well-being of the staff in the department.

Curricular and extracurricular activities: preserving the balance

Once immersed in the world of extra curricular music making, it can be difficult for music teachers to make sense of their role within school. They realize, perhaps with a sense of guilt, that they ought to meet the needs of all young people. However, they get praise, kudos and sometimes promotion from working with a small group of selected students. What is more this is a responsive and motivated group.

(Bray 2000: 5)

In addition to the responsibilities already outlined, the music department also has an important duty to the 'extracurricular' life of the school. This frequently requires the head of department to co-ordinate and organize multifarious musical activities involving many children. These activities can greatly enrich both the life of the school and the musical education of those involved in the activities. However, these duties can sometimes acquire an importance to rival or even overshadow the curriculum role of the department, representing real dangers for the quality of music education of the majority of children.

The consequence of such a situation is that the department becomes *isolated* from the central function of the school (that is, teaching and learning), *uninvolved* in the decision-making process that inputs into this, and that music is thus *marginalized* as a curriculum subject. Moreover, as HMI points out in the Ofsted report: 'some teachers have a combined curricular and extracurricular load which is unacceptably high, and are too busy with music to take on the pastoral or administrative responsibilities which might secure promotion in their school or elsewhere' (Ofsted 1995, par. 51).

The problem lies to some extent in the implications inherent in the frequently used title of Director of Music. Such a title undoubtedly has a seductive appeal. It sets the head of music apart from 'ordinary' heads of department and implies a special status within the school. However, it can also be something of a poisoned chalice, having consequences which are dangerously anti-educational. It suggests a

function akin to that of the organist and choirmaster of a cathedral or collegiate institution, and implies a style of didactic teaching that may be effective in producing
well-drilled performances from children with developed musical skills, but involves
them in little personal creative activity.

Here, music teaching and learning are not perceived as having inherent value but
rather valued only to the extent that they bring esteem to the school through concerts
and productions. Any educational value is derived as an incidental consequence of
the activity rather than as its *raison d'être*. Thus the end project assumes greater importance than the actual *process* wherein lies the educational experience. Furthermore,
the activity is restricted to those taking part – the 'musically able' – and is therefore at
odds with an inclusive ideal of music education: that is, the involvement of *all* children in the composing, performing, listening to and appraising of music from a wide
range of styles and cultures. It must be remembered that, however enriching for the
life of the school extracurricular music may be, it will 'touch only a minority of
pupils, and encompass achievement of a range narrower than the National Curriculum' (Ofsted 1995). A vibrant, relevant and effective extracurricular musical life
should celebrate and extend the achievements of the classroom as well as featuring
the choirs, orchestras, rock groups and steel bands developed outside of the formal
curriculum.

Heads of music who collaborate with a view of the role of the music teacher as
primarily a co-ordinator of extracurricular activities tend to do so from one of three
perspectives:

1   an attempt to compensate for lack of classroom teaching success by a com-
     mitment to extracurricular activities (HMI 1983: 22);
2   a narrow vision of the role of music in children's education;
3   a failure to perceive music as being part of the whole curriculum, and thus
     susceptible to those wider educational issues which affect all subjects.

The last two viewpoints are to a degree connected, and proceed from a view of the
function of music in schools that is embodied in the following quote from Peter
Fletcher: 'I am convinced that music is too powerful a subject to compromise its
individuality to education theory' (Fletcher 1987: v). Neryl Jeanneret, in whose
article this is quoted, criticizes such an attitude as supporting:

> the notion that music is an elitist area reserved for the cognoscenti. If music
> doesn't compromise its individuality to educational theory, it will continue to
> struggle for acceptance and recognition in the world of education. Music may
> well be unique in the curriculum, but its acceptance as such in the broader area
> of education will never come from nineteenth century Romantic notions that
> music is somehow removed from educational theory and research ... the recog-
> nition of music's individuality has to come from the marriage of solidly based
> philosophies of music, music education and learning theory, and general edu-
> cation theory in *the forum of the broader education audience.*
>
> (Jeanneret 1993: 24; my emphasis)

In an address given to a DES conference of arts teachers in Bournemouth, John Holden made the point that:

> Five hundred Headmasters and Headmistresses trained in Arts, Drama, Dance and Music as their main interest would make more difference in ten years [to the Arts] than all the White and Green Papers.
> (Holden 1977, quoted in Calouste Gulbenkian Foundation 1982: par. 123)

However, this is unlikely to happen until arts educators embrace whole-school and whole-education issues and involve themselves fully in the life of the school. Therefore, it is of vital importance that the unique contribution that the music department makes to the aims and ethos of the school occurs in the context of whole-school aims and objectives and is focused upon the quality of teaching and learning. Only by doing so will the uniqueness of the music department's contribution to the curriculum be recognized, and thereby the opportunity gained to influence issues that materially affect it.

> The profession of teaching demands not only enthusiasm and expertise within one's subject but also a deep commitment to the entire process of education … It is this, and the consequent philosophy, which will determine what we do and will sustain the curriculum teaching which is at the core of our responsibility. Without that conviction there are dangers for any teacher, but the music teacher is particularly vulnerable. For if the music teacher is not completely convinced about his [or her] role in general education, it is all too easy for him to divert his main energies to the extracurricular activities. It is then that the class music work either becomes a chore to be got through, or a nightmare of wondering how to maintain pupils' interests. Before long the law of diminishing returns begins to operate and music as a 'curriculum' subject becomes geared more and more towards the minority 'examination' group.
> (Paynter 1982: 90)

None of this is designed to discourage or denigrate the role of extracurricular music in schools. Indeed, its contribution to the ethos of the school and the delivery of a comprehensive music education is invaluable. It is just that, as Charles Plummeridge says:

> there is a serious danger of the arts becoming showpieces in a competitive education system increasingly subject to market forces. Throughout history, music and the arts have been used for extrinsic ends and this has frequently led to their being distorted and devalued. If this is allowed to happen in schools, arts educators will feel a loss of integrity. There is a possibility of a strong reaction against extracurricular activities if teachers and pupils believe that arts events are appreciated simply for their commercial usefulness. This would be extremely regrettable since there are good educational reasons why these activities should be supported and encouraged.
> (Plummeridge 1991: 115)

So why do we teach music in school?

The place of music in the curriculum is assured at least until the end of Key Stage 3 by its presence as a National Curriculum foundation subject. However, a Royal Society of Arts report on the arts in schools (RSA 1995) discovered that a substantial number of schools were 'allocating insufficient or ineffective space on the timetable'. Therefore, it is imperative that music departments are able to promote the place of music as a curriculum subject in schools. The only way that this can be done is by defining the unique contribution that music makes to the individual child's education. However, as John Paynter says, one of the problems of providing a rationale for music education lies in the nature of music itself: 'to the average person it is not generally clear what it does, beyond producing a (possibly) pleasurable effect' (Paynter 1982: 24)

When pressed to define why music is a 'good thing', many will suggest that it is a means of expressing individual emotions, some will point to the way it helps the development of social skills, while others will refer to the moral, Platonic characteristics of music:

> Education in music is most sovereign, because more than anything else rhythm and harmony find their way to the inmost soul and take strongest hold upon it, bringing with them and imparting grace, if one is rightly trained.
>
> (Plato; quoted in Watson 1991: 103)

These are undoubtedly important characteristics of music. However, they are not *specific* to music and therefore do not, in themselves, provide a rationale for the existence of music in the curriculum. The only justification for curriculum music is in terms of the unique contribution that it can make to the whole education of the child. A justification for music based on anything *other* than this will inevitably leave curricular music prone to marginalization, with its influence more and more restricted to the contribution it makes to the extracurricular life of the school, 'coming into prominence only once a year as part of the Speech Day or Founders Day' (Paynter 1982: 23).

Musical intelligence

Key to any argument in support of the place of music in the curriculum is an understanding of 'musical intelligence' as a discrete intelligence which contributes something unique to the children's holistic education. Frequently, 'intelligence' is assessed by reference to only a small part of what is taught: usually a form of the linguistic and mathematical/scientific. Thus an 'intelligent person' is defined as being one who is successful in these areas alone. In *Frames of Mind* (1983), Howard Gardner argues that intelligence *singular* is essentially a misnomer, and that we should begin to consider the concept of intelligences *plural*: a theory of multiple intelligences. Gardner (1994) defines seven different types of intelligence:

1   logical (mathematical);
2   linguistic;

3   spatial;
4   bodily-kinaesthetic;
5   musical;
6   interpersonal (the ability to notice and make distinctions between other individuals);
7   intrapersonal (access to one's own life feelings).

Gardner goes on to say that formal education only fully exploits the first two of these intelligences, labelling as failures those that don't succeed in their terms. The arts educationist Ken Robinson illustrates the illogicality of a singular (or dual) perception of the nature of intelligence in telling how, when remarking upon the beauty of a sculpture that adorned the entrance foyer of a school he was visiting, he was told by the headteacher that it had been created by 'one of our less able pupils' (Robinson 1995).

Gardner illustrates a similar point in his book *Creating Minds* (1993), a study of creativity through the lives of seven twentieth-century 'greats': Freud, Einstein, Picasso, Stravinsky, Eliot, Graham and Ghandi. He shows how all had great intellectual strengths in at least one intelligence but also all, with the exception of Stravinsky, had significant weakness in others.

	Strength	Weakness
Freud	linguistic, personal	spatial, musical
Einstein	logical-spatial	personal
Picasso	spatial, personal, bodily	scholastic
Stravinsky	musical, other artistic	
Eliot	linguistic, scholastic	musical, bodily
Graham	bodily, linguistic	logical-mathematical
Ghandi	personal, linguistic	artistic

Source: Gardner (1993) p. 363

The necessity of redefining what we mean by intelligence has a social as well as an educational imperative. Robinson (1995) has pointed out how our present system of defining intelligence reflects the model of education predicated in the 1944 Education Act. On the basis of an examination that focused exclusively on mathematical intelligence and linguistic intelligence, children were allocated places in grammar, technical or secondary modern schools. Although such selection took place ostensibly to provide an education which most closely accorded with a child's particular aptitudes, in fact the segregation of children was more a reflection of the needs of society of the time: the sponsored 20 per cent who were selected for grammar schools matching the numbers society needed for the 'professional classes' and the remaining 80 per cent fulfilling society's requirements for manual and blue-collar workers. Whereas the tripartite system of schooling has to a great extent ceased to exist, the *philosophy* upon which it was based still governs our attitudes towards the measurement of success in education. However, a recent European Commission report predicted that the requirement for the new millennium will be a 90 per cent graduate work force. This has implications for our education system and the way in which we define intelligence. It is obvious that if we are to achieve such a percentage, then it will be necessary to fully develop all intelligences, not simply the two hitherto deemed as relevant, and accord each intelligence parity of status.

Music learning and learning in other subject domains

Over the last few years there have been a number of conflicting research reports concerning the beneficial effects of music learning on, particularly, children's literacy and numeracy skills. Indeed, Gardner argues that not only is there a mode of intelligence specific to music but musical intelligence can also impact on other intelligences. Problems of learning in one intelligence can be solved by exemplification through another.

If learning in other subject domains results from the development of children's musical ability, then this is of course an added bonus. However, music teachers need to beware of making such incidental benefits (should they exist) a central plank of their rationale for music in the curriculum. In drawing parallels between music learning and learning in other subjects, we need to be careful not to overstate the case and consequently lose sight of the unique contribution music makes to the holistic education of the child, which is what justifies its place in the curriculum.

Connections have been drawn many times between music learning and mathematical learning: 'Mathematics is music for the mind. Music is mathematics for the soul' (Leibniz).

However, such connections have been predicated upon examples of composers' interest in numerology as a symbolic and/or structural device (for example the thirteen repetitions of the ground bass in the Crucifixus of Bach's *Mass in B Minor*), rather than evidence of there being similar cognitive processes at work.

Gardner argues, however, that the links between the two disciplines are tenuous:

> the task in which musicians are engaged differs fundamentally from that which preoccupies the pure mathematician … from the mathematics point of view music is just another pattern, [but for] the musician, however, these patterned elements … have expressive power and effects … . The formal patterns that are a mathematician's *raison d'être* are for musicians a helpful, but not essential, ingredient for the expressive purposes to which their own capacities are regularly marshalled.
>
> (Gardner 1983: 126–7)

There are, however, some parallels between music and language. Gardner describes how linguistic and musical intelligences can operate in two ways:

1   through the 'bottom-up' approach, showing how people 'process the building blocks of music: single tones, elementary rhythmic patterns' (Gardner 1983: 106) in ways similar to how they process the building blocks of language: words, phrases, sentences and so on;

2   by studying 'top-down' processes equally applicable to the study of language processes: 'where one presents to subjects musical pieces or, at least, healthy musical segments [examining] reactions to more global properties of music (does it get faster or slower, louder or softer?) … and metaphoric characterisations (is it airy or light, triumphant or tragic, crowded or sparse?).

(Gardner 1983: 107)

However, as with the mathematical correlation, Gardner warns that we should take care not to draw too close a parallel between music and language. He points out that studies 'have demonstrated beyond reasonable doubt that the processes and mechanisms subserving human music and language are distinctive from one another' (Gardner 1983: 117). Also, 'the whole semantic aspect of language is radically underdeveloped in music; and the notion of strict rules of 'grammaticality' is … extraneous in music, where violations are often prized' (Gardner 1983: 125).

He concludes that:

one of the great pleasures in any intellectual realm inheres in an exploration of its relationship to other spheres of intelligence. As an aesthetic form, music lends itself especially well to playful exploration with other modes of intelligence and symbolization, particularly in the hands (or ears) of highly creative individuals. Yet, according to my own analysis, the core operations of music do not bear intimate connections to the core operations in other areas; and therefore, music deserves to be considered as an autonomous intellectual realm.

(Gardner 1983: 126)

In *Music in the Secondary School Curriculum* (1982), Paynter makes a similar point and, in doing so, clearly articualtes the unique role of music in the education of the 'whole' person:

Music, unlike words, is not tied to precise meanings. It is therefore capable of almost limitless interpretation and re-interpretation. Thus it is ideally suited as a medium through which young people can develop skills of judgement and expression. This is not the same thing as self-expression, which is by and large an indulgent and inward-looking process, but rather an understanding of ways in which structure develops the inherent expressiveness of musical ideas in many different styles, creating coherent forms to reveal unexpected relationships of pitches, rhythms and timbres. Such understanding comes principally through first-hand experience of working in the medium of sound. And it is that – a symbolic seeking after order and integration – which is educative.

(Paynter 1983: 91–2)

References

Ash, M. (1992) 'In the pursuit of quality' in H. Tomlinson (ed.) *The Search for Standards,* Harlow: Longman.

Bailey, P. (1973) 'The functions of heads of departments in comprehensive schools', *Journal of Education Administration and History,* 5(10): 53.

Ball, S. and Lacey, C. (1980) 'Subject disciplines as the object of group activity: a measured critique of subject sub-cultures' in P. Woods (ed.) *Teacher Strategies*, London: Croom Helm.

Bray, D. (2000) *Teaching Music in the Secondary School*, Oxford: Heinemann.

Calouste Gulbenkian Foundation (1982) *The Arts in Schools*, London: Calouste Gulbenkian Foundation.

Department for Education and Science (DES) (1989) *Planning for School Development*, London: DES.

—— (1991) *Developing Planning*, London: DES.

Department for Trade and Industry (DTI) (1992) *Total Quality Management*, London: DTI.

Falk, G. (1980) 'The academic department and role conflict', *Improving College and University Teaching*, 27(2): 78–9.

Fitz-Gibbon, C. T. (1992) 'School effects at A level: genesis of an information system' in D. Reynolds, and P. Cuttance (eds) *School Effectiveness: Research, Policy and Practice*, London: Cassell.

Fletcher, P. (1987) *Education and Music*, Oxford: Oxford University Press.

Gardner, H. (1983) *Frames of Mind*, London: Heinemann.

—— (1993) *Creating Minds*, New York: Basic Books.

—— (1994) 'The theory of multiple intelligences' in R. Moon and A. Shelton Mayes (eds) *Teaching and Learning in the Secondary School*, London: Routledge.

Handy, C. and Aitken, R. (1994) 'The organisation of the secondary school' in R. Moon and A. Shelton Mayes (eds) *Teaching and Learning in the Secondary School*, London: Routledge.

HMI (1983) *Education Observed*, London: HMSO.

—— (1985) *Music from 5–16*, London: HMSO.

—— (1994) *Music at Key Stages 1, 2 and 3*, London: HMSO.

HMI (Wales) (1984) *Departmental Organisation in Secondary Schools*, Welsh Office: HMSO.

Hughes, M., Ribbins, P. and Thomas, H. (eds) (1985) *Managing Education: the System and the Institution*, Eastbourne: Holt, Rinehart & Winston.

Jeanneret, N. (1993) 'The preparation of secondary music teachers', *British Journal of Music Education*, 10, 1.

Marland, M. (1971) *Head of Department*, London: Heinemann.

National Foundation for Arts Education (NFAE) (1994) *The Arts 11–19: a Handbook for Teachers*, Oxford: NFAE.

Ofsted (1995) *Music: a Review of Inspection Findings 1993–4*, London: HMSO.

Paynter, J. (1982) *Music in the Secondary School Curriculum*, Cambridge: Cambridge University Press.

Plato, *The Republic* in *Chambers Music Quotations*, compiled by D. Watson (1991), Edinburgh: Chambers.

Plummeridge, C. (1991) *Music Education in Theory and Practice*, London: Falmer Press.

Ribbins, P. (1985) 'The role of the middle manager in the secondary school' in M. Hughes, P. Ribbins and H. Thomas (eds) *Managing Education: the System and the Institution*, Eastbourne: Holt, Rinehart & Winston.

Ribbins, P. and Burridge, E. (1992) 'Improving schools: an approach to quality in Birmingham' in H. Tomlinson (ed.) *The Search for Standards*, Harlow: Longman.

Richardson, E. (1973) *The Teacher, the School, and the Task of Management,* London: Heinemann.

Robinson, K. (1995) *Culture, Commerce and the Curriculum* (NFAE Conference).

Royal Society of Arts (RSA) (1995) *Guaranteeing an Entitlement to the Arts in Schools,* London: RSA.

Scheerens, J. (1992) *Effective Schooling: Research Theory and Practice,* London: Cassell.

4 Meeting special needs in Music class

Mary S. Adamek

The following scenarios are based on actual classroom experiences, and they are typical of events taking place in schools in recent years as educators are asked to open their classrooms to students with special needs:

Scenario No. 1: Ms Kelly, the school's music teacher, finds a note in her box on Monday morning. Three students from Mr Anderson's special education class will be coming to music today with the second-grade class. She knows that the students in Mr Anderson's class have severe disabilities, but she is unaware of their specific needs. Ms Kelly has an early rehearsal before the first class comes to music, so she does not have time to gather any information about these new students before they arrive.

Scenario No. 2: Sarah is a fourth-grade student who has an identified behavior disorder. She is fully integrated in the regular education class throughout the school day; however, she is frequently pulled out of class for special services. Sarah is difficult to deal with in music because she is aggressive toward others, damages instruments, and does not work well with the other students in the class. She has a one-on-one assistant with her most of the day, except during music, art, and physical education.

Scenario No. 3: The fifth-grade students at Henry Elementary are excited because they are finally old enough to participate in the band program. Joey, who has autism, wants to play the drums. The band director has never worked with a child with autism and is nervous about having him in the band program.

Principles for successful integration

In the USA before 1975, most students with disabilities were educated primarily in separate schools or classrooms.[1] Now, fully inclusive schools are structured under guidelines that provide the least restrictive environment for all students. Music educators have been greatly impacted by this shift as their students' abilities, disabilities and special needs increase. Some music educators feel unprepared to provide effective music instruction to such a broad range of students, leaving the teachers feeling frustrated, fearful, powerless, and sometimes angry.

Schools with successful integration efforts usually operate within a set of philosophical principles or beliefs relating to the education of students with disabilities. *Partial participation, normalization, interdependence* and *individuality* are important principles to consider when planning for integrated music experiences.[2] *Partial participation* means that the student can benefit from participating in some aspects of an activity, even if the student's disability prevents him or her from full participation. This principle opens up many activities to students with disabilities. However, teachers must strive to provide such students with full and enriching opportunities even when total participation is not possible. *Normalization* refers to the idea that children with disabilities should have experiences and opportunities that are as close as possible to those of students without disabilities. This does not mean that teachers should try to make these students 'normal' but, rather, should try to give them the best opportunities to learn and grow as members of the community. *Interdependence* refers to the value gained by each student through communicating, developing relationships, and cooperating with others in the classroom and community. *Individuality* refers to appreciating each student as a person with specific needs and skills upon which to base the best possible educational strategies. All these principles can manifest themselves in various ways throughout the school day. It is important to use them as a foundation upon which to develop the most effective interventions.

Communicating with teachers

The first step in working effectively with students who have special needs is to find out as much information as one can about individual students. Communication is essential. In large school districts that serve many students with special needs, music teachers may not be able to attend Individualized Education Plan (IEP) meetings for each child or even read each child's complete IEP. However, knowing key information from the IEP is fundamental to the development of effective instruction for these students.

Specific information from the IEP can be accessed quickly through a format developed to obtain IEP objectives and other pertinent student information. While music educators' primary focus is to teach and develop music skills, most would agree that non-music skill areas, such as cooperation, independence, classroom behavior and respect, can also be developed through music experiences. Knowing and understanding the non-music objectives upon which a student is working can help a teacher develop strategies for including the student in meaningful ways. In addition to the IEP objectives, one must also keep in mind each child's positive attributes in order to build on that child's skills and abilities.

A Student Information at a Glance form (see Table 4.1) can provide an overview of the student to aid in instructional development. Typical information includes:

1   strengths of the student, along with special skills and talents;
2   weaknesses or limitations of the student;
3   IEP objectives that the student is working on throughout the day;
4   strategies that are useful when working with this student.

These forms can be filled out by the classroom teacher, parent, and in some cases, the students themselves. Music educators can be pro-active in securing information about current or potential students by creating a form such as this and then asking the appropriate people to provide the information. This type of format provides a vehicle to develop common expectations for everyone who is involved with the student. Obtaining information before the student arrives in the class, or soon after, will help bridge the information gap and provide structure for planning effective instructional interventions.

Table 4.1 Student Information at a Glance form

Strengths, skills, and talents	Weaknesses and limitations
• participates actively in class • accepts leadership • shows good verbal skills • loves listening to music • reacts energetically • offers creative ideas in class	• has difficulty getting along with others • is easily frustrated • shows difficulty following complex directions • has difficulty sitting still for more than 5 minutes (hyperactive) • reads with limited ability
IEP objectives	**Strategies for success**
• follows teacher's directions • works with a peer during activities • asks for help when frustrated • focuses attention on task at hand • identifies letters and words	• uses trusted peer friend to help with tasks • teacher breaks down directions into small steps • teacher offers leadership opportunities as reinforcement • earns tokens in class for finishing work and getting along with others

Student: Sarah (from Scenario #2); Grade: 4th, Ms Jullian; Date: 1/99

Adapting for specific needs

The teacher who has information about student skills, IEP objectives, and strategies for effective instruction is now ready to develop adaptations that promote learning and success. There are many methods that teachers can use to adapt educational materials to suit the level of the student.[3] Music educators must be creative in using these techniques and applying them, wherever possible, to music materials already being used in the music class. The following methods of adaptation can be utilized in a variety of ways to meet specific objectives for the student.

Participation

Adapt the extent to which the student is involved in the task, based on the child's abilities. Keep in mind that partial participation must also be meaningful participation that is valued, respected and performed by peers. Avoid experiences that require a high level of assistance from adults or peers, or experiences in which the child with disabilities is the only student performing the task.[4]

A child with a physical disability who is unable to participate meaningfully in a circle dance could be part of a percussion section that provides rhythmic accompaniment for the dance. Other students would also be percussionists, a highly valued musical activity. The rhythmic accompaniment adds to the musical experience of the entire class.

Difficulty level

Adapt the skill level needed to perform the music task. This can be accomplished with multi-layered activities that offer a variety of possible responses. A student can participate as part of the whole music-making experience, yet have a very small, simple part to play.

> The teacher writes a part for a percussion student who is autistic and is unable to read complex rhythms. The original band part has crotchets, quavers and semi-quavers. The adapted part is all minims written using computer software so that it looks as professional as the original music.

Level of support

Increase the amount of personal assistance provided to a specific learner to promote success. Assign peer buddies, teaching assistants or cross-age tutors to assist the student in music class. Be aware of the level of independence that can be achieved by the student and encourage independence at the highest level. Do not allow helpers to 'do it all' for the student, but encourage them to offer assistance and encouragement when needed.

> Suzie, a child with behavior problems, always sits next to Marcia in music class. Marcia is an excellent role model for music behaviors, as well as appropriate classroom behaviors. Marcia helps Suzie find pages in the book, reminds her to put her instrument down when directed by the teacher, and gives her a 'thumbs up' sign when she is following directions. This close contact with a peer eliminates the need for constant teacher intervention or a high level of attention for inappropriate behavior.

Input

Adapt the ways in which instruction is delivered to students. Use a variety of visual aids, use concrete examples in your teaching, provide hands-on learning activities, and place students in cooperative learning situations. Children learn in various ways, some through visual input, some through auditory means, and others learn best through tactile or movement-based experiences. All children, not just children with special needs, assimilate information through different learning styles. By altering your teaching style to accommodate many types of learning styles, you will enhance the experience for all of your students.

> Josh has a severe hearing loss. In addition to using his assistive hearing device, he lip-reads to understand what the teacher is saying. Josh's music teacher uses visual aids to introduce music concepts, movement to help integrate the concepts, and rhythmic accompaniments to allow Josh an opportunity to feel the vibrations of the music. She also is aware of the need

to face the class when speaking, to speak slowly and clearly, and to keep her hands away from her mouth.

Output

Adapt how the student can respond to instruction by varying the types of responses expected. Instead of answering questions in writing, a student might give a verbal response or use a communication book/board to give a response. Other students might demonstrate their knowledge or understanding of a concept through hands-on experiences.

Paul has cerebral palsy. He is non-verbal and is unable to write legibly; however, he is at the same cognitive level as his fourth-grade classmates. He uses a communication board on his wheelchair to make requests and respond to questions. The music educator collaborated with the speech and language therapist to add music-related words to his communication system. Now he is able to request specific instruments independently and to answer questions related to musical concepts on his own.

Alternative goals

Adapt the goals or outcome expectations for the student, while using the same materials for all students. Success for one student might be playing on the beat, while success for other students might be to master a more difficult syncopated rhythm. It is important that the teacher identify these adapted expectations in a respectful way in order to avoid embarrassing the student in any way.

Kyle is in the sixth grade but has the cognitive abilities of a first-grade student. On a written test of musical terms, the teacher circles three questions that she expects Kyle to answer, while the rest of the class is expected to answer all thirty questions on the test. In this example, Kyle is doing the same test as the rest of the class, but the expectations for him are different.

Alternative materials

Due to physical or other limitations of a student, the music educator might need to use adapted instruments in the music class. Some instrument manufacturers have begun to develop lines of adaptive instruments to meet the needs of students with physical limitations. Wheelchair clips for paddle drums, instrument mounts that attach to a table or tray, and Velcro straps on mallets and rhythm instruments are a few of the recent innovations. With a little ingenuity, appropriate materials, and possibly the help of an industrial arts teacher, music teachers can create their own inexpensive adaptations. Always provide students with the best quality instruments, even when adapting instruments. Avoid using kitchen utensils as adapted instruments (i.e. using a spatula as an adapted Autoharp pick) unless the entire class is using kitchen utensils as sound sources or percussion instruments. In addition, keep in mind the need for utilizing age-appropriate instruments and materials. A student with disabilities should be playing the same type of instruments as the other students in the class. Even though the student can play the jingle bell easily, it might not be the best choice if the other students are too old to be playing that particular instrument. Whenever possible, make careful instrument choices so that adaptations do not need to be made. For instance, when the rest of the class is playing African percussion instruments, you might offer a light, easy-to-play African basket shaker to a child with limited strength or range of motion.

> Don has a physical disability that limits his range of motion and ability to play a variety of instruments. His teacher has been purchasing and creating adapted instruments for Don to allow him the highest level of independence in his music class. He enjoys playing the paddle drum that clips on to his wheelchair. He also loves to play the bass bar in Orff arrangements because it is large, easy to hit with his built-up mallet, and adds to the musical experience for the entire class.

Today, more than ever before, schools are structured to educate a wide variety of students, each having their own strengths and weaknesses, abilities and disabilities, and unique gifts and needs. Teachers have a right and a responsibility to know as much as possible about the special needs of the students in their classes. This process takes time and patience, but teachers can start by gathering information on one or two students, talking with other teachers to find out what strategies they use with specific students, and then developing adaptations to promote richer and more successful music experiences for all students.

Notes

1   Adamek, Mary S. 'In the Beginning: A Review of Early Special Education Services and Legislative/Regulatory Activity Affecting the Teaching and Placement of Special Learners' in *Models of Music Therapy Interventions in School Settings: From Institution to Inclusion,* ed. B. Wilson (Silver Spring, MD: American Music Therapy Association, 1996), 3–12.

2   Beninghof, A. *Ideas for Inclusion: The Classroom Teacher's Guide to Integrating Students with Severe Disabilities* (Longmont, CO: Sopris West, 1996).

3   Deschenes, C., Ebeling, D. and Sprague, J. *Adapting Curriculum and Instruction in Inclusive Classrooms: A Teacher's Desk Reference* (Bloomington, IN: Center for School and Community Integration – Institute for the Study of Developmental Disabilities, 1994).

4   Judith Jellisson, 'Principles for the Inclusive Music Classroom: Guidelines for Developing, Selecting, Adapting, Implementing, and Evaluating Lessons and Activities' (paper presented at the 12th National Symposium on Research in Music Behavior, Minneapolis, MN, 1997).

5 Gender identity, musical experience and schooling

Lucy Green

Introduction

This chapter represents a résumé of some of the main arguments in the author's book, *Music, Gender, Education*. Inevitably, this involves a broad overview and a level of generalization concerning large-scale norms and trends in musical practices, which are treated in more detail in the book itself, along with many references to further readings.

Two brief working definitions

Musical meaning

I wish to sketch a theoretical distinction between two virtual aspects of musical meaning. The first operates at the level of musical materials, the syntactical organization of which gives rise to the listener's sense of whole and part, opening and close, repetition, difference, and all other pertinent functional relationships. I call this *inherent meaning*, not to indicate that there is anything essential or ahistorical about it, but rather that both the materials which form the signifying part of the process of identifying structures, and those which are being signified as structures in some way, are made up of musical materials; the meanings are inherent, then, in the sense that both the sign and that which it signifies are a material part of the music itself. Listeners' responses to and understanding of inherent meanings are dependent on the listeners' competence in relation to the style of the music. A piece of music whose materials are highly meaningful or very rewarding to one person might be relatively meaningless or lacking in interest to another.

This aspect of musical meaning is only partial, and can never exist on its own. We have become accustomed to the idea that the social or cultural images of performers make an important contribution to their commercial survival. But the manipulation of performers' images is not a mere marketing strategy, for clothes, hair-styles or posturing on the sleeves of recordings are all details of a broader, necessary aspect of any music: its mediation as a cultural artefact within a social and historical context. This context is not merely an extra-musical appendage, but forms an instrinsic part of the music's meaning during the listening experience. Without some understanding of the fact that music is a social construction, we would ultimately be unable to recognize any particular collection of sounds as music at all. When we listen to music, we cannot separate our experience of its inherent meanings entirely from a greater or lesser awareness of the social context in which it is produced or received. I will therefore suggest a second category of musical meaning, distinct from the first, and called *delineated meaning*. By this expression I wish to convey the idea that music metaphorically sketches, or delineates, a plethora of contextualizing factors. As with inherent meaning, listeners construct the delineated meanings of music according to their individual identity in relation to the music's style. Delineated meanings are at some levels, conventionally accepted, and, at others, personal.

Whenever we hear music, we are affected to some extent by both types of meaning, and both must always be present in all musical experience. But each type of meaning operates very differently, each acting in various ways upon the other, to affect our total musical experience, our musical practices and the construction of our discourses on music. It is through the mutual interaction of the different aspects of musical meaning that we learn, amongst other things, our gendered relationships with music.

Sex, gender and sexuality

In current usage in the English language, the term 'sex' normally refers to the biological characteristics of men and women, whilst 'gender' refers to culturally-acquired characteristics and practices that tend to be associated with masculinity and femininity. For example, reproductive organs are a function of 'sex'; wearing skirts in most western countries is a function of 'gender'. It is important to recognize that there is no necessary connection between sex and gender: a 'feminine' man or a 'masculine' woman are readily conceived. However, through history, a conceptual congruence of femininity with women and of masculinity with men has developed, such that men and women are to a large extent expected to behave in ways that correspond with masculinity and femininity respectively. Not only that, but certain qualities and attributes have come to be accepted as characterizing features of masculinity and femininity. In a nutshell, and polarized into extremes, masculinity is understood to characterize a person who is active, productive, rational, inventive, experimental, scientific, technological, cerebral and creative; femininity suggests one who is passive, reproductive, caring, subject to the body, emotional and diligent. The term 'sexuality', as distinct from 'sex' and 'gender', denotes sexual practices and sexual orientations such as homosexuality, heterosexuality and others.

Gendered musical practices and meanings

I have suggested that the social context of music's production or reception becomes a part of its delineated meanings. I now want to suggest that, amongst other contextualizing factors, the gender of a performer or composer becomes a part of their music's delineations. I will discuss this notion with reference to women musicians. (For historical work on women's roles in music, I would recommend Bowers and Tick 1986.)

Affirming femininity: women singing

The female singer in a public arena performs on an instrument which *is* her body, without recourse to the manipulation of any palpable physical object in the world. In so doing, she enacts a scenario which affirms an enduring understanding of femininity as both in tune with, and subject to, the natural givens of her body, whilst at the same time being alienated from, and needless of, technology. In this highlighting of the body away from technology, vocal performance is akin to a type of display, and indeed, the singing woman has been associated in many cultures with sexual temptation or sexual availability. But the woman singer is not only linked with sexuality, for in her private capacity she conjures up an inversion of this public image, symbolizing instead the idealized mother singing to her baby. Engaged in a type of bodily display, and pivoted upon the contradiction between whore and madonna, the woman singer re-enacts some of the fundamental defining characteristics of femininity.

When we listen to a woman sing, we do not just listen to the inherent meanings of her music, but we are also aware of her position with relation to these defining characteristics of femininity. Her femininity becomes an affirmative part of the music's delineations. The affirmation of femininity and its delineation in women's vocal music is, I would suggest, one of the reasons why, throughout the history of music, women have been more abundant and successful in singing than in any other single musical role.

From affirmation to interruption of femininity: women playing instruments

The woman instrumentalist is on display, and she does to that extent participate in the same processes as the woman singer. But in certain respects, her display takes on rather different connotations. For example, in an early nineteenth-century domestic setting, a woman pianist would have given rise to delineations that were just as affirmative as those of a woman singer; but on a public stage of the same era, a female trumpeter in the ranks of an otherwise entirely male orchestra would have incurred radically different display delineations, and in fact, was quite unheard of. Why is it that, like singing, some instruments have been seen as acceptable or even desirable feminine accomplishments; whereas unlike singing, certain other instruments have at various times been shunned by women, frowned upon or even prohibited? I will approach this question, for short, through a comparison of extremes, suggesting some fundamental, qualitative differences between the delineations of women's singing practices, and those of their instrumental practices.

In the case of instrumental performance, particularly in a public arena, the presence and manipulation of the instrument to some extent *interrupts* the appearance of the woman's natural in-tuneness with and susceptibility to her body. The more unwieldy and loud the instrument, the more technologically demanding for the performer, and the more public the performance scenario, then the more problematic is the construction of a 'safe', affirmatively feminine display. The effects of this problematic relationship between femininity and instrumental performance are decipherable throughout the history of women's musical practices, which reveal that women have mostly played plucked string and keyboard instruments, often to accompany the voice, always in demure postures, to begin with in private, domestic surroundings, only in the last couple of hundred years on public stages, and even then, relatively sparingly. Contrastingly, unwieldiness, high volume or technological complexity in public venues have tended to characterize the instruments and the performance situations from which women have been most vehemently discouraged.

Threatening femininity: women composing

Femininity also enters delineated meaning through the composer. I am using the word 'composition' to include improvisation, notated and unnotated methods of recording, and solo or group work. Clearly there is no display of the composer's body, but composition requires a level of knowledge and control over technique, distinct from the physical motor-control of performance; and through this type of control, mind features in any composition-related delineations. As we listen to music, one of the elements of which we are more or less aware, an element that we are prone to marvel at in some musical experiences is the mind behind the music. 'How *could* Beethoven have *conceived* of such a thing?' the classical admirer is liable to say; or 'Just how far was Hendrix blown out of his mind during that solo?', the rock fan is wont to wonder. In such cases, whilst we listen, it is not just the inherent meanings that occupy our attention, but the idea of Beethoven's or Hendrix's mind.

There is a *metaphorical* display of mind in composition, which becomes a part of the music's delineated meanings. When it is not a male but a female composer to whom we are listening, such a response is liable to be marked by an even greater level of interruption than that caused by the problematic type of female instrumentalist. When the composer is known to be a woman, the fact of her display of mind conflicts with her traditional, 'natural' submission to the body, going so far as to *threaten* conventional definitions of femininity. This is part of the reason why women have, throughout music history, been even more vigorously discouraged from composition than from instrumental performance.

Gendered musical meaning and experience

I have suggested some ways in which the femininity of the performer or composer enters delineated musical meaning. Clearly, by my definition of inherent musical meaning as purely to do with musical materials, inherent meaning itself can have nothing to do with gender. But the gendered delineation of music does not stop at delineation: it continues, from its delineated position, to affect listeners' perceptions of and responses to inherent meaning.

Here I wish to look more closely at some of the possible interrelationships between the two types of musical meaning.

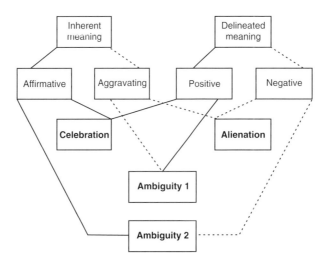

Figure 5.1 *Two types of musical meaning*

Sources: Adapted from 'Music on Deaf Ears', p. 138, and 'Music, Gender, Education', pp. 133, 251

Imagine a music listener who is familiar with and enjoys the inherent meanings of Mozart or of the Spice Girls, and who is also positive about the delineations of the music. This will engender an overall experience of what the chart refers to as 'celebration'. By contrast, imagine a listener who is unfamiliar and negative concerning the inherent meanings of the music, and also feels negative about the delineations. Such a listener will have an experience of 'alienation' in response to the music. More interesting are cases where there is a conflict between the listener's responses to the inherent and delineated meanings. On the one hand, a listener is positive about the inherent meanings: has sung or played a lot of Mozart, listens to a lot of charts music; but at the same time, is negative about the delineations: hates operas, finds the Spice Girls aggressive. Such a conflictual response is denoted on the chart as 'Ambiguity 2'. On the other hand, a listener is negative about the inherent meanings: finds Mozart filligree and superficial, considers the Spice Girls raucus and uninteresting; but is positive about the delineations: loves going to the opera, or finds the visual aspects of the Spice Girls considerably more appealing than their auditory aspects. Such a response is denoted as 'Ambiguity 1'.

The influence of gendered delineations over the perception of inherent meanings

One of the central points I wish to make is that the gendered delineation of music does not stop at delineation. It continues from its delineated position to affect listeners' responses to and perceptions of inherent meaning. Firstly, how does it affect the listener?

> There was this young girl on stage, and this enormous drum kit. I couldn't believe that she was going to play it: but she walked across the stage and sat down behind it, and she did play it – and she played it well too!
>
> (A comment by an audience-member at a school concert)

Innocuous though it is in many ways, this comment illustrates some significant features of the interface between gendered musical meaning on the one hand, and musical experience on the other hand. The idea of the girl's femininity had fleetingly become a problematic part of the music's delineations in the experience of this listener. This interruptive feminine delineation then affected the way he listened to her controlling the inherent meanings: he was 'listening out' to discover whether she could play well. Not only for him, but for all of us, the gender of the female instrumental performer in such circumstances enters into delineated musical meaning, as an interruption to traditional definitions of femininity and, from there, acts to affect the way we listen to inherent meaning.

Rather than a female performer as in the example above, when listeners are aware that the *composer* is a woman, a long history shows that they tend to perceive the inherent meanings of the music in terms of delineated femininity. For example, a Scandinavian music critic was in the habit of writing rave reviews about a particular composer. After many reviews, the critic found out that the composer was a woman. He carried on writing good reviews, but his language changed; he ceased to describe the music with words like 'strident', 'virile' or 'powerful', and began to include words like 'delicate' and 'sensitive'. What had happened was that his new knowledge that the composer was a woman, or in the terms I am suggesting, the delineation of the femininity of the composer, affected the way that he also heard the inherent meanings. Throughout history there are numerous examples of criticisms of women's work. A great deal of music by women has been denigrated for its alleged effeminacy; other music (such as the example above) has been more favourably received as displaying positive feminine attributes such as delicacy or sensitivity; and a tiny amount of music by women has been incredulously hailed as equal to music by a man.

Gender-identity and musical experience

History makes it reasonable to assume that the composer behind nearly all the music that most people hear is a man, and on top of that, as I have already suggested, the compositional delineation contains the notion of mind, which is associated with masculinity. When we discover a woman, or a woman's min,d behind the music, her femininity then problematically enters the delineations, from which position it acts to alter our perceptions of the inherent meanings. If you are a 'man', or if you are a 'woman' – using those words advisedly to include the different combinations of gender and sexuality that are available to all individuals – then I would suggest it is likely that the masculine meaning of music will affect you differently.

In the case of the listener, most music will quite reasonably be assumed to have been composed by a man. It is therefore reasonable to suggest that the male listener may be more able to 'find himself', find his gender, expressed in the normative delineations of the music, regardless of whether he has positive or negative responses to specific inherent or delineated meanings. The woman listener, by contrast, is more likely to be 'thrown off'. In the case of the performer, most of the music performed will normally have been composed by a man. Therefore likewise, the female performer is more 'thrown off'. Increasing numbers of women today are specializing in performing music by women; perhaps female listeners are more receptive to it, and female performers are less thrown from this music. In the case of the composer, the male composer is creating something which 'always-already' carries a normative historical, and a normative ideological masculine delineation. As he composes, his own music comes back to him, with this meaning which is congruent with his gender. For the woman composer, she is also creating something which 'always-already' carries a normative historical and a normative ideological masculine delineation. As she composes, her own music comes back to her, with this meaning which is *non*-congruent with her gender. As I mentioned earlier, women's works have nearly always been judged in terms of their composer's femininity, understood in either a positive or a negative light, as if their femininity somehow gets inside the music. But men's music is never judged in terms of their masculinity; rather, masculinity is assumed as normal.

I would suggest the above as possible ways of understanding why there are relatively few women performers compared to men, particularly on certain instruments and in relation to certain styles of music; and so few women composers, particularly of certain genres such as large-scale symphonic and operatic works. Behind historical conventions, concerning what are seen to be acceptable behaviours or activities for men and women, are gendered musical meanings. But not only that, for I am also suggesting that the gender-identity of the listener or the musician himself or herself affects our motivation and individuality in relation to music, our musical practices and our self-conceptions as musicians.

Summary

My suggestion is that music delineates gender in a variety of ways according to the gender of the performer and/or the composer, in combination with the music's style, its historical context, and the individual identity of the listener. Musical delineations are not closed, but they affect our perceptions of inherent meanings. When music delineates femininity through a female performer or composer, we are liable to also judge the handling of inherent meanings by that performer or composer, in terms of our idea of her femininity. Moreover, as listeners, performers and composers, individual gendered subjects position themselves in relation to an overarching masculine delineation of music. It remains to indicate that the gendered meaning of music is both restrictive in the sense that it can confine us to particular spheres, but also liberatory in the sense that it can reveal to us something about our gender and present to us the possibility of alternative gender-positions.

The reproduction of gendered musical practice, meaning and experience in the school

I now wish to explore the idea that the historical gendering of musical practices is carried on in schools, not only through the different practical musical opportunities which education offers to girls and boys, but moreover, through musical meaning and, most significantly, musical experience itself.

I conducted a questionnaire-survey in different parts of England, involving seventy-eight secondary school music teachers who gave their views about boys' and girls' musical practices, abilities and inclinations. I also conducted two case studies involving tape-recorded interviews with sixty-nine pupils aged 11–16, in small, single-sex friendship groups in two mixed inner London comprehensives. In both the questionnaires and the interviews, I asked open questions with the aim of digging beneath responses to seek out teachers' and pupils' implicit assumptions, values and expectations. I have no intention of attributing particular psychological states to teachers and pupils. Rather, I aim to illustrate patterns in the ways in which teachers and pupils talked about themselves in relation to their musical practices.

Affirming femininity in the school: girls and boys singing and playing

The teachers overwhelmingly characterized girls as willing vocalists who enjoy singing lessons and who volunteer in large numbers for extracurricular choral and other group singing activities, often to the total exclusion of boys. The pupils agreed. A large number of girls expressed a readiness to sing, and many said that singing was seen as a girls' activity, or, in the words of one 11 year-old, 'singing is girls' jobs'. Teachers also said that far more girls than boys play orchestral instruments,

especially the flute and violin, and keyboard instruments, all of which were associated mainly with classical music. Again, the pupils' responses were entirely
commensurate. For example:

LG   Do you think that girls like to play the same instruments as you?
Boy 1   No.
Boy 2   Most girls like to play the violin and the cello.
LG   Do you think girls have a similar approach towards their music lessons as
          you do?
Boy 3   No, not at all.
Boy 4   Mostly they, like, they take music lessons, they play flute, violin.
Boy 5   They don't branch out much from classical music.

Teachers linked girls' attitudes and approaches with a desire to express their feelings,
with delicacy, or with decoration. Girls were regarded as lacking confidence and
being disinclined to 'show off'. They were also seen to be more co-operative and
open-minded, more mature, hard-working and reliable than boys. Overall there was
a clear impression that girls are seen to *conform* to the teacher's and school's values,
expectations and standards of behaviour. The same perceptions were again echoed in
interviews with pupils. Firstly, they said girls like love songs, soft or slow music,
which was sometimes associated with classical music. For example:

Boy 1   There are two girls in our class who play the cello I think it is.
LG   Why do you think that is?
Boy 1   'Cos they like slower music.

Secondly, some of the boys characterized girls as shy or embarrassed, and this was
also more than once associated with classical music.

Boy   Most of the boys I know like to express theirself, and the girls, like
          Kerry-Ann, they're too shy, but I say if they're too shy, they should learn
          classical music.

Clearly there is a strong relationship between these comments on girls' practices, and
empirical reality, because it is partly empirical reality that the teachers and pupils
were describing. But that is not the end of the story, for teachers and pupils are also
operating with meanings and values surrounding their notions of femininity, linked
to the musical practices and the music itself in which girls are seen to engage. Classical music, slow music, and music which is sung or played on keyboards and orchestral instruments in schools, delineates an affirmative concept of femininity. Through
this affirmative delineation, girls are able to adopt certain musical practices and
musical styles, like a mantle or a piece of clothing which helps them to affirm their
gender. At the same time, in their musical practices there is a reproduction of the
historical legacy of music, in which women's roles as singers, keyboard players and
players of certain orchestral instruments have, for varying lengths of time, been
common and affirmatively feminine.

Interrupting femininity in the school: girls, boys, technology and popular music

In general, girls actively avoid performance on highly technological or electric instruments, especially those associated with popular music, most notably drums and electric guitars. But boys are responding very differently to the relatively recent entrance of popular music and jazz into English schools. Boys in every 11–14 age-group to whom I spoke, without exception, chorused that either they already play the drums, or that they would like to play the drums. Many complained that they were not given the chance. This interest in drumming was associated with a desire to be involved in other popular music instruments and in sound-reproduction technology. Just as girls' music was understood as 'slow', so popular music in which boys expressed interest was characterized as 'fast' or to 'have a beat'.

Boy 1	I asked Miss if I could play drums 'cos I'm really good at it. But she says 'later', but she never gives us the chance.
Boy 2	I'm already good at drums 'cos I got some things at home.
Boy 3	'Cos we like putting a beat into it.
Boy 4	I like playing the drums but it's just that we never get a chance to express ourselves. It's just xylophones, xylophones. We would like to play drums, we would like to play guitar, we would like to play lots of things.
Girl 1	Boys don't like music lessons.
LG	Why do you think that is?
Girl 1	Well basically in the music lessons all we do is listen to classical music … and that sort of thing.
Girl 2	It might make a difference if the music they [the teachers] played was more for our age group.
Girl 3	Yes, so the kind of things they played were sort of electric guitar and that sort of thing.
Girl 4	Like not orchestras and that sort of thing.

Whereas, as we saw earlier, girls are understood to use music to express their feelings, boys are understood, by both teachers and pupils, to emphatically denunciate most musical activities as 'cissy' and 'unmacho', and to be keen on keeping up to the minute in their tastes.

LG	Do boys feel the same way about music as you feel?
Girl 1	No.
Girl 2	The kind of music they like is different.
Girl 3	Most of the boys that I talk to they don't really talk about music and that; but when you put on your kind of music you like, they say 'Oh turn that off, that's rubbish' and so on.
LG	What sort of music are they likely to say 'That's rubbish' about?
Girl 1	Reggae and things.
Girl 2	Slow songs, yeah, MoTown, love songs and that. They don't listen to that.
LG	Why do you think they don't like slow music and love songs?
Girl 3	People might think they're soppy.

Girl 4   They don't like showing their feelings.
Girl 5   Bit of an unmacho image.

Many teachers and pupils also said that boys were anti-conformist and over-confident in music lessons, refusing to take part and 'mucking about' with instruments, in ways that contrasted starkly with the characterization of girls as shy and co-operative.

For a boy to engage in vocal or orchestral music, 'slow' music, or music that is associated with the classical style in school, this involves taking a risk with his symbolic masculinity. If these activities provide a suitable mantle for girls, then for boys, they are rather like putting on a dress. Just as girls negotiate a feminine gender identity through music, so boys negotiate a masculine gender identity; and they are often under a great deal of pressure to appear 'macho'. In the context of the school, just as 'classical' music delineates an affirmative, conformist femininity, so 'popular' music interrupts femininity; and in this interruptive fissure a delineation of masculinity is able instead to assert itself. This interruption of femininity and the assertion of a masculine delineation again reproduce the historical legacy of women's roles in music.

Threatening femininity in the school: girls and boys composing

The most striking thing about teachers' responses was that, despite their almost unanimous characterization of boys as uninterested, unco-operative and negative towards music lessons, they regarded boys as excelling at composition. Contrastingly, they saw girls as dull and lacking in creative spark. For example:

Teacher 1   On the whole, boys produce more imaginative work than girls.
Teacher 2   Boys are not so afraid to be inventive, and experiment. Girls tend to stick to set forms.
Teacher 3   Girls tend to be more traditional and conservative in their compositions.
Teacher 4   Girls seem to have to work harder and don't have as much natural ability.
Teacher 5   Boys seem to have a greater creative spark than girls … The girls seem often to be devoid of ideas, and have a problem developing musical ideas.

It is helpful to compare these responses with Valerie Walkerdine's (1990) analysis of gender in the mathematics classroom. Here, she shows, girls have been *constructed* as failing, through being attributed with qualities such as perseverance, obedience and hard-working attitudes, which are then used as *causal explanations* for their failure: as examples of lack of autonomy, creativity, initiative. When girls do succeed, this is attributed to rule-following and rote-learning, which are distinguished from and even opposed to understanding. But 'naughty' boys can 'break set', think independently, 'reason'. Thus, even though their actual attainment may be poor, they are seen to 'understand' properly.

When talking about composition to *pupils*, I concentrated on the 14–16 age-group, because they are engaged in more focused composition than their younger colleagues. They did not use the same terms as teachers, 'conformity', 'creativity' and so on, but they adopted these same characteristics through other means. Some of the girls expressed a strong dislike of and a debilitating lack of confidence in composition. Others viewed their compositional work with pleasure and pride. But in both cases they operated within the bounds of traditional conceptions of 'femininity'. For example, they opposed themselves to theory, using composition as a way of expressing their feelings:

Girl 1   Well, I like composition, when it's doing what you feel and everything, but I don't so much like the theory because you've got to learn it.

Girl 2   When you look at the piece of paper and think that, you know, you've written that, and it's not come from a book, it's come from you, and actually you know it's yours, yourself.

Girl 3   When I like a piece [of mine] it's more, like I get this feeling, I know it's really silly but I get this feeling I think, you know, ah, self-satisfaction, and I sort of like have this big glow on my face.

They shrank from putting themselves forward as composers:

Girl 1   Well, I don't really like playing my compositions to the class, but if it's something that I feel is good, like other pieces composed by other people, famous or not famous, then I feel more confident than when I do my own.

Some of them characterized themselves as 'incompetent' or 'confused'. All of them indicated a reliance on the teacher. Even those who liked composition were prone to denigrate at least some of their own work or their own feelings about it in numerous asides when they described their work as 'silly', 'boring', 'horrible' and 'terrible'.

Boys displayed a completely different attitude. All but one of them were positive, confident and carefree in their attitudes to composition, whether or not they saw themselves as 'good' at it. They demonstrated not merely a confidence in their ability and a lack of reliance on the teacher, but a rejection of the teacher's advice and values; they presented themselves as less hard-working, yet more 'clued up' about what they needed and what they were aiming for. Rather than having 'done their best' they all indicated that they 'could have done better'. None of them mentioned his feelings.

As with the affirmation and interruption of femininity in the realms of performance, once again I would suggest that the symbolic threat posed to femininity by the compositional delineation of a male composer and of mind as a masculine attribute is here being re-enacted in the musical practices and the common-sense attitudes of teachers, girls and boys.

Resistance and desire in the music classroom

Thus far, I have made it seem as though the reproductive mechanisms of the school work rather too smoothly: girls and boys seem to negotiate their musical practices in close accordance with the history of music. But the school does not straightforwardly reproduce wider societal relationships. On the one hand, resistance to musical gender-roles is sometimes offered to pupils by teachers, who themselves take up critical practices. On the other hand, although pupils do largely share the same assumptions as their teachers, they also have alternative perspectives, and take part in different practices, of which teachers are often either disapproving, dismissive or unaware. For example, the interest of girls in classical music and singing is, as I have indicated, linked to a notion of their conformity to the teacher's values. But 'naughty' girls, who may be sexually active, subculturally involved or generally disaffected, are liable to find singing, orchestral instruments and classical music less inviting.

For such girls, one musical practice that is available is the singing of popular music. Many schools, of course, nowadays include popular music in their curriculums; but what often happens is that the music then takes on the same conformist characteristics as its classical counterpart; and, in fact, it is often not even perceived by pupils as being 'popular music' at all. Therefore, when girls resist the *mores* of the school through singing what they regard as 'popular music', they often do so outside the officially sanctioned limits of 'what counts' as music in the classroom: in youth groups, perhaps, in the playground, at home. By taking this route to musical practice, some girls may be sending overtly resistant signals to the school; but they are a long way from resisting the wider and more powerful definitions of femininity which have been handed down through the affirmative delineations of women's singing for hundreds if not thousands of years.

When it comes to the more interruptive practice of playing instruments in popular music, even though a minority of girls and women do play drums and electric guitars, the overwhelming finding of my empirical research was that in schools, such girls are still perceived as very rare; but, more significantly, that the delineations carried by popular music instrumental performance practices are almost exclusively masculine.

In the case of the threatening delineation of a female composer, teachers and pupils alike closely guarded the concept of the creative genius as a male-only preserve. There was very little, if any, evidence of a challenge to this conception by the compositional practices of girls, or the expectations of teachers.

Even though some girls may resist the authority of the teacher, in general, girls do not resist the symbolic aspects of femininity carried by the delineations of different musical practices. Likewise, boys who wrest their musical roles away from the surface values which they understand to be propagated by the school – who refuse to take part in classical music, who assert a 'macho' and nonconformist allegiance to popular music – are nonetheless conforming to wider conventions of masculinity. This deep conservatism in the realm of gender and sexuality is expressed because of a desire: a desire to *be* a 'girl', a desire to *be* a 'boy'. At the same time, music is available as a symbolic means to cross over gender: girls and boys do not only use music to affirm conventional sex-gender associations, but to express challenges to them, an expression which may be particularly poignant in the realm of sexuality.

Conclusion

The school reproduces enduring historical patterns in musical practices according to gender. But it does not achieve this through a raw offering of opportunity. Rather, it perpetuates subtle definitions of femininity and masculinity as delineations of different musical practices and musical styles, in which pupils invest their desires to conform, not necessarily to the school, but to the wider social construction of gender. Most significantly, gendered delineations are not just extra-musical append-ages, but they affect perceptions of musical inherent meanings. It is in musical experience as an undifferentiated whole, when delineated and inherent meanings come together as one apparently unified apperception, that some of the deepest power of music resides.

When we sing, play, compose or listen to music, we don't normally analyse our experience, or declare: 'Oh, yes, that's an inherent meaning (or some such category); and that's a delineation, (or the like)'. On the contrary, the two types of meaning come to us as if they were one. Therefore delineations, including gendered delinea-tions, appear to arise, not from the social context of the music's production, distribu-tion or reception, but, mysteriously, from within the 'music itself'.

In this way, delineations can come to us with the impact of apparent, unmediated, or immediate truth. It is therefore in musical experience itself – in music's apparently unquestionable symbolization of how things are and of who we are – that gender identities are symbolized and reproduced at some of their most effective and most profound levels.

A number of avenues are open to music teachers who wish to combat the gendering of musical practice and opportunity. These include ensuring that works by women composers are represented in the curriculum; providing role-models of both male and female musicians who play instruments that are unconventional for their sex; setting up a variety of mixed-sex and single-sex groups for different musical activities; making sure that equal numbers of girls and boys have the oppor-tunity for instrumental lessons, especially on those instruments that are strongly gendered; attending to our own assumptions so as to avoid, for example, unfairly labelling girls as lacking compositional spark; there are many other possibilities. However, I believe that the strongest single way in which teachers can make a differ-ence is through being sensitive to our pupils' musical abilities and interests, in full awareness of the embeddedness of gender in musical practice, meaning and experi-ence, and its effects, not only on our pupils, but also on ourselves.

References

Bowers, J. and Tick, J. (eds) (1986) *Women Making Music: the Western Art Tradi-tion,1150–1950*, Urbana: University of Illinois Press.

Green, L. (1997) *Music, Gender, Education*, Cambridge: Cambridge University Press.

Walkerdine, V. (1990) *Schoolgirl Fictions*, London, New York: Verso.

6 How far do tests of musical ability shed light on the nature of musical intelligence?
Christopher Murphy

If the aim of intellectual training is to form the intelligence rather than to stock the memory, and produce intellectual explorers rather than mere erudition, then traditional education is manifestly guilty of a grave deficiency.

(Jean Piaget 1970)

Cogito, ergo Sum.

(René Descartes)

'I think therefore I am,' I announced. There was a pause. 'I feel therefore I am,' he replied quietly. I knew there was a beginning to the matter.

(Robert Witkin 1974)

Introduction

Recently, while working as a supply teacher in a failing London secondary school under special measures, I was required to attend a series of in-service training seminars run by the Assistant Director of Education on the subject of promoting intelligent behaviour in our pupils. This, rightly or wrongly, was, for him, the ultimate aim of education. At these seminars it became apparent to me that many experienced teachers held quite clear and fixed ideas about what they considered constituted intelligent behaviour in their specific subject area, particularly when this subject dealt almost exclusively with more propositional and cognitive forms of knowledge (i.e. facts). It also became clear that many senior teachers and educational administrators still hold fast to traditional conceptions of intelligence that really only represent half the story in terms of psychological debate.

As a music teacher I found it difficult to make any clear correlation between some of the definitions of intelligence put forward and what I might define as musically 'intelligent' behaviour. Apart from some Craft Design and Technology and a small amount of Drama offered as part of English, Music stood alone in the curriculum as the only essentially aesthetic 'arts'-orientated subject. This seems to be an increasingly common occurrence at secondary level where relatively few subjects deal with affective responses and concentrate almost exclusively on cognitive propositional (i.e. factual) modes of thinking and knowing.

The oft-cited remark of Cardinal Newman, that music is nothing more than an 'elegant pastime', still seems to persist in the minds of some heads and senior educational administrators. In a society increasingly conscious about 'accountability', I often find myself in the position of having to 'justify' the place of music in the National Curriculum as a subject that is as much concerned with developing the mind as it is with subjective emotional responses.

While I feel it is inherently wrong to assume that knowledge is only that which can be stated in propositions, or that subjective responses are of no educational value, I still feel that it is possible to be musically intelligent. If I were to attempt to define what I mean by 'musical intelligence', I would describe it as 'a way of knowing'. To be able to think 'musically', whether as a performer, composer or listener, is to be musically intelligent. Traditional conceptions of musical ability, in my view, shed little light on the nature of musical intelligence and how it is developed. This article explores the reasons behind my convictions and shows the context in which music can be considered to be an 'intellectually' as well as aesthetically worthwhile subject.

It also provides a broader perspective on the question of whether musical ability is learned or innate. As an instrumental teacher I have often been asked if there are any potential drawbacks in a student beginning specialist instrumental studies who does not come from a 'musical' background. Parents are often at pains to point out at the start of tuition that they either have no family history of musical achievement or that someone, no matter how remote in their family history, was particularly musical and that this explains the musical motivations of their child. While there may be nothing essentially wrong with such convictions, traditional conceptions of 'musical' people having some special genetic predisposition to music have often tended to undermine the confidence of beginners and deterred others from even starting.

The view of innate musical ability has, in my view, tended towards a proliferation of élitist practices in music education in which many children have been denied access to worthwhile musical encounters. I have, for example, lost count of the number of students I have taken for private instrumental tuition who were initially turned down by their school on the grounds that they had failed a musical ability test or were considered 'unmusical'.

Some of these students went on to achieve a remarkably high standard in performance. I have also taught handicapped children and others with learning difficulties who, although severely restricted in what they could realistically achieve, gained huge personal fulfilment from active music-making and were tremendously well motivated to learn.

The role of motivation in the acquisition of musical skills has, I feel, been underestimated in the psychometric approach. I therefore examine some theories of learning which attempt to explain this process and explain why some mentally handicapped children may display prodigious musical talent.

Shuter-Dyson and Gabriel (1981) have comprehensively reviewed some twenty-four tests of musical ability. Sloboda (1985) also evaluated most of these. As Hargreaves (1986: 167) observes, psychological research within the psychometric tradition represents by far the most extensive area of psychological enquiry on creativity. It is not therefore my intention to look in detail at the tests themselves or to show how each one may or may not shed light on the nature of musical intelligence. Rather, I intend to examine and explore the overall concept of intelligence advanced in the psychometric tradition and contrast this with other psychological theories. In this way I hope to demonstrate different approaches to the development of musical ability and establish the context in which we can talk of musical thinking as a distinct form of intelligence.

My focus will be essentially psychological and primarily concerned with psychological theories of learning and intelligence, rather than with aesthetic or philosophical questions about the nature of musical knowledge. I do, however, recognize that, in the broader view and within the context of some psychological approaches also, these are undoubtedly important considerations in examining the nature and context of musical intelligence.

The psychometric tradition

Psychometry is a branch of psychology dealing with measurable factors. It is from this field of psychology that we get the concept of the Intelligence Quotient (IQ) and the subsequent development of tests of musical ability. One of the problems for psychometricians has been defining what they set out to measure and an abundance of different terms has been used to describe various musical traits. The scope of this article does not allow a more detailed analysis of these definitions and I must therefore take them as read or refer the reader to the body of literature for further clarification.

For example, the terms 'musicality', 'musical talent', 'musical ability' and 'musical capacity', as Lundin (1953: 174) points out, are often used indiscriminately. In his view, musical talent refers to the capacity for musical performance, whereas musicality is the capacity for musical reception. Musical capacity and ability, on the other hand, refer to 'inborn traits', a view shared by both Seashore (1938) and Schoen (1940) (also see Lundin 1953: 184). This concept of musical ability advanced in the psychometric tradition, particularly by Seashore and Bentley, has had a considerable influence on the practice of music education over the past fifty or so years. However, as Bentley (1966: 9) observes, there has been considerable disagreement about the nature of musical ability:

> It has to be accepted that the measurement of musical ability has not moved beyond a rather rudimentary and unsatisfactory stage. Nor could it be otherwise whilst there exists no agreement on what musical ability is. We may be able to recognise it, or think we can, but we cannot as yet define it.

In my view, this position pertains equally to the term 'musical intelligence'. Despite this, or perhaps because of it, there has been a considerable amount of work in the psychometric tradition concerned with the application of techniques for testing and measuring various musical traits or abilities.

As Mursell (1937: 287) observes, this has developed along three principal lines:

1   attempts to measure musical capacities or aptitudes;
2   attempts to measure musical achievement, such as aural perception, technical abilities and skill in reading music;
3   attempts to measure knowledge about music.

All three could loosely be termed 'tests of musical ability', but what might these tests tell us about the nature of musical intelligence?

Concepts of intelligence and musical ability

Entwistle (1988: 147) comments that:

> What intelligence tests have in common does at least represent a consensus of what psychometricians understand by intelligence.

This, in my view, is also the underlying assumption of musical ability tests. Generally speaking, however, the core subjects of the National Curriculum tend to reflect a widely held view of what intelligence is: to be good at Maths, Science or English is to be intelligent. The media also tend to advance this narrow view with programmes such as 'University Challenge', 'Master Mind' and other increasingly abundant quiz shows which reinforce the propositional view of knowledge which Langer (1957), Reid (1986) and others have all challenged.

While I feel it is inherently wrong to assume that knowledge is only that which can be expressed in propositions, can we talk of being 'musically intelligent' or is intelligence a general phenomenon confined only to propositional realms of thought? If we can talk of 'musical intelligence', do tests of musical ability identify this trait let alone reliably measure it? What might such tests tell us about the individual or groups' 'potential' for musical 'achievement'? To answer some of these questions, we must first look at some contrasting theories of intelligence and how they relate to the concept of musical ability.

The relationship between general intelligence ('G') and musical ability

Seashore (1938), Bentley (1966) and others saw no correlation between musical ability and intelligence as a general phenomenon whereas Schoen (1940), Mursell (1937), Farnsworth (1958) and others have all reported a positive relationship. More recent psychological research, however, presents an alternative perspective that could radically alter our perceptions of human intelligence and our approach to teaching music, as Entwistle points out:

> For teachers, assumptions of intellectual consistency might have unfortunate consequences for their approach to teaching.

Theories of multiple intelligence

In recent years, traditional conceptions of what constitutes human intelligence have been challenged and, according to Plummeridge (1991), it is only recently that we have come to talk of musical 'thinking' as a distinct or even 'autonomous' form of intelligence. In my view, these theories are of far greater significance when related to the aesthetic theories of Langer, Reid and others mentioned earlier.

In the field of psychology, Howard Gardner (1984) and J. P. Guilford (1967) have advanced theories in which human intelligence is viewed as a multidimensional phenomenon. The 'Structure of Intellect' model advanced by Guilford proposes some 120 different forms of intelligence, or 'vectors of mind'. Here, 'abilities' are seen as an integral part of a general intelligence ('G') rather than as a combination of varying amounts of general intelligence and some content-specific factor as proposed in the 'two-factor' theory of C. E. Spearman (1927 and 1930).

As Hargreaves (1986) observes, Guilford's theory of cognitive abilities is the main theoretical model for psychometric approaches to the testing of creativity. This is a 'person-based' approach that centres on tests of 'convergent' and 'divergent' thinking in which creativity is viewed purely as a cognitive operation. While Guilford, like Thurstone (1938), advances a pluralist or multifactoral approach, abilities are still conceived as being part of a 'general' intelligence and are theoretically conceived within the psychometric tradition.

Alternatively, Gardner (1984: 320), who refers to the two major schools in the psychology of intelligence as 'Hedgehogs' and 'Foxes', posits only six (more recently, seven) relatively autonomous 'intelligences' of which music is but one type. These views are of singular importance to music educators and musicians. As Gardner (1984: 4) points out:

> Only if we expand and reformulate our views of what counts as human intelligence will we be able to devise more appropriate ways of assessing it and more effective ways of educating it.

In this specific context, do tests of musical ability shed any light on the nature of musical intelligence? Are ability tests of any use to us as a diagnostic tool in telling us something about an individual's potential for progress and achievement in music? As a large proportion of work in the National Curriculum is done in groups rather than on an individual basis, their educational utility in this context would seem to be limited.

Mursell (1937) believes their practical utility as educational instruments to be rather slight but their 'psychological' significance to be very far reaching due to the underlying assumptions about the nature and functioning of the musical mind on which they are based. Sloboda (1985: 233) points out that the purpose of musical ability tests is quite different from that of examinations in music:

> Whilst examinations presuppose intensive preparation of specific materials, tests of ability involve no foreknowledge of test content. Indeed, such tests are invalidated by extensive practice on the task they contain. This is because of the rationale which underlies their construction.

This underlying rationale is, as Hargreaves (1986: 25) points out, designed to assess an individual's 'potential' for skilled musical behaviour 'regardless' of previous musical learning experience. In this view, children are initially considered to have a relatively common exposure to and involvement in music. However, as Sloboda (1985) explains:

> Because of differences in innate potential, motivation or experience at certain critical periods, the 'take-up' of musical knowledge varies from child to child. Thus, even before some children are selected for specialist training, they have come to differ from one another quite widely in the stock of underlying skills and sensitivities they possess.

This view places emphasis on the individual's environmental and innate predisposition to musical stimuli, but what might this 'stock of underlying skills and sensitivities' be? Swanwick (1988: 54) believes that the observation of children's spontaneous musical behaviour is likely to tell us much more about such phenomena than the limited activity of testing will allow. I will return to this point later when discussing theories of musical development. However, Gardner (1984: 104) argues:

> there is very little dispute about the principal constituent elements of music, though experts will differ on the precise definition of each aspect. Most central are 'pitch' (or melody) and 'rhythm' … next in importance only to pitch and rhythm is 'timbre', the characteristic qualities of tone.

From this we might start to suspect the type of reductionist argument advanced in the psychometric view. However, in defining these central elements, or 'cores' as he terms them, Gardner places the 'affective' aspects of music very close to these cores:

> From the point of view of 'hard' positivistic science, it would seem preferable to describe music in terms of objective, physical terms: to stress the pitch and rhythmic aspects of music. … Yet hardly anyone who has been intimately associated with music can forbear to mention its emotional implications.

Shuter-Dyson and Gabriel (1981: 254–5) cite a number of tests which have attempted to measure the ability to discriminate between musical meanings in which ability was related to neither intelligence nor musical ability test scores, but to enjoyment.

Again this raises more philosophical and aesthetic questions about musical ability. Is it appropriate to conceive of it as a set of hierarchically ordered skills? While Gardner concedes the role of audition as being crucial to all musical participation, he argues that there may also be other aspects of musical experience accessible even to those who cannot appreciate its auditory aspects. The musician Evelyn Glennie, despite being profoundly deaf, maintains that she can 'hear' music through her body. By 'hearing', Glennie means that she is able somehow to sense vibrations and rhythm through her body rather than aurally.

This would seem to support Gardner's view that, not only rhythmic organization, but also many other aspects of music exist apart from purely auditory realization and where synergistic interaction of other 'intelligences' may also be significant factors in the development of musical ability. However, many standardized musical ability tests in the psychometric tradition tend to focus on individual performance over a relatively narrow group of core skills in auditory aspects of music, such as the discrimination of pitch and pulse. Entwistle (1988: 148) comments on the concern many psychologists have expressed at the rash of tests of narrowly defined specific abilities. This concern could equally apply to tests of musical ability.

Mursell (1937: 49–98) points out that while identifying and discriminating between sounds in terms of their pitch component is an important consideration for musical ability, it is not so exclusive as is often supposed. Responsiveness to pitch, rather than being a fixed innate ability, as Seashore maintained, may be susceptible to improvement through aural training. Like Gardner, Mursell (1937: 72) maintains that responsiveness to pitch, as with response to other musical elements, is by no means confined to the ear alone but is also a characteristic of the central nervous system.

Furthermore, Mursell (1937: 152–3) considers the concept of rhythm advanced by some psychologists to be incorrectly based on assumptions about innate or instinctive tendencies. While he concedes the legitimacy of some claims concerning instinctive rhythmic proclivities, he argues:

> such views as ordinarily understood involve a far-reaching error which results in mistakes both in interpretation and practice. Perception does in fact tend to fall into simple intelligible forms, a consideration of the greatest importance which we have seen formulated in the Law of Pragnanz by Gestalt psychologists. But that the organisation of perception is due to an instinctive drive which operates apart from learning is untrue.

Gestalt theory and its development and elaboration with reference to music through the work of Meyer (1956), particularly with regard to the principles of pattern perception and 'The Law of Good Continuation', have had a seminal influence in this field. However, as Meyer (1956) observes, the Gestalt school, in reacting against the sensationist concept of perception and associationist theory of learning, has tended to minimize or deny the role of learning in the perception of musical structures.

More specifically, Mursell (1937: 162) maintains that the ultimate foundation for rhythm is to be found in mental activity rather than in instinctive semi-voluntary motor responses to music. He argues that the muscles that control movement are operated by the higher nervous centres and are therefore susceptible to training. In an earlier paragraph, however, he qualifies this by stating that there is also some truth in the following argument:

> that interest in and response to rhythm, whether in music, poetry, dance, the visual arts, or anywhere else, is due to an instinctive demand for beauty or simplicity or proportion, for order as contrasted with disorder, and that this is an innate tendency on the emergence of which, apart from learning, we can rely.

This seemingly intractable dichotomy between 'nature' and 'nurture' has established a paradigm central to the psychological dialectic of musical intelligence and its development during the past fifty or so years. Is musical behaviour learned or is it innate? If it is not innate, how is it acquired? Is there an identifiable pattern or sequence of developmental stages through which the musical progress of children can be traced? In addressing these crucial questions we need to examine some of the theories advanced in the field of developmental psychology.

The development of musical intelligence and ability

A considerable amount of psychological research on the musical development of children has been undertaken in recent years, particularly in the United States, which has attempted to map out developmental models of music based on Piagetian theories generated in other areas such as mathematics. One of Piaget's main critics with regard to artistic development was Howard Gardner whose work has already been briefly discussed.

Swanwick (1988: 54 and 1994: 95) has expressed his concern with approaches that attempt to approximate musical experience and development to models generated in areas other than music. Similar criticisms have been levelled at the indiscriminate application of Piaget's theory of Genetic Epistemology to the field of music. Piaget himself never wrote on this topic.

Swanwick (1988) advanced the theory of a developmental spiral in music which is also, to some extent, based on Piagetian concepts, though fundamentally different in its conceptual framework from the American research reviewed by Hargreaves (1986). Their work was based on empirical research directly related to music and draws on Piaget's theories of play, rather than on his analysis of 'scientific' thought structures. However, Swanwick (1988: 53) has this to say with regard to the developmental sequence theory:

> I want to suggest that there is a sequence, an orderly unfolding of 'musical' behaviour, that there are cumulative stages through which the musical behaviour of children can be traced. It would be unwise to be too dogmatic about identifying broad developmental changes to a fairly standard timetable, especially to generalize this to almost 'all' children.

Gardner (1984: 108) also proposes a rough-and-ready portrait of early musical competence. Here, the majority of children make little significant progress after school years begin due to the relatively low niche which musical attainment, in comparison to linguistic competence, occupies within our culture and where musical illiteracy is the accepted norm.

It is widely accepted, for example, that a person can have a 'reading age' above or below their chronological age, or that their numerical ability is above or below average for their age. It is not quite so clear what levels of competence we should expect at different ages in music, although the National Curriculum, for example, is largely based on assumptions regarding 'stages' of musical development. The reality, of course, is that children's musical development at any given age can vary enormously between individuals.

Shuter-Dyson and Gabriel (1981: 171–93) review a plethora of psychological research on the genetic heredity of musical ability that would seem to run in families and tends to support the view that musical ability is largely innate. However, Lundin (1953: 184–91) maintains that studies of family histories can support a view that musical behaviour is acquired just as well as they can support the theory of inheritance.

Similarly, Gardner (1984: 113) cites examples of famous musicians such as the renowned pianist Artur Rubinstein who came from a family in which nobody, according to Rubinstein, had the slightest musical gift. His home did, however, contain a piano, which he felt 'motivated' him, and was encouraged to play from an early age. What factors might be involved in providing the motivation for children to acquire and develop musical behaviour? In addressing this question it is necessary to examine some theories of learning.

Theories of learning

In considering the role of motivation in the development of intelligence, Furth (1970: 140) equates Piaget's concept of intelligence with creativity:

> because in Piaget's view, intelligence is identical with development, with going beyond present structures and an active transformation of present situational data. I have consistently argued that our traditional view of intelligence is too limited in scope and impoverished by its failure to integrate intrinsic motivation.

Gagne (1977: 243) working in the behaviourist/associationist tradition, observes that conditioning in the classical or Pavlovian sense can produce learned emotional responses to stimuli and that it is often the reward which provides both reinforcement and motivation for learning. This is what he calls 'Stimulus Response Learning'.

In Rubinstein's case this reward was undoubtedly his ability to impress his family and overcome the speech problems he experienced during his childhood. This would seem to support the theory that musical ability is learned rather than innate. Gardner (1984: 120–2) observes that unusual musical talent is a regular feature of certain anomalies such as autism where the child may cling to music because it represents an island of preservation in a sea of impairment.

The way in which people with various disabilities tend to compensate by a heightened sense or ability in other areas seems to be a common enough feature to speculate that such adaptation in the evolution of human intelligence was needed for survival.

Conclusions

Generally speaking, the circular argument that is often levelled against IQ tests is that they retain the assumption about the nature of intelligence built into the test; that 'intelligence' is what intelligence tests test. This, in my view, applies equally to tests of musical ability. Whether or not they shed light on the nature of musical intelligence would then depend on how the particular tests define and accurately measure this trait.

The general validity of such tests, as Sloboda (1985: 236) observes, lies in the selection of sub-tests used, the age-group for which they are designed and the standardization procedures and reliability of validity studies. This would invariably involve trying the tests out on a broadly representative sample of the population in order to gauge the average test score or 'norm'. This, as Mursell (1937: 327–30) observes, might not be as scientifically accurate as some would assume:

> In spite of the astonishingly, not to say arrogantly overconfident statement by certain self-styled authorities, our actual knowledge concerning the distribution of musicality in the population … is exceedingly slight.

In discussing IQ tests, Entwistle (1988: 141–6) also points out that, in practice, even the best psychometric tests rarely have a reliability coefficient in excess of 0.92 and that this margin of error could only ever be acceptable if the tests really do measure the elusive quality of 'intelligence'. The following passage that he quotes from Vernon (1970) is, in my view, as relevant to tests of musical ability as it is to IQ tests:

> Far too many psychologists and sociologists assume that test scores, and the psychological lay term 'intelligence', are interchangeable. But tests are merely a (particular) sample of cognitive abilities.

The extent to which some tests of musical ability, based as they are on reductionist assumptions regarding the uniform auditory components of music, are truly representative of musical intelligence is open to question. In any event, such tests may not measure those specific abilities that they purport to with any accuracy, if at all.

While some tests in the psychometric tradition have attempted to measure affective aspects of musical experience they have assumed that this is primarily a cognitive operation. As Hargreaves (1986: 50) observes, the arts may transcend the distinction between affect and cognition as, for Gardner, aesthetic objects are the objective embodiment of subjective experience. Gestalt theory as advanced by Meyer (1956) may go some way towards explaining such phenomena in cognitive terms but there are also other more aesthetic perspectives relating to the work of Witkin, Langer, Reid and others, in which feeling and emotion can be regarded as 'intellectual' traits.

Furthermore, musical ability tests may not take sufficient account of the ways in which individuals are initially exposed to or encounter music or the ways in which various aspects of musical intelligence interact with each other as Gardner (1984: 119) observes:

> there is a tremendous range of types and degrees of musical skill found in the human population; since individuals differ so much in what they can do, it is conceivable that the nervous system can provide a plurality of mechanisms for carrying out these performances.

How can we know which tests, if any, might shed light on the nature of such 'mechanisms'? Here I am in agreement with Swanwick's belief mentioned earlier, that we are likely to learn more about such phenomena through the observation of children's spontaneous musical behaviour than we are from testing.

It might also be argued that classroom teachers, being concerned with broader educational goals, are more inclined to be concerned with musical 'achievement' (at least initially), than with musical 'ability'. Unlike instrumental music teachers, who might wish to use some form of testing in the selection of pupils for specialist instrumental tuition, classroom practitioners are required 'by law' to teach music in the National Curriculum to 'all' 7–14 year-olds, 'regardless' of their abilities. In this context, the educational utility of musical ability tests is strictly limited and inappropriate. Their 'psychological' implications, however, as Mursell earlier noted, may be highly significant in terms of understanding how different aspects and component parts of music may be 'perceived' by the brain in different individuals.

However, it has also been suggested that social and cultural differences may account for variations of performance in ability tests and, for this reason, Shuter-Dyson and Gabriel (1981: 204–15) review a number of tests that attempt to take these factors into consideration. It might, nevertheless, be argued that the vast majority of musical ability tests are conceived in terms of western tonality and that environmental factors conducive to the early development and reinforcement of musical behaviour are more likely to be found in homes of higher socio-economic status.

There is also the question of how we might interpret the results of musical ability tests and whether these scores do in fact measure innate or learned abilities, as Vernon, who I quote here from Entwistle (1988: 146), observes:

> intelligence scores are achievement measures just as much as are reading or arithmetic scores, and they are equally required to be 'explained'. The former does not cause the latter … (but they do) sample the more general conceptual and reasoning skills which a child has built up largely outside the school, and which he should therefore be able to apply to the acquisition of more specialized skills in school.

All classroom teachers have a statutory duty in the National Curriculum to ensure that adequate provision is made for less able students and that Programmes of Study are sufficiently differentiated to take account of pupils needs, backgrounds and 'stages' of musical development. As has been shown there is considerable disagreement amongst psychologists as to what these stages of development might be and whether they conform to a uniform pattern in all children of a similar age and maturity. This, in my view, is one of the primary reasons why music, as a general school subject, does not conform so readily to current educational theory and philosophy. It has not proved practicable to establish a 'differentiated base-line on which to monitor musical achievement' (DES 1991) in 'all' children.

On the other hand, the psychometric concept of musical ability has exerted a powerful influence on the practice of music education over the past fifty or so years and, to some extent, continues to do so. The concept of the 'genius' with the high IQ is still perpetuated in the media through their emphasis on quiz shows, and the like, requiring mental recall of facts rather than the ability to use knowledge 'creatively'. This tends to reinforce traditional conceptions of human intelligence as being founded on only one form of knowledge – the propositional.

Of all areas of human endeavour, music above all others seems to have suffered from a potentially damaging and commonly-held belief amongst the beginner musician and lay-person, that in order to achieve anything worthwhile in music, you must first have some special innate ability or God-given talent and be born into a musical family. That is not to deny that 'gifted' people certainly do exist, but does it necessarily follow that music is a no-go area for the vast majority of the population? If this were so, what would be the point of music in the National Curriculum?

I believe there is a sense in which, to a degree, we are all musical and possess the potential for 'intelligent' and 'worthwhile' engagement in music. I feel it is our duty as educators to develop these abilities and sensibilities, in whatever shape or form they may manifest themselves, to the fullest in 'all' our students. Having said this there is an important distinction to made between music 'in' education and music education, as Plummeridge (1977: 57) points out:

> that we differentiate between concepts that lead us to an understanding 'about' the arts (i.e. propositional knowledge) and the perceptual abilities and skills (concepts in the second or musical sense) that are necessary for the practice of performance and understanding in the arts.

In considering the place of music as a general school subject, can we really expect anything other than a rudimentary understanding of music when, so often, students are given neither the time nor appropriate resources with which to develop the necessary skills, techniques, procedures and methods, and make them their own?

The fact, as Gardner observes (1984: 109), that music is not generally valued in western society accounts for the rather underdeveloped state of musical competence in which assumptions about innate musical abilities tend to further undermine and inhibit the confidence of the uninitiated. In African tribal societies, for example, music is much more highly valued and, while they still have their 'virtuoso' musicians, almost everyone will be a competent musician and take part in musical activities from an early age. Indeed, music is an essential and integral part of tribal life through which the young are educated in the *mores* of their community.

As Gardner (1982) rightly observes:

> For most of humanity, and throughout most of human history, the process and products involved in artistic creation have been far more pervasive than those employed in the sciences. In fact, logical scientific thought can be considered an invention of the West in the wake of the Renaissance – an invention which is still restricted to a small enclave of thinkers; participation in the literary, musical or graphic arts, on the other hand, has been widespread for thousands of years.

Despite this, music still occupies a marginal position as a foundation subject in the National Curriculum that is often low on the list of educational priorities when it comes to allocating time and resources. This position has not been helped, at secondary level, by the drive for stronger vocational links in education and changes in emphasis in subjects like Craft Design and Technology and English Literature. This has further marginalized the arts to the extent that music often represents the only essentially aesthetic subject in the curriculum in some secondary schools.

In challenging the traditionally narrow view of human intelligence, based only on certain types of cognitive operations, Gardner's Theory of Multiple Intelligence provides an alternative perspective to the question of musical ability in which musical behaviour can be considered as a distinct and autonomous form of intelligence. Drawing, as it does, on other fields of enquiry such as medicine, philosophy, neurophysiology, biology and anthropology, it makes a valuable contribution to our understanding of musical behaviour as well as broadening our perspectives on the value and significance of the arts in education and society generally. In this view, music can be seen, not only as an aesthetic subject concerned only with subjective affective responses, but also as a worthwhile 'intellectual' pursuit.

References

Bentley, A. (1966) *Musical Ability in Children and its Measurement,* London: Harrap.
—— (1975) *Music in Education: a Point of View,* Slough: NFER.
DES (1991) *Music for Ages 7 to 14 yrs,* London: HMSO.
Ellis, A. (1982) *Normality and Pathology in Cognitive Functions,* London: Academic Press: 299.

Entwistle, N. (1988) *Styles of Learning and Teaching: an Integrated Outline of Educational Psychology,* London: David Fulton Publishers.

Farnsworth, P. (1958) *The Social Psychology of Music,* New York: Dryden.

Furth, H.G. (1970) *Piaget for Teachers,* New York: Prentice Hall.

Gagne, R. (1977) *The Conditions of Learning* (3rd edn) New York: Holt, Reinhart & Winston.

Gardner, H. (1982) 'Artistry following damage to the human brain' in A. Ellis (1982) *Normality and Pathology in Cognitive Functions,* London: Academic Press.

—— (1984) *Frames of Mind: the theory of multiple intelligences.* London: Heinemann.

Guilford, J.P. (1967) *The Nature of Human Intelligence,* New York: McGraw-Hill.

Hargreaves, D. (1986) *The Developmental Psychology of Music,* Cambridge: Cambridge University Press.

Langer, S.K. (1957) *Philosophy in a New Key,* Cambridge, MA: Harvard University Press.

Lundin, R.W. (1953) *An Objective Psychology of Music,* New York: The Ronald Press Co.

Meyer, L.B. (1956) *Emotion and Meaning in Music,* Chicago: University of Chicago Press.

Mursell, J.L. (1937) *The Psychology of Music,* Westport, CT: Greenwood Press.

Piaget, J. (1970) *Science of Education and the Psychology of the Child,* New York: Orion Press: 51.

Plummeridge, C. (1977) 'Music, knowledge and the curriculum', *Journal of Further and Higher Education,* 1/2, Summer: 55–64.

—— (1991) *Music Education in Theory and Practice,* London: Falmer.

Reid, L.A. (1986) *Ways of Understanding and Education,* London: Heinemann.

Schoen, M. (1940) *The Psychology of Music,* New York: Roland.

Seashore, C. (1938) *The Psychology of Music,* New York: McGraw-Hill.

Shuter-Dyson, R. and Gabriel, C. (1981) *The Psychology of Musical Ability,* London: Methuen.

Sloboda, J.A. (1985) *The Musical Mind. The Cognitive Psychology of Music,* Oxford: Oxford University Press.

Spearman, C.E. (1927) *The Abilities of Man,* London: Macmillan.

Spearman, C.E. (1930) *Creative Mind,* London: Nisbet.

Swanwick, K. (1988) *Music, Mind and Education,* London: Routledge.

—— (1994) *Musical Knowledge: Intuition, Analysis and Music Education,* London: Routledge.

Thurstone, L.L. (1938) 'Primary mental abilities' in *Psychometric Monograph,* no. 1, pp. 8, 10–11, 13.

Witkin, R. (1974) *The Intelligence of Feeling,* London: Heinemann.

7 Assessment in music education
David Bray

There are some aspects of assessment where music education has a long tradition and most people feel reasonably comfortable:

- marking GCSE or A level coursework;
- instrumental/vocal examinations;
- music competitions.

There are, however, other areas where teachers seem to be less confident and there is less agreement about the right way forward:

- Key Stage 3;
- National Curriculum End of Key Stage Level Descriptions.

There is also sometimes a prevailing feeling that music is one of those subjects difficult to assess; more difficult than subjects such as mathematics, for example, where things are perceived as being right or wrong.

It is not uncommon to hear comments such as:

Comment 1 It is difficult to assess compositions.
Comment 2 Assessing music is a subjective thing and you cannot be objective about it.
Comment 3 Aesthetic education is to do with feelings. You cannot assess these.

There is certainly something in these views.

Why is it that the assessment of compositions can seem to be difficult? For example, when assessing compositions:

- should we consider originality – and if so how do you assess this?
- should we take into account the complexity of the composition?
- what if the composition is the work of more than one student?

The assessment of GCSE compositions may help to answer some of these questions, since we have already noted that there is a fairly high level of confidence amongst teachers in this area. One of the reasons for this may be due to the fact that examination boards publish assessment criteria. Following these criteria helps us to feel that we are doing the 'right thing'. It may be helpful therefore to have some similar criteria when we assess compositions at Key Stage 3. The End of Key Stage Level Descriptions go some way towards this but are not really suitable for use each year, or even each term. They are generally not specific enough.

There is a sense then in which performance and listening are more straightforward to assess than composing, especially at KS3. Composing is an activity, not an outcome. This is a very important distinction and can lead to confusion. A helpful way of thinking about this may be to consider the difference between:

- the **activity** (composing); and
- the **outcome** (composition).

They are not the same thing. The **activity** (composing) is what students do in order to learn things or practise particular skills. The actual composition they produce may not be important and, if we focus all our assessment intentions onto the finished composition, we may be missing some very important factors in the whole process.

Once we start to consider the composition as an **outcome** (which therefore requires assessment) we will need to make judgements about things like:

- the structure of the piece;
- how effective it is;
- the technical skills used;

and a range of other things which can make the whole thing seem more complex and difficult to manage. Therefore, a way to avoid this problem is to consider that, on some occasions, it may be helpful not to assess the **composition**, but to focus on the skills and understanding the students demonstrate whilst **composing**. The finished composition was actually less important than the skills that students demonstrated whilst they were composing. These skills will be much easier to assess than the finished composition.

Finished compositions will need to be assessed from time to time, perhaps every term. When doing so it is probably most helpful to consider them as end points in a process (i.e. outcomes) and to use GCSE-type criteria.

However, when teaching GCSE students in Years 10 and 11 *it is not always helpful to only assess against the criteria supplied by examination boards*. The teacher will need to use these criteria (and will hopefully share them with students so that they are familiar with them). However, effective assessment will need to be more subtle than just using these criteria. The same principle applies to using the National Curriculum End of Key Stage Descriptions and A level specifications.

There are then two types of assessment in this model:

Type 1

Activity → e.g. composing → teacher assesses the skills, knowledge and understanding demonstrated as students compose (but not the composition)

Type 2

Outcome → e.g. composition → the teacher uses specific criteria (such as those used by GCSE examination boards) to assess a composition

---

An important principle worth remembering is that *assessment is more difficult when it is added at the end of a planning process.* If the teacher plans the curriculum and then plans how to assess it, assessment will seem hard to fit into the process, especially as other factors such as the National Curriculum or examination specifications will need to be put into the equation.

Therefore it makes more sense if the teacher decides what the students are to learn before planning the curriculum. Assessment will mean either seeing how far the students have met this aim (summative assessment) or offering students targets, written comments or verbal suggestions in order to help them to achieve the desired aim (formative assessment). There will be more information on these terms later.

Why is it that assessment sometimes seem difficult?

Often, difficulties can arise through a lack of clarity over terms and concepts. Confusion over terminology can make things seem more difficult than they perhaps are. Putting assessment at the start of the process and making sure we focus on the outcome (rather than the activity) can help.

There are other aspects of assessment where a confusion of terms can be unhelpful; for example, there are three common processes used in assessment:

- assessment;
- recording;
- reporting.

When talking about assessment, it is quite common to discuss marks or grades. This is part of the assessment process but there is far more to it than this. We might talk to someone about our assessment 'system' by showing them the mark sheet we use and as a result actually end up discussing the way we *record* assessments. Once again, the two are linked. They must be. However, designing an elaborate system which records our marks and grades may not lead to effective assessment. *It is the process, which leads to the record, which is most important.* Sometimes an enormous amount of time and effort is put into a system which records a great deal of information but which does not help students to learn. We want to devise a system that is:

- clear;
- easy to use;
- has a beneficial effect on learning;
- does not take up enormous amounts of time.

In fact it can be quite revealing to match the assessment activity in a school against these criteria and to discard any part of the process which does not make a suitable contribution.

If there are aspects of assessment in music where we feel comfortable why not just use these?

We have noted that some aspects of music education have built up a strong tradition of assessment methodology. In graded instrumental/vocal examinations, assessments are regularly made and there are things that we can learn from this system. There are, however, a number of points we will have to bear in mind:

- assessment in instrumental/vocal examinations is often 'summative' only;
- a lot of the assessment may be quite subjective;
- it often assumes a particular performance style which may be appropriate for only a small minority of students and which is therefore not going to have relevance for other students.

This kind of system therefore has relevance for a few students but cannot be applied to all. It will probably be most relevant to performing and not to composing or appraising music.

Why do we assess?

It may be helpful to remind ourselves of the reasons why we want to assess, so that we are working from important principles. If there were no reason to assess, we could dispense with the whole process immediately. However, teachers realize that assessment is important and often devote large amounts of time and effort to it.

We assess in order to:

1   gain information on the development, progress and achievement of students. This sort of information is required for parents. A parent will want to know:

- where her child is in relation to the attainment of his peers and what might be expected for his age group;
- how much effort her child has been putting into his work;
- how much progress her child has made since the last feedback;
- what her child needs to do in order to make progress;

2   evaluate the teaching and learning which has taken place, in order to see how effective a project has been and whether it should be adjusted in the future;

3   increase motivation and individual responsibility for learning.

The differences between assessment, recording and reporting

We have already noted that assessment, recording and reporting are closely linked and can easily be confused. For example, we may start our work on assessment planning by drawing up assessment forms. Before doing this, we perhaps need to ask:

- what it is we are trying to assess;
- how we intend to go about it.

Careful consideration of whether we are dealing with assessment, recording or reporting can be helpful.

Assessment

In lessons, assessment is actually a process by which the teacher (or student) makes judgements about teaching and learning within music lessons. There are four common types of assessment activity:

1   Giving marks or grades. This is usually summative.
2   Observation of activity in order to try and assess understanding. This is usually formative.
3   Question and answer techniques used to elicit understanding. This is usually formative.
4   Making comments to students about targets for improvement. This is usually formative.

All assessment types are relevant in music education and a balance will give secure information for planning future work. Most schools have a policy on these areas and it is helpful if the techniques used for assessment match what is happening in other subjects (i.e. the whole-school policy). A common approach will help students to understand how their work is assessed throughout the school.

What might we find in a music lesson where these techniques are working effectively?

- students' work is regularly evaluated (probably once every half term);
- the criteria for these evaluations are clear (to the teacher, students and parents);
- the criteria used are consistently applied;
- students are encouraged to use assessments as indications of how to make improvements in their work;
- there is evidence in the teacher's planning of a response to individual students (differentiation).

Recording

Once assessments are made, they need to be recorded so that they can be used for future reference. The emphasis should be on 'knows and understands' (outcomes) rather than 'has done' (activity). Accurate records give secure information, which can be used for the purposes of report writing.

Over-emphasis on the method used for recording information can lead to ineffective and time-consuming assessment.

The records kept by a teacher will probably follow a whole-school format. They should try to give information about what a students knows, understands and can do (i.e. skills) rather listing activities that a student has completed.

There are numerous ways of recording information. There are some good principles to follow:

- only collect information which is useful;
- make records regular (e.g. every half-term or term);
- be clear about recording effort or attainment;
- make the process manageable or it will not happen.

Do not make the process too general; it stands more chance of working if it is specific. For example, instead of just recording activities such as performing, composing and listening, make the recording process more related to a specific topic. If the class is going to do a project on chords, then decide what you want them to learn, by when and record it. Don't just record what they have done.

Reporting

Once a year, teachers are required to give a report to parents on a student's progress in all subjects. At key points the report will contain information on the National Curriculum Level Descriptions (e.g. for students aged 14). These are essentially summative statements about a student's work. *They should also describe the progress that has been made since the last report.*

Ideally students should be made aware of the methods used to assess their work and should be encouraged to become involved in the appraisal of their own work. Some schools use report banks, where a statement is selected from a range of possible options. These can be effective provided there is a sufficient range and variety of statements available.

What is the difference between formative and summative assessment?

The terms 'formative' and 'summative' assessment have already been used and are probably familiar. However, clarity here can really help. Summative assessments provide teachers, students and parents with information about the stage a particular student has reached at a specified time. We have already noted that instrumental graded examinations are one example of assessment with a strong summative element. This is the mark or grade given (the comments made will often be more formative in nature and may give information about how the student can improve). Usually, summative assessment information is related to peer group, age-related expectations or a particular grade or mark. A common form of summative assessment might be found in an end-of-year report. The student is given a grade and a comment.

Name	John Green
Class	7d2
Attainment	B
Effort	2

Plus the comment:

> John has worked well this year and I was pleased with the way that he has learned about chords during the reggae project.

The students and the parents know how John has done in terms of attainment. He seems to have done better than average (because the school uses a grading system which goes from A–E and John has scored a B). John also has quite a good grade for effort. The effort grade may mean that he has quite a good attitude in the lessons. These grades are summative. The report also includes a comment, which gives some formative information. However, although we know the teacher was pleased with a particular topic, we do not know what John needs to do in order to improve and get A for attainment and 1 for effort in Year 8. The report therefore lacks formative content. Nor do we have much information about the progress that John has made. There are two important points which need to be considered:

1   If the teacher has been making a series of formative assessments during the year and John already knows what was good about the reggae project and how he can improve, the information provided on the report is perfectly adequate.

2   If the student or parent were to ask the teacher how a decision had been reached to award a grade B for attainment, would the teacher be able to show the evidence which had led them to the decision? Did John Green get a grade B because, over a period of time, it was the average grade that he was awarded for various projects and so a grade B would be about what he might expect?

Julian White	
Effort	1
Attainment	C

Even less helpful are reports that comment mainly on attitudes:

> I have been pleased with some of the work that Julian has done this year. He is a conscientious student and has a good attitude to his work.

The report gives little information about what Julian has done, what he was good at and how he can improve. It certainly gives no information on the progress made since the last report (which is a statutory requirement).

There is little formative assessment. Julian might like to move from a grade C to B or A. However, it is hard for him to improve without clear information about what needs to be done. Over-concentration on summative assessment can therefore be de-motivating for students. It can also lead teachers to think that assessment is point-less and appears to be taking them away from the task of teaching.

Formative assessment

Formative assessment is more diagnostic and gives information to teachers, students and parents about how a student is progressing and which areas need to be improved. It can help to motivate students. Formative assessment consists of:

- comments made by the teacher to a student about how to improve a partic-ular aspect of their work;
- written comments on a piece of work which give information about how work could develop and improve (particularly important for examination classes);
- diagnostic comments which enable a student to improve their work.

Formative verbal comments:

Example

A Year 9 student is working on a piece with contrasting textures. The teacher listens to the piece and identifies that the piece might benefit from a clearer structure. The student is encouraged to consider how two clear textures can be used to contrast ideas and provide a sense of tension and resolution. The student is asked to develop these ideas further.

Formative written comments:

Example

A Year 10 student is composing a piece based on a chord structure. The teacher does not give a mark for the work but writes comments on the student's notes and suggests some ideas for the student to try. Over the next two lessons, the student works on these ideas and the teacher refers back to his comments when he re-evaluates the piece.

What about involving students in self-assessment?

With careful planning and management, the involvement of students in assessment can have a significant impact on motivation and the quality of work produced. It is clearly important that the students have an understanding of *what* they are doing and *how* they are doing. Some activities are not appropriate for self-assessment and the teacher will need to use discretion. However, self-assessment should be encouraged because it can:

- improve motivation;
- lead to better communication between the teacher and student;
- provide the teacher with useful insights into how a student perceives an activity;
- enhance the validity of teacher assessment.

A weakness of self-assessment is that students are sometimes asked to evaluate in an unfocused and uninformed way.

Example

I liked it when we played the keyboards and made up the piece using the drum beat. I worked well on this.

The teacher has been helped in assessing the students' attitudes. The problem with this self-assessment has arisen due to a lack of communication between the teacher and the students.

At the end of a project the teacher might decide that he wishes to make a final assessment of the students' work. It is once again important to give clear information about how the work is to be assessed. The teacher may say, for example, that the compositions are going to be assessed using grades A–E for attainment and that, in addition, each group, or each individual, will receive an effort grade of 1–5. This information is useful for the students and they might be asked to make an assessment of the grade they think they should be given.

Perhaps even more useful would be for the teacher to try and give some kind of criteria to go with the grades. For example, when working on a project which focuses on semitones and chord clusters, students could be asked to assess themselves using the following criteria:

---

1   In this project I made effective use of semitones and clusters and it is imaginative and interesting.
2   In this project I made effective use of both semitones and clusters.
3   In this project I made some use of semitones and clusters.
4   In this project I made some use of either semitones or clusters.
5   In this project I did not make use of semitones or clusters.

In practice there may be too many statements. Most projects will probably only require three. They will probably describe:

- the expectation (achieved by the majority of students);
- attainment above expectation;
- working towards the expectation.

Criteria can easily be devised for effort and these will probably be applicable to most projects.

By the time end-of-year reports come to be written, the teacher might have records of a number of effective self-assessments. It is particularly helpful if this sort of information is given to students before they start the project and if they are reminded of the criteria as they go. In this way, the self-assessment can become formative as well as including a final summative process.

The key to making this successful will be the criteria that are given to students for their self-assessment. If they are too open-ended, they are unlikely to be successful.

What are learning outcomes in music and how should I plan for them?

Learning outcomes are what a teacher expects students to achieve. They are the end result of a process. It really helps the assessment process if this is the starting point for the curriculum. We have already noted that it is preferable to plan these *before* the activities that are intended to achieve them. So what do learning outcomes look like? They are commonly expressed in terms of attitudes, knowledge, understanding and skills.

Attitudes

Attitudes are important. For example: it is pointless planning a curriculum if students end up disliking music at the end of it. Attitudes are relatively easy to assess since all the teacher has to do is ask the student for information about their attitudes to a particular topic.

> ### Example
>
> In a Year 8 class, students have been working on rhythm. As part of this, they have looked at rhythmic devices from a number of cultures. Some of the students have listened to a piece by Sheila Chandra and decided that they like the use of Indian-influenced 'talas'.

Knowledge

Knowledge in music is facts about pieces, people or things. Facts (and therefore knowledge) are easy to assess:

- how many symphonies did Mozart write ?
- how many strings are there on a cello?
- what notes are they tuned to?
- rearrange these letters, GORAN, into an instrument.

Although easy to assess, these sorts of facts can be a pitfall within the music curriculum. Teaching facts can result in time-consuming and peripheral activity. Students will usually fill in missing words or complete work sheets quite diligently. They will probably not develop good attitudes to music and they will certainly not experience really musical events at work. The teacher may wish students to acquire a particular piece of knowledge and may want them to know certain facts about music or musicians. However, he needs to be aware of the dangers of constructing a curriculum based around knowledge. For example, when planning lessons on Stravinsky's *Firebird*, lessons might consist only of writing information about the composer, the piece of music and then listening to it. The project may contain a lot of activity, but it is divorced from the students' own practical exploration of music. Knowledge about music has been allowed to replace understanding of music. This sort of activity may be devised in order to show how music can contribute to literacy skills.

Understanding

Understanding is harder to define and therefore harder to assess. *It is, however, the most important outcome of any musical interaction in a classroom or in an out-of-class activity.*

In the example quoted above, we mentioned Stravinsky's *Firebird* as an example of a piece which is often written about in music lessons. What are the features of the piece that we wish to concentrate on with the students? It can sometimes be useful to refer to the musical elements. The teacher might decide to start by looking at timbre and decide to pose some questions to the students:

- which instruments can be used to create the tension felt in the Infernal Dance?
- what special effects can we get from the instruments that we have available in class so that we can enhance the effect we want to create?

Having explored the idea of timbre and its effects, the teacher might move on to get the students to use some of these effects in their own music. At the point where they are using particular instruments to create an effect, they are approaching musical understanding. If they can also start to recognize this in the works of others (from different styles and cultures) they are probably well on the way to showing understanding.

Understanding can be assessed through:

- listening to compositions to see how effective students have been in using the musical material we are working with and whether they have managed to create the desired effect;
- asking them questions whilst they are composing or rehearsing pieces of music;
- asking them about what processes they can hear going on in a piece of music they listen to.

Their answers will give good information about the level of their musical understanding. Both of these procedures require the teacher to be astute and to make effective use of questioning.

Skills

Students will need to develop skills in each Key Stage. These will include:

- performing pieces on an instrument/voice;
- developing a sense of ensemble;
- ICT skills;
- improvisation skills;
- playing by ear and from memory;
- the ability to develop and extend compositions;
- being able to communicate with an audience;
- working together in a group;
- presentation skills.

Some skills are relatively easy to assess. For example: information on summative performance assessments can be found in examination specifications and instrumental examination schemes. There is a long tradition of assessing these skills. Others are less regularly assessed: for example working together in a group or presentation skills. More thought may need to be given about how to assess these. Clarity over the intended outcome should make assessment in all these areas possible. These outcomes can be shared with students, who can be asked to make their own self-assessments and helpful verbal and written formative comments can be given.

Using the National Curriculum Level Descriptions for Key Stage 3 students

Towards the end of Year 9, students will need to be assessed against the National Curriculum Level Descriptions. This will be a summative assessment and will be based on information that has been obtained and recorded about what a student knows, understands and can do (i.e. learning outcomes). Because the Level Description is a summative assessment, it is probably not helpful to plan your assessment system around it. This is a similar point to the one already made about not necessarily using terminal examination criteria with students during the early part of their course. For example, it may be helpful to put into place an assessment system which is mostly related to your scheme of work and then to assess against the Level Descriptions at the end of Year 9.

Provided your scheme of work addresses the National Curriculum Programme of Study, this should not pose too much problem. For example, during Years 7 to 9 students will control sounds through singing and playing, create and develop musical ideas, respond to and review music, listen to music and apply knowledge and understanding. Therefore, by the end of Year 9, students will have covered all the relevant sections of the music KS3 National Curriculum Programme of Study.

Some teachers may want to divide their assessment methodology into five strands, based on the paragraphs in the music National Curriculum document (pp. 20–1). This is certainly a possibility. The danger of this process is that the assessment might be added on at the end, rather than being an integral part of the process. This is why careful planning of the scheme of work is so important and why it can save a lot of time and confusion when it comes to thinking about assessment.

Whichever way it is done, the teacher should end up with quite a lot of information about the student:

- marks or grades in a mark book;
- pieces of work that have written comments;
- verbal comments that have been made to the student;
- targets for improvement that have been set;
- other information that the teacher knows about the student.

This information will now be used in order to inform the level that the student can best be described as working at.

Using Level Descriptions

Most 14 year-olds will be working at levels 5 or 6. In order to help make a decision about which level to apply it is possible to break the statements in the Level Description down into their separate parts and give examples by each statement of how students have demonstrated this achievement. The students could be involved in this process themselves.

Level 5	Give examples of how students have achieved this
Students identify and explore musical devices and how music reflects time and place.	
They perform significant parts from memory and from notations with awareness of their own contribution such as leading others, taking a solo part and/or providing rhythmic support.	
They improvise melodic and rhythmic material within given structures, use a variety of notations,	
and compose music for different occasions using appropriate musical devices such as melody, rhythms, chords and structures.	
They analyse and compare musical features.	
They evaluate how venue, occasion and purpose affect the way music is created, performed and heard.	
They refine and improve their work.	

Level 6 Give examples of how students have achieved this
Students identify and explore the different processes and contexts of selected musical genres and styles.
They select and make expressive use of tempo, dynamics, phrasing and timbre.
They make subtle adjustments to fit their own part within a group performance.
They improvise and compose in different genres and styles, using harmonic and non-harmonic devices where relevant, sustaining and developing musical ideas and achieving different intended effects.
They use relevant notations to plan, revise and refine material.
They analyse, compare and evaluate how music reflects the contexts in which it is created, performed and heard.
They make improvements to their own and others' work in the light of the chosen style.

Of course, some students will be at higher or lower levels. Some of these statements could be broken down still further. For example:

Level 6 Give examples of how students have achieved this
They improvise and compose in different genres and style,
using harmonic and non-harmonic devices where relevant,
sustaining and developing musical ideas,
achieving different intended effects.

This process is very thorough, but may end up being too cumbersome.

Summary

- Assessment is made easier by clarity over terminology.
- It is easier if assessment aims are set out before planning the activities that will be undertaken.
- Give students information about expectations for each project, use these to set targets and keep records of how well they do. Provided this information is well-focused, it can be useful to involve students in a certain amount of self-assessment.

Reference

Bray, D. (2000) *Teaching Music in the Secondary School*, London: Heinemann.

2 Musical activities

8 Putting listening first
A case of priorities
Philip Priest

Within every view of musicianship we will find those perceptions, skills and responses that we refer to as 'aural'. The need for a label is the result of music having become a subject, an activity to be trained in. For it is only because we refer to printed scores, because we can study music silently, that the need is felt to stress the fundamental and overriding place of the ear in music. The totally aural tradition of most musics of the world means that they would have no need of the arguments reviewed here, though we can learn much from them. Even for formally-educated, British musicians, the idea of listening as 'the normal mode of all musical experience' is surely undeniable, though Brian Loane's argument (1984) that 'listening is the whole of music education' may be too strong for some.

George Pratt (1990) has challenged the common practice understood by 'aural training' with ideas, developed from a research programme, which broaden and perhaps deepen our understanding of the term. We must all develop a better understanding of what is meant by 'aural' in music education. The use of the term is odd, despite its familiarity to music teachers. Programmes of Study in music, particularly those leading to examinations at GCSE or A level or instrumental grades, are broken up according to a syllabus and one section is allocated to aural. Imagine periods of 'visual' training in art education, or 'visual' tests appended to drawing examinations. We have aural culture, aural training, aural skills and, of course, aural tests. The word is used as a noun – even a plural noun, and has developed an organic life of its own. Here are a few reactions by PGCE students to the aural lessons they received in schools, colleges and universities:

Comment 1 The aural that we were subjected to was either too difficult or too easy.
Comment 2 I had no idea how inflexible the teaching of aural would be … limited to trying to write down rhythms, melodies and chord progressions as required by exam boards.
Comment 3 As soon as they say aural I go deaf … notes swim about in my head.

The dissection of aural acuity in music into rhythm, pitch, amplitude and so on, in the 1930s, while helpful in an academic sense, has held sway ever since in the form of compartmentalized testing. Worse still, the emphasis on tests has been tied inextricably to notation. 'Aural' has usually meant writing. An assumption of literacy skills is always present, with 'co-ordination of ear and eye' given as the most useful skill of a musician. This link between aural and literacy is strong: it is said that the 'aural

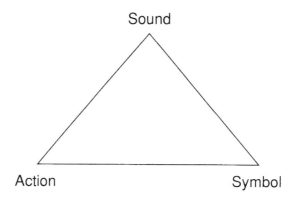

mental-image' gives the power to 'hear' printed music silently; and that sound or action can be enough to recall the symbol (see the above diagram).

This view of 'aural' forms the basis of books of 'aural method', examination syllabuses and common practice in schools and colleges. The fact that young instrumentalists can read is taken for granted; that many of them seem to have difficulty in hearing is merely regretted; and individual response to music as art does not feature generally in work under the 'aural' heading. As another student said about his aural class at a conservatoire: 'It seemed ridiculous to have a music college full of people who thought they couldn't hear very much'.

To be able to write what is heard accurately enough for another performance is of course a useful skill. But to see aural development in music education in this limited way not only ignores the musician who does not read and music which has not been written; it also means that the concentration on accuracy of pitch and rhythm marginalizes any other quality of music. Yet the idea persists. Of course it is important to encourage children to develop their 'inner ear', as it is called – the ability to recall in silence music that has been heard previously; but the idea that true understanding of music is reserved exclusively for those who can read notation is preposterous. (For those who need reassurance about the value of non-literate intelligence I recommend Howard Gardner's *Frames of Mind,* especially the chapters on 'Music' and 'Kinaesthetic intelligence'.)

Even the widely-used tests of musical ability have been seen as subtly assuming a knowledge of notation, whilst one of the standard aural tests of the examining boards demands an oral description of notation. Small wonder that so many parents and other adults consider themselves to be non-musicians, or even unmusical, because they cannot read.

Notation implies conscious analysis and can lead to an assumption that memory depends on this. This is not true. Tunes we know are not 'coded in memory' by differences in pitches and rhythm alone, and are not recognized like this either. Memory and recognition are complete experiences: the meaning of music is conveyed by the interaction of its parts. By Swanwick's (1979) use of the terms 'materials' and 'elements' of music, we may recognize the familiar problem of students battling with traditional aural testing: not being able to see the wood for the trees, and oblivious to the beauty of either.

Some music educators, trying to move away from a dependence on reading when discussing hearing, acknowledge the fundamental place of aural ability, referring to it as 'thinking in sounds'. They imply that literacy may not be involved at all, but regret that this would make an incomplete musician. Others have been well aware of the need to develop perception and imagery and 'auditory feeling' in order to avoid a mechanical approach to reading. If musical understanding is the objective, different from 'knowing about music', then the ability to use operations in music is clearly more important than knowing the formal names for them: terms such as 'dominant', 'perfect cadence', 'legato', or the note names of pitch or rhythm. All of these familiar materials of music can be understood, and are used, by musicians who do not know these names. There are musical operations which do not have adequate terminology or signs, which cannot be expressed adequately in words. These are much more interesting and challenging because they represent much less secure territory in formal teaching.

Confusion has always been apparent between aural awareness of music as an expressive power and notation and names. Three hundred years ago Christopher Simpson was baffled by 'hard words and obscure terms' and how these related to the 'tuning of a song' (Lawrence 1978). And Carl Seashore (1938–67), who writes of sensing and imaging sounds and of 'sustained thinking' in them, is very blunt about so-called musicians who cannot do this: 'Some musicians are not musical,' he writes.

Fifty years ago, writers on music education in this country and in America were enthusing about the need for ear-training to aim for a grasp of phrase and tonality rather than a sort of drill with tests of separated aspects of sound. Yet the response by teachers to the aural tests of examining boards is so often a form of drill: coaching for particular tests; dealing in materials rather than elements, for the most part unrelated to the pupils' instrumental playing and to music they know; and using only the piano. A former student, recalling her first experience of an ABRSM aural test for a grade exam, said, 'It didn't sound like any other music I knew.' The task of practice in these tests is in some cases left to someone – anyone – else:

Comment 1 'I couldn't do aural, there wasn't a piano.'
Comment 2 'I don't deal with aural – I leave that to your class teacher.'
Comment 3 'I had heard other people talking about aural but I had never really understood what it was. When I asked my teacher whether we would be doing some she said: "Oh no, we don't need to do any because you are not taking any exams yet".'

'Aural', in the experience of those we teach, should be concerned with sounds in the head and responding to them practically. These can be remembered sound patterns or new, imagined ones. We might depend on some prop or mental reference point which could be aided by notation, but need not be. If such imaging of sounds is considered to be an essential part of behaving like a musician, it should be integrated with other aspects. Then the aural experience would be seen and felt to be at the heart of musicianship, at the heart of performance, at the heart of composition and at the heart of listening, rather than the appendage it sometimes is when the following of notation is insisted on, and for many absorbs all their attention.

Some teachers' work is as soundly based as this; but what is equally true is that children are still emerging from the formal education system as musicians lacking skills and perceptions identified as essential for musicianship. Included among these children are some who became teachers, primary and secondary, class and instrumental. And so the system can so easily perpetuate a cycle of deprivation among formally-taught musicians.

Aurally-based methods do exist in the UK and are used widely, commonly, of course, by musicians learning outside the formal education system. They are used too by those teachers fostering jazz- and rock-inspired groups in schools, by Suzuki teachers for certain instruments, by many of those who train steel bands and by many vocal groups. All of these, however, lean towards the learning of a fixed or teacher-chosen repertoire by rote, with less attention, or perhaps none, given to imaginative exploration of sound: using your instrument to make your own music. Now that such exploration is considered to be an essential feature of the curriculum, we should ask whether this is fostered best by aurally-based methods, and whether it may be frustrated by the habit of using notation.

The influence of reading on the development of skills and musical understanding is very strong. To many, reading notation is such a basic part of musicianship that it hardly needs to be mentioned. Can you imagine the art of choreography developing in the way that musical notation has, to the extent that literacy in it takes over in dance in formal education? In order to learn to dance at school you must read the notation.

Some class teachers believe that literacy skills have been overstressed in the past, but among instrumental teachers there seems to be no choice for those they teach *but* to read. If children who learn instruments, and their teachers, are never seen to operate without reading, a strong impression is given to all other children.

Research studies highlighting the negative aspects of an insistence on musical literacy have been ignored. Many students wishing to pursue music at degree level, and graduates applying to become teachers, view with suspicion and alarm the idea that they should play at all without notation. This is regrettable, but it can be overcome. The effect on those children still struggling with basic technique who are expected always to read while playing is even more unfortunate, for they may be discouraged and give up. In the classroom, the eighth-year pupil trying to learn two or three chord shapes on keyboard would become fluent in them much more quickly without books or work sheets to decipher. And in the practice room, pupil and teacher of cornet or clarinet could more usefully have their eyes free for each other rather than fixed constantly at the tutor-book.

Materials for use in school have been criticized for the imbalance shown between the over-stressed learning of symbols and the more necessary aural discrimination. 'Sound before the sign' seems to be interpreted by some as 'sound illustration before the inevitable and obligatory sign'. The intention is surely that sounds should be enjoyed, worked with, chosen and arranged independently of any signs, until the children feel the need to fix their musical ideas graphically. And when they do, increasingly there is available a machine that will do it for them. As a breed, we music teachers are slow to help children realize the inadequacy of musical notation to convey the essentials of music – anything beyond the nuts and bolts. The very basic sheet music produced for chart songs may be an acknowledgement that, since one cannot convey the original in print, a sort of blueprint is best: a ground plan on which to build.

Arguments for the importance of music literacy include the claim for the 'social discipline' of reading and playing a part in ensemble. But this is too often practised at the expense of listening, which tends to be hindered or even obscured completely – especially by the habitual concentration on counting rests. In any case, literacy is only necessary for certain groups playing certain kinds of music.

Before moving on to consider how teaching and learning can take place without omnipresent notation, it may be useful to glimpse how music is taught and caught in some other societies, and to see what can be learned from them.

In Afghanistan there is a form of oral notation, with names for pitch and rhythm, but it is known and used only by professional musicians (Baily 1979). It is part of the secret science of music, kept secret because it is not written down. The children of professionals are encouraged to observe, learn and join in as soon as possible with their parents' public performances. Amateur music-making is done in private, for the performer's own enjoyment. A more accurate translation of the word for amateur is 'enthusiast'. Children are actively discouraged from wanting to play. A determined teenager has to learn by stealth, creeping out after dark, watching other players from a distance, even denying that he has learned in this way, and practising secretly. Do we distinguish between intending amateurs and intending professionals? Should we? Who is more enthusiastic? Do we offer too much instruction? Should public performance be the goal for all?

The music of the Japanese puppet theatre has been systematized for over 200 years, but apparently without recourse to standardized notation (Motegi 1984). Traditionally, aural methods are used, based on listening, watching and imitating; though some teachers or schools have developed their own system of notation as an *aide-mémoire*, scribbled in the margin of the script. For performance, however, both libretto and cues must be memorized. It is claimed for these methods that they develop a clear understanding of the music's structure, foster musical imagination, and allow – even demand – freedom of interpretation. Recent attempts to revive wider interest in the genre have been on different lines, resulting in uniformity through the use of tapes and notation from the outset. Pupils who learn by this modern method can perform more quickly, it is acknowledged, but they are said to 'master the form' without being able to 'express the content'. Are these musicians in our schools who have 'mastered the form' but fail to 'express the content'? We refer to such playing as 'unmusical' (or 'playing without the music', as Busoni wrote, in contrast to 'playing without the copy'). Would we be willing, as teachers, to marginalize notation?

A similar form of rudimentary notation was discovered by Colin McPhee for the Balinese gamelan. It was never intended to be read in performance, serving mainly as a reminder of the 'nuclear tones' for specialists. Traditional music was – is – kept alive by group-memory, and new compositions are taught direct to the players by the composer. In McPhee's colourful account some methods of teaching are described, including the singing of tunes before playing them, all depending on acute listening and copying someone else – the teacher or a more advanced player. 'The teacher explains nothing, since for him there is nothing to explain' (McPhee 1955). Yet the music is not simple – nothing like as simple as some parts our children play in brass and wind band marches, or 'Tunes for strings', which have to be read. Every rehearsal had the pitched instruments accompanied by the 'exuberant' rhythmic drive of the gongs and cymbals. McPhee says he thought it was this background that gave impetus, 'that made these rehearsals go, made these children coherent from the very start'. Have we anything to learn? Music literacy serves music teachers well in so many ways. We may deny that it hinders our own aural awareness at all and this may be the case. But the argument here is made from the perception of what music is to those who do not read, and to some – the majority – who never will.

Peter Ustinov tells how, on a train journey, he was reading the newspaper, looking across occasionally at a man sitting opposite who was reading an Eulenburg miniature score. The man smiled from time to time and even chuckled with delight as he turned a page. Ustinov says he never felt more inferior in all his life.

Yet if we are to encourage music teachers to downgrade the importance of notation, to defer its introduction, even to do without it or at least put it in its place and concentrate on aural awareness and still to pursue children's development through performance and composition, then some will feel a prop has been removed. It is a useful prop. The trouble is we tend to rely on it too much, because we can, and maybe to insist on it because we know it and they don't. What else do we put in its place? How else can we refer to music? What is there of substance children can learn and be seen – and heard – to learn?

How do trombonists know how far to move the slide? How is it that pianists seem to know where to put their fingers? How do kit drummers become so well co-ordinated with hands and feet? These are the questions in the minds of children, sometimes put to teachers, and the answers all have to do with the psychomotor element in the process of playing a musical instrument, which has been undervalued by teachers.

Kemp (1990), writing on kinaesthesia in music, reminds us that we are dealing with both the sense of touch and of movement; with both the physical feeling – through fingers, mouth or feet – of an instrument, poised to produce a certain known sound, and with the movement of various parts of the body to change this sound – its duration, timbre, dynamic or pitch. The distinction is between the tactile and the kinaesthetic.

Analyses attach much importance to 'mechanized processes' in the development of musical skills on instruments (Priest 1989). These are developed through repetition, with 'each isolated action in the series becoming a stimulus to the next'. There is general agreement among psychologists that musical performance must be based on the 'mechanization of the sound-action relationship' (Mainwaring 1951). Some music teachers might react to the use of the term 'mechanized' and confuse it with 'mechanical' performance. 'Mechanized' refers to the way in which basic common patterns of sound (for example scale passages, chords) are produced on instruments – how they are learned and how executed. The player is still free subtly to change the way they are played – in tempo, gradation of tone, or in any other way. The point is that he is not having to concentrate on the basic action of fingers, arms and mouth, but on the sound and its effect. If a player's conscious mind is to be on the aesthetic aspect of the music then there must be a large degree of 'automatic performance'. In the early stages of learning, both teacher and learner must consciously attend to physical skills. Physicians, particularly neurologists, give very detailed accounts of the fine changes in all forms of physical movement and sensation in singing and playing that must be experienced and learned (Phillips 1977).

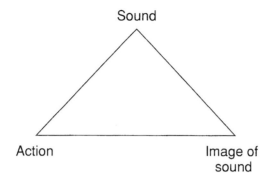

In most analyses the eye is involved, responding to notation. But there is a suggestion that the aural image of the sound might be enough to stimulate the action, once learned. Now, if this image of a sound can be experienced without a visual (notation) symbol, either real or imagined, and if this is sufficient to be able to reproduce that sound on an instrument, then we seem to have a different triangle. We now have a similar link between an aural image, the action to produce it and the sound itself – playing by ear (see the above diagram).

But how can we best develop in young beginners this familiarity with the instrument; this concentration on sound shapes rather than on their graphic representation, on the thing itself rather than pictures of it? By acknowledging ways of learning kinaesthetically.

Among others (see Kemp 1990), here are two. First, by valuing experiment. Interest in soundmaking activities through experiment is often thought of in connection with very young children, but such interest can be observed in people of any age; and perhaps could be allowed, or encouraged, more by music teachers, because the feedback of the sound produced by the action is the greatest aid. Once a sequence of movements, different in some degree from our previous attempt, produces a sound that pleases us, our classmates or our teachers, then we can repeat it, return to it and remember it like Skinner's pigeons.

Second, by accepting the importance of the 'image of an action' (Priest 1989). This can include all forms of pretend or imaginary action springing from musical performance – voluntary or involuntary. One example is the extrovert members of a Year 7 class miming the action of a trombone as soon as it is mentioned. Another is the silent 'bowing' (arm movements) that usually accompanies the marking of string parts. It is the common experience of instrumentalists, when listening to others play, to 'feel' the actions of the players, to share the sensation of playing. In its most gross form, this might include very definite movements of limbs and digits, clearly perceptible and even disturbing to others. Usually there will be only tiny muscular changes to various parts of the body, involving the diaphragm and the larynx, even though they need not result in a sound. Instrumental teachers may recognize in this the way they are ready for action as a pupil plays – breathing with the phrases even with stringed instruments, ready to burst into a vocal version of the music being attempted. The teacher's 'ghosting' action is supposed to encourage the player.

But a fundamental point has been made about imaging the action: 'the instrumentalist is apt to use fingers, etc. in cognizing music' (Vernon 1933). Or to use

Kemp's words, 'knowing through whole-body experience' (Kemp 1990). Here we have the idea of cognition that comes from practical action associated with sound but independent of signs and labels. 'Doing is active, analytic, critical and objective.' Kinaesthesis is valuable in drumming fingers on thighs with, say, trumpet fingering, or forming the shape of chords for an imaginary keyboard on the table, as an aid – tactile or kinaesthetic – in the same way that a visual cue is an aid. And by 'visual cue' in this context, we should think not of notation or other written instructions, but of seeing the teacher or another player. The learner sees an action which produces a sound – a hand position, arm movement or inclination of the head – and imitates it, hoping for the same result. Aural, visual, kinaesthetic and tactile senses operate together, and an attempt can be made to produce a similar sound to the teacher's model. The development or growth in skill and powers of expression through experience will be with the continued aid of a model, usually the teacher. Close imitation of the action of others is a common trait, forming the basis of the work of mimics, actors and dancers. Kinaesthesis has been described as the 'sixth sense': 'the capacity to act gracefully, to apprehend directly the actions or the dynamic abilities of other people and objects' (Gardner 1983).

All musical performance, then, has an important psychomotor element. Playing without notation, in its many forms, is likely to be especially dependent on this element. The action of playing is real, and needs no intermediary between it and the aural image. The sounds themselves, and the means to produce them, form the only substance necessary to play. Even if the name and sign are known, still the physical means to produce the sounds might give a stronger identity to that sound for some players. The *feel* of playing low F on trombone, or of grabbing a diminished seventh chord on a keyboard, is important to the player. For some it may be the strongest image of the sound, or even the only one. The image of the action can conjure up the image of the sound. The skill of playing is acquired, at least in part, experimentally and in imitation of a model. But however important the psychomotor element, the aural image comes first. If a child is about to play a tune or chord sequence from memory, s/he might go through the note-names, or might rely on 'motor memory'; but the most important thing is that she should recall the sound of the tune.

References

Baily, J. (1979) 'Professional and amateur musicians in Afghanistan', *World of Music* 212.

Gardner, H. (1983) *Frames of Mind*, London: Heinemann.

Kemp, A. (1990) 'Kinaesthesia in music and its implications for developments in microtechnology', *British Journal of Music Education* (7)3.

Lawrence, I. (1978) *Composers and Music Education*, Aldershot: Scolar Press.

Loane, B. (1984) 'On "listening" in music education', *British Journal of Music Education* (1)1.

McPhee, C. (1955) 'Children and music in Bali' in Meade and Wolferson (eds) *Childhood and Contemporary Cultures,* Chicago: University of Chicago Press.

Mainwaring, J. (1951) 'Psychological factors in the teaching of music', *British Journal of Educational Psychology* XXI, Part II.

Motegi, K. (1984) 'Aural learning in Gidayu-bushi music of the Japanese puppet theatre', *Yearbook for Traditional Music* 16.

Phillips, C. (1977) 'Brains and hands' in Critchley and Henson (eds) *Music and the Brain*, London: Heinemann.

Pratt, G. (1990) *Aural Awareness*, Milton Keynes: Open University Press.

Priest, P. (1989) 'Playing by ear: its nature and application to instrumental teaching', *British Journal of Music Education* (6)2.

Seashore, C. (1938/67) *Psychology of Music*, New York: McGraw Hill/Dover.

Swanwick, K. (1979) *A Basis for Music Education*, Slough: NFER-Nelson.

Vernon, P. (1933) 'The apprehension and cognition of music', *Proceedings of the Music Society*.

9 Developing vocal skills in the secondary classroom

Nicholas Bannan

Introduction

This chapter is about vocal skills in classroom Music teaching, focusing on Key Stage 3 of the National Curriculum. I make the assumption throughout, based on research into the nature of interpersonal vocal communication in the human species, that the skills to be developed are both those of the pupils and those of the teacher; and that this is a shared and continuing process. The majority of activities outlined in the chapter are based on the idea of *teaching through* rather than *teaching about;* and make the assumption that everyone, teacher and pupil alike, has a potentially expressive singing voice the development of which can yield pleasure in its own right while also providing a powerful underpinning to other aspects of musical learning. Teachers who are well-informed about the nature of the vocal instrument and how to employ it confidently are the more likely to act as effective vocal leaders in the classroom.

Singing is prescribed in the National Curriculum (1999):

> ### Controlling sound through singing and playing – performing skills
>
> 1   Pupils should be taught to:
>   ▪   sing unison and part songs developing vocal techniques and musical expression

It is additionally implied that all creative tasks can employ the voice. Vocal work has also featured as an activity present in schools whose inspection in Music has received praise, and snapshots of good practice have been published in the Ofsted *Review of Inspection Findings 1993/4* (HMSO 1995) and *The Arts Inspected* (1998), excerpts from both of which will be drawn on to illustrate this chapter. What is clear from the former is that lessons based on vocal participation represented amongst both the best and the least successful teaching observed. This 'black and white' picture is consistent with individuals' responses to whether or not they enjoy singing: it can be either amongst the most pleasurable and fulfilling activities for some pupils, or an apparent purgatory for others. Given the social and physical nature of singing, it cannot flourish as a passive activity: so the foremost challenge to the teacher is the creation of the right psychological environment in which to encourage universal participation. In turn, the quality of vocal leadership of teachers plays a key role in whether pupils respond to them expressively and with confidence.

At KS3, singing is subject to the additional challenges, at least in modern western society, that physical growth brings about vocal change which can undermine progress; and that peer-consciousness and adolescent attitudes to matters of repertoire and style can stifle creativity and inhibit the development of performing skills. Research and inspection evidence would suggest that this poses greater problems for boys, and that the effects are noticeable even before the completion of Year 6. The change of school which occurs between KS2 and KS3 represents the critical point at which pupils' vocal development needs to addressed effectively if the potential of each child is to be realized. Unfortunately, inspection evidence reveals that this is not always accomplished:

> in the majority of schools the achievement of all pupils, but particularly those of middle and upper ability, is limited seriously by the low challenge of the tasks set. Singing of a technical and expressive quality which would rarely be tolerated in Y6 is often welcomed in Y7.
>
> (Ofsted 1995: 8)

> Lacklustre singing is accepted, and sometimes praised.
>
> (ibid.: 12)

On the other hand:

> a large minority of the more successful lessons focus on singing; such lessons occur in all year groups of the Key Stage, and in co-educational schools, boys' schools and girls' schools.
>
> (ibid.: 12)

What are the teachers of these classes doing right?

The roots of this variation in teachers' perfomance would seem to go back a generation or so to a world in which singing was largely abandoned as elitist, reactionary or unpopular in comparison with creative work on instruments (see Bannan 1994, for a discussion of this). For some teachers, the requirements of the National Curriculum may have come as something of a shock. Consider what, in 1995, was described as expected within KS2 (Year 6):

> At age 11, pupils should be able to sing in tune over a range which exceeds an octave. They perform complete songs from memory in a range of styles, demonstrating awareness of audience and occasion. They sustain parts in rounds or simple songs. They talk constructively about their own singing, and that of other pupils … . They improvise vocally and instrumentally on sets of notes, including pentatonic scales.
>
> (ibid.: 32–34)

Note particularly *they talk constructively about their own singing and that of other pupils*. What is described here is a context in which singing is engaged in through imaginative teaching which takes account of the responses of the pupils. It would not be unfair to state that singing has traditionally been managed in a manner which leaves little or no room for self-expression. On the one hand, we have the hangover from the community singing ethos, wherein song suppressed individuality in the interests of group identity through the lusty performance of religious, national or moralist material. This tended towards a confrontational style whereby pupils were coerced into singing by the sheer volume of the teacher's own voice or, worse, explosive pianism. On the other hand, there is the condescension of the *sotto voce* singalong, a kind of lobotomized karaoke in which repertoire is worked through to little audible effect. In both cases, 'low challenges of tasks set' are part of the problem. But so is the severe lack of that fundamental of good teaching, effective interaction with the children: in short, education. The touchstone should be: is the activity enhancing the singing ability of the class? If class-singing teaches children to sing less well, or not at all, there is something wrong!

This chapter will propose that the means of matching the excellent practice divulged by the Ofsted reports are available to every prospective music teacher who is prepared to explore the exciting resources which can inform a modern and enticing approach to classroom singing: varied material, including multicultural music from a wide variety of cultures and songs from the whole gamut of western art and folk traditions; appropriate use of ICT; practical knowledge of the workings of children's voices and how they develop during adolescence; consciousness of the social and personal development associated with successful vocal performance; and foremost, a curiosity and desire on the part of teachers to employ their own prime resource, the singing voice with which they were born and which they, as a musician, should be able to exploit to the full.

Knowing your tools

How voices work

Pupils have every right to assume that anyone who asks them to sing will know how to help them overcome any problems which might arise when they do: this ought to be true of both classroom teachers and choral conductors. The turn of the twenty-first century is a pretty good time at which to think about how the voice works. Clinical research into both the anatomy of the vocal organ and the neurology of oral communication has revealed more than has ever been known before about how the voice develops, how varieties of vocal production are achieved, and what constitutes healthy singing and, in turn, 'safe' teaching. A growing literature is developing from works for the specialist teacher and clinician (Bunch 1982; Miller 1986; Thurman and Welch 1997) to those intended as accessible to the individual singer (Kayes 2000; Laurence in Potter, 2000; Sundberg in Potter 2000) to teachers and choral directors working primarily with vocal groups (Ashworth Bartle 1988; Hill *et al.* 1995; Jordan and Haasemann 1991; Rao 1994; Brewer 1997; the *Singing Matters* books, Allen 1997 and 1999). What has emerged more forcefully than ever before is a converging consensus on what happens when we sing which is supported by scientific evidence; and a new spirit of assumption that resonant, expressive singing can be achieved by everyone open to the methods these authors outline. Singing need only remain a mystery where these sources of authority and inspiration are left unread; prospective teachers should equip themselves with this knowledge if the practical work they are to do in the classroom is to be based on correct assumptions and procedures. The ideas shared below are largely based on testing in a variety of teaching contexts the pedagogical influences of these sources. The best outcome of scrutiny of my brief overview would be to become moved to consult the originals.

Singing is an acquired skill developed through harnessing sound-producing reflexes endowed as instinctive in early infancy which need to be practised for them to be fully maintained as we grow and mature. Many of the factors which inhibit effective singing develop out of a combination of unfamiliarity resulting from under-use of the singing voice and lack of confidence associated with a negative self-image. It is very easy for carers, peers and teachers to dampen the confidence to sing. The most important first step is to establish that this is an activity in which people cannot fail. I stress this as the best possible argument for beginning singing sessions with exercises which promote a sense of progression and achievement. There is no point in starting out with songs for which voices are not first made ready: it is a recipe for imposing failure.

Yet exercising ('training') the voice has tended to be seen as the province of the expert. I will provide a further spur to those who need convincing: suitable vocal exercises can simultaneously develop healthy singing *and* lay down some of the fundamentals of musical practice on which creative tasks can draw heavily. They sensitize the *musician* in partipants as much as they develop skills.

Vocal development thus depends both on setting up expectations at the beginning of the learning process, and continually monitoring that they are being met as further work builds on these foundations. Most of all, pupils should perceive for themselves that the buzz they get from singing well is its own reward. Much of what will be covered next has as its goal this achievement of physical sensations: of power, pleasure, strangeness, fun.

To begin with **posture** may seem to convey none of these, but it is basic to further progress. An approach borrowed from the drama department may help: experimenting with how others perceive ('read') our intentions from the way we stand. Do we believe in a singer who looks awkward either because he is in a collapsed posture, or because he has artificially overcome this by standing like a guardsman? Or we could borrow from our colleagues in PE and consider the assembly of a straight back by having the class lean forward, head lolling towards the floor, and then move vertebra by vertebra to a position in which the head sits over an elongated spine. This combination of the credibility of a performer's stance and the athletic readiness it permits can provide an agreed model to which one can subsequently refer as frequently as necessary. It is assumed that singing will not normally be carried out with children sitting at desks.

Relaxation can be difficult to reconcile with upright posture, especially where the latter is so unfamiliar that it takes work to achieve. But tension must be exorcised if the vibrations on which resonant singing depends are to be released, and in order to avoid discomfort and maximize efficiency. A 'shake-down' routine can be useful: working up from the floor, and always matching movements symmetrically so as to avoid overworking one side of the body.

exercise the toes

go onto tip-toe and back down

shake each foot loosely from the ankle

bend the knees gently, like a skier: and keep them 'unlocked' thereafter

rotate the hips a few turns in each direction (the Elvis pelvis)

move the fingers as fast as possible

add a shaking of the wrists

add a shake from the elbow

add a shake from the shoulder

lift the shoulders high up around the ears, then let them go

look four times along each shoulder in preparation for looking all the way behind

Once your classes are used to these exercises any one of them can be used at any time to help retain relaxedness and keep fatigue at bay in class and rehearsal.

Phonation comes next, though many would deal with breathing at this point. I just feel it is important to get on to singing, and address matters related to breathing while making sounds which can be heard to improve as a consequence.

With new groups, the first pitch I get them to produce is never specified. Why give a piano note, from which it may be clear that some have failed to match its pitch? The same is true even of singing a starting-pitch at this stage. I would suggest requesting everyone to hum any note they like for as long as they can. Then begin moving their notes around through calling upon different meanings we associate with the shape of hummed sounds:

the hum of satisfaction

the hum of anticipated pleasure

the hum of confused questioning

the hum of affirmative discovery

These should be tried out at ever slower speeds ('slow motion singing'), which will make their contribution to developing breathing as well as promoting confidence and aural sensitivity. All this could easily become a composing exercise and the outcomes transferred to instruments.

To return to singing: the transition between humming and making vowel sounds is often a point at which problems arise, because vowels require opening the mouth, and not everyone is used to doing that. The consequences of simultaneously opening the mouth and wishing you weren't doing so tend to tighten the tongue or result in tension in the jaw, akin to trying to suppress a yawn. So rather than go straight to singing 'Ah' sounds, I introduce an exercise which helps develop or achieve the independence of jaw and tongue which will promote open, resonant vowels and easy transitions between them. Beginning with the relaxation exercise at the end of the list above (stick your tongue out, and touch your top and bottom lips alternately), but now making a continuous singing sound at the same time (the apparent vowel will vary from person to person, and does not matter at this stage), move your tongue gradually faster and faster without moving your jaw. It may help to advocate placing a finger lightly against the chin to monitor that the jaw is still; or suggest practising with a mirror. The result will sound like: 'lebble-ebble-ebble'. Mastering this can be really helpful in achieving a relaxed and agile tongue.

The next stage beyond this would be to move this 'lebble-ebble' sound around in pitch: either adopting the same kinds of generalized contours as in the humming exercises given above, or via introducing simple scalic patterns:

Doh-ray-doh
Doh-ray-mi-ray-doh
Doh-ray-mi-fah-mi-ray-doh etc.,

in whatever key feels comfortable (again, beginning from vocal modelling rather than giving notes from the piano). Whether one goes for accurately pitched material of this kind at this stage or not depends on assessing whether it will be effective. On the one hand, I always listen to judge whether generalized contour work is beginning to focus spontaneously towards a natural unison, as it often will, rather than risking exposing too early anyone who is finding pitching difficult; on the other hand, the very practices which have characterized the approach taken so far (establishing effective posture and relaxation; introducing 'risk-free' phonation) can often remove many of the physical and psychological factors which one has to address in order to promote in-tune singing in participants for whom this is initially difficult.

I would strongly advocate that teachers investigate and ponder the properties of a group vocal unison which is reached instinctively by social interaction in practical tasks in this way, rather than relying on singing being a response to an 'external' pitch–response yardstick. It works every week on the football terraces. Amongst strategies I have observed for dealing with so-called 'tone-deafness', this is one of the most effective. It requires musicians to, perhaps, put aside some of their assumptions momentarily in the interests of focusing on the physicality, drama and implied emotion of sound-production, rather than principles dependent on specifically musical values. These can come later!

Resonance is what efficient singing is all about. I remember vividly the sensation I had as a 7 year-old when participation in class singing yielded a new sensation which 'blew my mind': a feeling that something special and dizzying was happening when we were encouraged to enjoy singing the highest notes of the tune. If one thing motivates me as a teacher and researcher, it is the desire to endow this experience on every child: the right to have a voice which not only deserves to ring out, but also gives pleasure to its owner in doing so.

My approach to aiming for the achievement of resonance in young and inexperienced singers is to guide them in where to locate the sensations they can associate with releasing their voices in this way. Three simple procedures can open up this brave new world of enhanced sensation.

---

1 **Vibrations in the sternum**
Participants put one hand flat on their chests just below the collar-bone and feel for vibrations here associated with low notes and confident middle-range pitches.

2 **Vibrations in the back of the skull**
Participants place a hand against the base of the skull just above where it joins the back of the neck, and sense how this becomes more active with middle-range and higher notes.
[Before moving onto the third procedure, it can be particularly useful, when pupils are ready for it, to incorporate simultaneously feeling for vibrations in the sternum and skull, one hand in each location. The ideal here is to experience the voice as spread over the whole area between the two hands, giving the impression of a large and powerful 'virtual' instument similar in scope to a clarinet or horn.
It is all too easy for students to perceive their voices as very localized and limited, and this image can be very helpful in giving the valid impression that the entire upper body is involved in the experience of the sound we produce.]

3 **Vibrations at the front of the skull**
This should be reserved for when participants are ready, but can yield exceptional results once relaxed and confident phonation is evident. Participants pinch the nose so that it is closed when singing vowel sounds, and focus on maximizng the impression that the sound is occurring in the space in the roof of the mouth behind the top front teeth.

Again, procedures of this kind can be drawn on in response to specific challenges at any stage subsequent to participants having got used to them.

This section has, as it were, been about assembling the instrument. The voice has an energy source, the lungs; a sound source, the vocal folds; and a capacity for resonance and filtering in the pharynx and mouth, which we have just illustrated. These procedures dealing with posture, relaxation, phonation and resonance have set out to act as a checklist for identifying that the bodies of our participants are ready for effective singing. No lesson should address all these matters in one go. Instead, an expectation should develop in which good practice is developed sequentially, in relation to creative and performing work. But it cannot be stressed too strongly that singing is a whole-body, athletic activity in which responsible teachers will take the trouble to ensure that healthy practice is promoted; and that these exercises and procedures, once learnt, remain available for diagnostic and developmental purposes. Above all, pupils should be encouraged to *listen,* not just as an aspect of monitoring their vocal performance, but also in order to internalize the harmonic, dynamic and textural experiences which will remain available to inform their composing.

Your own voice as a teaching resource

As the designated leader and enabler of all the above, the teacher needs to feel confident to demonstrate anything and everything which might arise in a vocal lesson. A helpful model for developing your own voice as a teaching tool is to practise employing it as a means of establishing and making personal and real the elements of music. From this position, pupils will become aware of and respond to the idea that *anything* they might conceive musically can be carried in their voices. It helps enormously if the same is, without limit or inhibition, true of their teacher. I would recommend the BBC 2 programme *Never Mind the Buzzcocks* as an illustration of this!

The four irreducible elements of music are: pitch; volume; duration; and timbre. Our practice of simultaneous development of vocal flexibility and creative awareness benefits from exploration of these.

Pitch can best be investigated from a starting point motivated by its extreme physical manifestation, after which everything becomes a controlled choice within a personally-experienced continuum. Beginning with the lowest comfortable note you can produce, glissando evenly and smoothly on an 'Ah' up to the very highest and back again. This is your total range – at least, it is if you have been daring and honest in the attempt! Now try to decide what feels like the point half-way between these extremes. Sing the glissando:

Lowest – Middle – Highest

Now add further 'mid-points':

Lowest – Medium Low – Middle – Medium High – Highest

Work at accessing these points as freely and efficiently as possible, without dislocations or audible 'gear changes'.

Now return to the middle note and practise simple fluctuations above and below it, beginning with semitones, then branching out via whole tones to minor and major thirds, etc. Everything about your singing should be as calm and effortless as possible for your performance to send out the right signals to your pupils.

Working in this way with classes, you can investigate the building-blocks of vocal harmony, refining over time the confident clusters which permit every singer to contribute without fear of failure to develop aural and productive sensitivity out of which triadic harmony and pure intervals will emerge. Teaching pupils through the use of the voice to select intervals which sound effective promotes tuning and confidence in part-singing far more effectively than resorting to the out-of-tune and unvocal resource of the piano.

An additional resource many teachers find aids pitch sense and their efficiency in teaching is the use of Kodály hand-signs. These work best where *Doh* is moveable. In a similar manner which does not employ a gestural component, participants can learn to locate pitch-relationships based on a scalic numbering-system. Whether using Kodály signs or numbers, it is possible for teacher and pupils to develop a language of harmonic analysis and pitch location which is of inestimable help in devising arrangements and composing.

Volume means so much more than loudness, especially in the context of vocal performance in which evolution has endowed us with the ability to attribute meaning to perceived effort as much as to relative amplitude. In developing your own ability, focus especially on being able to control pitch while altering loudness: for many pupils, even aged 11+, the attempt to make a crescendo will be accompanied by a rise in pitch. Once this has received attention, the excitement which can be generated by controlled crescendo and diminuendo will communicate itself vividly. Again, it can help to do this first with a cluster on which every pupil is singing a note they find comfortable. Another effect which can be highly influential is alternating loud and soft staccato sounds.

In describing preparation for working with volume, it is inevitable that we have focused on group effects: harnessing the power of simultaneous chorusing with other members of our species is a universal and defining characteristic of human culture, and its capacity for generating loudness is much older and more socially cohesive than using a microphone!

Duration has already made an appearance in the difference between alternating staccato notes and making crescendi on sustained pitches in our consideration of volume. Here, too, is a link to developing breath-management: we can compare the maximum duration of notes we can sing on a single breath and see if this can increase with practice. Conversely, controlling the pitch and volume of very short notes is a skill to develop, where the exact co-ordination of breathing and voice onset will yield clear, open sounds. It is important that the control of stopping singing is achieved with the breath and not from the mouth or throat, which creates tiredness and fails to allow notes to ring.

Timbre is in many ways the most fascinating element of all, and can be investigated in a great number of highly stimulating ways. It lends itself to exploring the differences between speech and song, and all the stylistic features of singers' performances which plough this furrow, between rap and punk, a variety of ethnic styles, opera, 'belt', etc. Our ability to understand language depends entirely on perceiving timbral differences:

The Main Vowels in English
illustrated by words and names beginning with the phoneme B and ending with T:

Boot (english)   [Boo-wot (geordie)]
Boat
Bought
Bott
Bart   [Bite]
Bat

Bet
Bate
Bit   [Birt/Burt]
Beet
Boot (scottish)   [Bute]

Each of these vowels represents a different harmonic filtered by the actions of our tongue and lips to vary the colour of the sound produced as a fundamental by our vocal folds. We all have a built-in graphic equalizer which allows us to assign linguistic meaning to tiny variations in perceived harmony: every human being able to understand and mimic language does so on the basis of this fundamentally musical skill.

If we sing the vowels from the above list in order

oo – oa – or – o – ar – a – e – é – i – ee – ü

it should be possible to refine this musical element and produce a set of distinct harmonics. This is the technique used in Stockhausen's *Stimmung* and in several vocal styles from cultures as different as South Africa, Mongolia, Tibet and Japan; and in Australia, where it is a component of performance on the didjeridoo. Harmonic singing of this kind is thought to have magic and healing properties. It can certainly prove infectious in the classroom once the basic skills have been acquired.

A further aspect of timbre which relates to vocal development is to explore the properties of consonants. 'Noise' consonants such as the sounds represented by k, sh, s, f, h, t, ch can be assembled rhythmically into vocal drum-tracks:

t – tss – t – t – tss – t – t – tss – t – ch – t – t – ch – t – t – ch – t-t-hhhhhh

Several consonants sustain as effectively as vowels: try vocalizing melodies on the following:

v, l, m, n, ng, j, r, z, th

Sonic resources of this kind lend themselves well to presentation in graphic scores.

A further aspect of timbre is to consider variation in vocal style and emotional motivation:

Sing *Happy Birthday to You* (or any other song everyone knows) in the following ways:

• like a country 'n' western singer;
• as if dying of thirst;
• impersonating the current Prime Minister;
• as if you think it's a very rude song;
• with operatic wobble and intensity;
• as if underwater;

- like it's punk;
- to send a baby to sleep;
- etc. (an important part of this task is for participants to come up with their own ideas).

A great many connections can be made between these vocal development procedures and issues arising in composing and listening contexts. Carefully chosen examples of vocal styles can influence performing and develop appraisal skills. Exploration of the elements of music can contribute to the development of notation skills, especially those related to conveying articulation and dynamics. Where pupils acquire confidence to use their voices in this way in ongoing musical study, the investment of time and personal energy will always repay the effort.

Acquiring resources for voice-based teaching

In support of the programme of practical development represented in the previous sections, a streetwise and effective vocal practitioner needs to build an extensive library of resources. Be encouraged that you need not feel alone! A variety of agencies have responded during the last decade to the commitment required by the National Curriculum to involve and maintain singing in the classroom. These include: the consciousness-raising efforts of organizations such as the British Federation of Young Choirs, Sing for Pleasure, the Association of British Choral Directors and the Voices Foundation; increasingly realistic and supportive policies of enlightened publishing houses; the stimulus brought about by the popular success of the Sainsbury's Choir of the Year competition; and, not least, the efforts made by publications such as *Music File*, *Music Teacher* and *The Singer* to promote good practice and educational initiative in the field of classroom and extracurricular singing.

Foremost in my own stock of resources is a wide selection of recordings which I find help to influence pupils' creative imagination regarding the use of the voice while also providing enticing technical models. What works for me might leave others cold, and I would advise that this is a fairly personal matter. However, my criteria for the choice of material are:

- the music is principally *a cappella* and features small groups of singers or soloists, so that responses in group work can allow identification with the roles taken by the performers;
- the style and character of the original can be accessed without overmuch reliance on language and verbal meaning;
- the music contains easily-grasped features which can influence creative work.

The following, then, are a brief sample of the recordings I have found helpful:

- The Balinese *kejak* ritual
- The Beatles songs which feature *a cappella* singing (*Michelle; She's leaving home*)
- The Cuban groups *Vocal Sampling* and *Exaudi*

- The Swingle Singers, especially arrangements such as *Claire de Lune* and *Flight of the Bumble Bee;* and *Bolivian Getaway* from *Butch Cassidy and the Sundance Kid*
- Barbershop: *The Gas House Gang*
- Stockhausen's *Stimmung*
- Allegri's *Miserere*
- Inuit vocal games form northern Canada
- Subharmonic singing from Tuva
- David Fanshawe's *African Sanctus*
- South African choral music; *I Fagiolini* with the Sdasa Chorale

Developing teaching materials

As will have become apparent from the methods proposed in the sections above on technique as well as the recorded resources I use, my message is that vocal development works best where it is fully integrated into creative aspects of musical learning. I would rarely advocate that groups learn songs in isolation. Again, this is very much an aspect of teaching style; but it remains my reason for not, at this stage, giving a list of songs I would propose pupils learn.

What I will do is outline some of the criteria which I try to bear in mind regarding repertoire choice:

- some songs have a limited lifespan, while others appear timeless: one has to allow pupils' reactions to inform you of which is which;
- choose songs for what they can deliver by way of vocal development: i.e. don't be apologetic if they contain challenges: they provide an opportunity for learning;
- by contrast, avoid songs which fail to stretch, even if the pupils like them: they can just reinforce ineffective singing;
- choose material which allows differentiation. Unison singing is not a prime candidate for this. Songs which allow some pupils to sing an ostinato or perform a vocal drum-track (as in *Vocal Sampling*) or which have, say, call-and-response elements are far more effective in this respect;
- similarly, choose repertoire which allows participation to pupils having vocalizing problems during voice-change: musical speech is far preferable to unmusical singing, so have resources available such as John Paynter's spoken round on railway station names, or Ernst Toch's *Geographical Fugue*;
- in the same spirit as the Swingle arrangements, advocate vocal versions of instrumental pieces.

To sum up: while voice change as a physical phenomenon is a significant factor in singing at KS3, one also needs to consider aesthetic and sociological considerations if progress is to be made. Pupils who may have been happy to sing pop cantatas and songs about animals at junior school will be looking for something new. But a complete rupture between what they are used to and what you offer may do more harm than good. In the spirit of the 'spiral curriculum', the best policy may be for a proportion of classroom work to build in new and enticing ways on what they already know:

locating, or creating (or giving them the responsibility to help create) arrangements in two or three parts of songs learnt previously. Bridging the gap between KS2 and 3 can benefit from links between schools:

> Coseley School, near Wolverhampton, uses curriculum materials devised by primary and secondary teachers and advisers in Dudley LEA to smooth the transfer between primary and secondary school … The self-consciousness that often arises when Year 7 pupils are asked to start singing at secondary school by learning a new song in new surroundings and seated among pupils they do not know is avoided.
>
> (Mills 1998: 69)

Allowing pupils to feel convinced by their own performance should be the aim:

> The pupils learn to sing in a range of styles. During the inspection visit they sang *Blue Suede Shoes* with uncanny authenticity.
>
> (Mills 1998: 69)

The role of ICT in creative singing development

ICT resources can have a highly stimulating influence on vocal work. I tend to steer away from workstations which promote sedentary singing, though there are some useful programs which allow the addition of recorded or sampled vocal material to tracks which can be created and edited in the computer. It will help if pupils using such resources are encouraged to place microphones in positions which allow good posture and free expression: all too often ICT resources tend to be associated with confined spaces in which the voice sounds dead. Of course, reverb and other effects can be added to give body to recorded vocal sounds: but there is no substitute for capturing the best-produced vocalization in the first place.

The resources I have found most effective are those which promote vocal experimentation, both individually and in groups (Bannan 1998). I use a Lexicon Jam-Man, which can sample up to 32 seconds of performance of reasonably high fidelity. Set to an 8-second loop in 'echo' mode, it can stimulate uninhibited layering of sounds in a manner which often yields exciting results even from reluctant singers.

Video can also play its part in vocal development, both as a resource for showing singers how they look and sound, and for developing responses to existing material: recording 'new' vocal soundtracks to old films in the manner of *Whose line is it anyway?* can allow pupils to experiment with varied styles and timbres.

Whole-school aspects of vocal development: towards a 'singing culture'

While the focus of this chapter has been singing in KS3, the outcome and concomitant of work of this kind need to be the development of voice-based musical opportunities throughout a school. Classroom work at KS3 will flourish where pupils can be inspired by what GCSE and A level pupils are doing as composers and performers, and where work in the classroom is related to opportunities in choirs and music/theatre ensembles.

> Some secondary schools emphasize the acquisition of vocal skills. The Duchess's County High School, Northumberland, is a 13–18 school that emphasizes singing. The pupils learn to sing unison song, and in up to four parts. They are taught to sing in a range of styles and how to improve the quality of their singing … . The school promotes the image of singing as an adult activity. It is clear to the pupils that the music teacher enjoys singing. Pupils who are taking A level music attend some Year 9 music lessons, and lead some of the singing.
>
> (Mills 1998: 75)

Where pupils can initiate such extracurricular activities or take ownership of them, so much the better:

> The gospel singing at St Saviour's and St Olave's, Southwark … began with a group of enthusiastic pupils who wanted a room to rehearse in at lunchtime. Over the years, teachers have been drawn in, public performances organised, and more pupils of all ages have started to participate.
>
> (Mills 1998: 80)

Where the foundations for vocal participation in the classroom are laid down in Year 7, they will not desert students in later life:

> The lesson opened with the pupils singing a Bach chorale at sight securely, and without an accompaniment. This shared practical experience was used as a springboard for starting to analyse the chorale … . One of the set works was Schubert's *Death and the Maiden* quartet. After some work on the second movement, the two pupils and teacher rehearsed the *lied* that serves as its theme. One pupil played the piano, and the teacher and other pupil sang.
>
> (Mills 1998: 83)

Continuity and progression are, then, the watchwords of teachers involved in effective vocal development. While KS3 teachers inherit pupils at age 11+, the process begins at birth. The more we are able to diagnose what pupils can do and facilitate their vocal development from the first week of Year 7, the deeper and surer the foundations we can lay for lifelong vocal participation.

References

Allen, P. (1997) *Singing Matters,* Oxford: Heinemann.
—— (1999) *Developing Singing Matters*, Oxford: Heinemann.
Bannan, N. (1994) *The Voice in Education,* London: Rhinegold Publishing.
—— (1998) 'Aural feedback, vocal technique, and creativity' in B.A. Roberts (ed.) *The Phenomenon of Singing,* Newfoundland, Canada: Memorial University Press: 11–19.

Bartle, J.A. (1988) *Lifeline for Children's Choir Directors,* Toronto: Warner/Chappell Canada.

Brewer, M. (1997) *Kick-start Your Choir,* London: Faber Music.

Bunch, M. (1982) *Dynamics of the Singing Voice,* New York: Springer-Verlag.

Haasemann, F. and Jordan, J. (1991) *Group Vocal Technique,* Chapel Hill, NC: Hinshaw.

Hill, D., Parfitt, H. and Ash, E. (1995) *Giving Voice: a Handbook for Choir Directors and Trainers,* Rattlesden: Kevin Mayhew.

Kayes, G. (2000) *Singing and the Actor,* London: A. & C. Black.

Laurence, F. (2000) 'Children's singing' in J. Potter (ed.) *The Cambridge Companion to Singing,* Cambridge: Cambridge University Press.

Miller, R. (1986) *The Structure of Singing,* New York: Schirmer.

Mills, J. (1998) 'Music' in *The Arts Inspected (Ofsted),* London: Heinemann.

Ofsted (1995) *Review of Inspection Findings 1993/4,* London: HMSO.

QCA (1999) *The National Curriculum for England: Music,* London: HMSO for the Department for Education and Employment/Qualifications and Curriculum Authority.

Rao, D. (1994) *We Will Sing!* London: Boosey & Hawkes.

Sundberg, J. (2000) 'Where does the sound come from?' in J. Potter (ed.) *The Cambridge Companion to Singing,* Cambridge: Cambridge University Press.

Thurman, L. and Welch, G. (1997) *Body, Mind and Voice: Foundations of Voice Education,* Collegeville, MN: Voicecare Network.

10 Teaching composing in secondary schools
The creative dream
George Odam

> What though the dream crack!
> We shall remake it.
> Staring with those startled eyes at what we are –
>   (Michael Tippett, Third Symphony, final movement)

Background: how the creative dream emerged

Surprisingly little has been written on the teaching of composing in schools. There had been early experiments in the first decades of this century. Emile Jaques-Dalcroze, who visited London to teach composition in conservatoires in the first years of the century wrote in 1914, 'The study of solfège teaches the pupils to hear and mentally envisage melodies, and all sorts of melodic combinations, to identify and vocally improvise them, to notate and compose them'. In the USA, Satis Coleman's early work in New York with children and composing stated that it seems rather inappropriate to let anything so formal as a fixed method stand between the little child and his experiences in so elemental an art (Coleman 1922). The basis of her work was with individual pupils as was that of Walford Davies whose mission through early BBC broadcasts was based on 'a belief in the ability of children to compose their own melodies' (Cox 1997: 45). One of the first written records of the early practice of composing in an English secondary school is that of the young Peter Maxwell Davies where he states: 'It was here that the *creative* work with music in the school began – born of sheer necessity' (Davies 1963: 108).[1] Books on classroom composing published in Canada and taken up by Universal Edition here in England brought the views and experience of composer R. Murray Schafer to the attention of music educators in the mid–1960s. Schafer was influenced greatly by the New York group of composers centred on John Cage. George Self's Cage-inspired work written from the experience of working with lower ability secondary children was published as *New Sounds in Class* (1967) by Universal Edition. This publishing house did more than many to awaken interest in and support the practice of composing in schools, largely due to the enterprise and enthusiasm of Bill Colleran.[2] There was a growth of publications around 1970 including Wilfrid Mellers's composition and philosophical schools material, *The Resources of Music* (1969), which preceded Brian Dennis's *Experimental Music in Schools* (1970) and Paynter and Aston's *Sound and Silence* (1970) by one year. It shows Mellers to have been a powerful influence on music education from his York University base.

At the same time a movement in developing creativity was strongly evident in primary education. It is not insignificant that many of the leading activists working in teacher education, such as the young Paynter himself, spent some of their professional lives supervising students and teachers in primary schools. In the late 1950s, the principles of Carl Orff's *Schulwerk* were brought to the attention of British schools through the work of, amongst others, Margaret Murray and Doris Gould. Creativity in music received special mention in the Plowden report, *Children in Their Primary Schools* (DES 1967), and two further government papers, *Music and the Young School Leaver* (Schools Council, 1968) and *Creative Music in Schools* (DES 1970), encouraged composing practice throughout our school system. Composing at secondary school was the focus of the NW Region Development Project's report, *Creative Music and the Young School Leaver* (1974).

Two films were made which had considerable impact in the profession. For television, the *Monitor* Unit film was made on Peter Maxwell Davies's work at Cirencester in 1961[3] and the BBC 2 in-service training film, *Discovery and Experience*[4], co-ordinated by Walter Drabble HMI in 1965. Both showed direct evidence of classroom methods.

The York University Schools Council Project, *Music in the Secondary School Curriculum* (1973–82), gave rise to a huge amount of practice-based material on tape, slide and film and was followed up by the book, *Music in the Secondary School Curriculum*, in 1982. Paynter gives a more comprehensive picture here of methodology in composing than in the earlier book, and continues to see small-group workshops as the main way of organizing things. His advice on the problems of noise and group-work could be construed as less than helpful and he feels that part of the problem of motivation and control is teachers' lack of experience in making music themselves (Paynter 1982: 82). These issues will appear as important elements in our findings.

Research focus

In the 1970s, *Sound and Silence* (Paynter and Aston 1970) provided a practical educational focus for composing, which eventually coalesced into the previously mentioned Schools Council Secondary Project based at York University (1973–82). The ideas developed through this work were profoundly influential on a whole generation of music teachers and represented what I have chosen to call the 'Creative Dream'. A great deal of idealism and lateral thinking was built into the original concept. For instance, in *Sound and Silence,* Paynter and Aston recommended that creative work should take place in the lunch-hour and break times. New generations of teachers have struggled with the reality of trying to adapt their inadequate teaching environments, equipment and training opportunities to accommodate and develop this work. At the heart of the problem is the difficult balance between co-operative learning techniques which encourage groups of children to work with minimum supervision in order to maximize limited resources in a mixed-ability environment, and individual learning needs.

Composing was a dominant and revolutionary feature in the revision of the General Certificate of Secondary Education (GCSE) in England and Wales in 1987. The formulation of the National Curriculum for England and for Wales (1992–5) confirmed the teaching of composing as a requirement, not just for secondary music specialists, but for all primary teachers as well. The challenge this provided both to teachers and their pupils was far reaching and its consequences enormous. It brought music education officially into the realm of arts education where pupil-centred learning, creative work and problem-solving techniques in other arts disciplines had been the norm for decades. For many teachers it has become the vehicle not only for composition itself but also for the delivery of listening and performing. In many classrooms composing has become the dominant working mode. 'Composing is … the surest way for pupils to develop musical judgement and to come to understand the notion of "thinking" in music' (Paynter 1997: 18). Effectively, the promotion of composing as a central curriculum activity has changed the balance of what is traditionally called 'musicianship'. It requires skills which have not been universally practised by musicians in the last century or so, and draws on models of practice more common in the seventeenth and eighteenth centuries in our own culture. It challenges the notion of the specialist musician and looks to a more holistic model much more common in other cultures.

Composing as a national requirement is also to be found in Scotland, where the guide-line approach to 'inventing' at primary level is very similar and rather more formal in outlook at secondary level. The new National Curriculum requirement to teach composing within the music curriculum in 1992–5 in England, Wales and Northern Ireland, although unfamiliar to many generalist primary-phase teachers, was not unfa-miliar to most music specialist teachers, particularly those at secondary level. However, as acknowledged by Paynter in 1982, the majority of these teachers lacked composing in their training and for many it was and is quite outside their own experience of music-making. New teaching skills were needed of an order very different from standard music education practice. Without any co-ordinated or strategically planned in-service education, teachers had been left to learn on the job. The demands of a secondary music post leave little time for reflection on practice. As a result, teaching methodology in composing has become fixed and highly dependent on a dominant teaching method using small group-work.

As a music-educator who has been implicated in the promotion of composing in the curriculum in the UK over the last thirty years, I felt that it was time for a good, hard and critical look at what we do. As a teacher-trainer my main concerns leading me to this research project were focused by a new government emphasis in the last five years on teacher-led initial teacher training.[5] One direct result of this initiative has been that student teaching programmes have also become heavily dominated by group-work approaches. This style of teaching demands the practice of highly advanced teaching skills in the classroom by inexperienced trainees. Also there is worrying evidence of an unbalanced music curriculum practice emerging as a direct result of an emphasis on composing, despite clear national guidelines to the contrary. At secondary level, through personal observation in schools, I identified the following problems to be of most concern especially at Key Stage 3 (ages 11–14):

- group-work in composing seriously dominating curriculum time;
- attendant problems of pupil discipline and stress accumulation in trainees;
- evidence of 'burn-out' in good and experienced teachers;
- recruitment into secondary music teacher-training was continuing to drop;
- lack of evidence of skills development in composing;
- little evidence of progression in composing either from primary to second-ary or within secondary until examination work took over at KS4;
- inadequate resources in many schools even though nearly all used elec-tronic keyboards;

- inspection evidence which suggested that non-specialist primary-phase teachers were more successful in teaching music than were the specialists in secondary schools (Mills 1997).

Aims of the 'Creative Dream' research project

The most immediate aim of this project has been to search out and identify good and effective teaching of composing in secondary schools and to make information on this available to teachers nationally. The ultimate aim is to revitalize and remake the 'creative dream' through a clear and thorough investigation of current practice. The new 'dream' is to continue to find composing firmly at the heart of music education practice in the UK and for it to affect all stages of our national music education process from nursery to higher degrees in the first decades of the new century.

Objectives

- To observe, investigate and document effective methods used to teach composing in the secondary classroom for 11–18 year-olds with special emphasis on KS3;
- to undertake an in-depth appraisal of the use of keyboards and associated equipment for composing, since they are the most commonly used equipment;
- to develop understanding of the effectiveness of whole-class, group, paired and individual pupils' work in composing;
- to identify, document and define progressive learning in composition;
- to recommend developments and to disseminate ideas of good practice.

Presenting our findings

Although the initial impetus and bias of the above basic questions came from me as a composer and teacher-trainer in discussion with my Research Fellow, Anice Paterson, it must be understood that she has been my ears and eyes in carrying out the fieldwork. My analysis of the data she has gathered may present a different view from hers. Anice is an experienced teacher, adviser, INSET leader and inspector. What we present is the product of many hours of discussion, letters, telephone conversations and emails. We do not claim to have arrived at any particular theory and are both aware that we analyse what we have with different experiences and priorities. This chapter presents my interpretation of the results of our work. Hers is available in a different form through a publication by the National Association of Music Educators in July 2000.

Neither of us believes that it is possible to present our readers with simple objective facts about the practice of composing in the KS3 classroom. Such objective information is unavailable. Although we used a questionnaire as the only feasible way of testing pupils' reactions to what they do in class, we are very wary of suggesting that the results of this survey are an objective statement of fact. The questionnaires used were given to pupils by their teachers. We had only limited control over how this exercise was presented and could not be certain that teachers had provided any bias intentionally or unintentionally. Results should be read as indicators and readers can take from the figures what they may.

Composing and the individual: the unanswered question

> It [composing] should be child-centred and start from the needs of the individual.
>
> (Paynter and Aston 1970: 2)

The above list of aims and objectives gives the overall emphasis of our enquiry and the reasons why I have been worried enough about the way composing is taught to invest so much time in this study. What it does not make clear is an underlying concern I have about the place of the individual in creative work.

About twenty-five years ago I was involved in one of the summer school courses run by the Music Teachers' Association at York University. I remember clearly being challenged then by a sceptical West Country music adviser who could not grasp how any teacher could get round a class, in the time given, to view and comment upon each pupil's composition. His comment was greeted at the time with laughter and derision from the floor, most likely encouraged by me. But the real concern behind his question has stuck in my mind and remains unanswered. 'How do you promote individual creativity in pupils when their total experience of the work is corporate?' is a question that so far remains unanswered by practice up to and including KS3. 'What is creative music?' asks Paynter in *Sound and Silence*; 'First of all it is a way of saying things which are personal to the individual' (Paynter and Aston 1970: 7).

Of course, as soon as they meet examination work at KS4, pupils are expected to become individual creators. But where is the experience of self-expression and of being totally in charge of what you create before examination work begins? Does any other arts subject expect creativity to be totally corporate, and why has group-working been so exclusively promoted in the music classroom? Is it inherent in the subject or has it arisen, as I believe, from more practical priorities?

My concerns over the effectiveness of group-work, embodied in the research questions, are very much driven by these unanswered questions. As will be obvious, the questions remain unanswered for me by observation of current practice and form, the area in most need of development. If these difficult questions remain unaddressed or unanswered, I fear that composing, as a central classroom activity, may be under threat in the longer term. So far, just as in Charles Ives' vision of the unanswered question, the ancients remain mute and immobile.

Effective educational activity depends ultimately on the motivation and commitment of the individual learner. Although other cultures provide us with a few models of co-operation in creative music-making, the most common practice all over the world stems from the individual's response to sound and what it can express. The experience of drama and sports education specialists could well be helpful to musicians in this area. There are now, at last, encouraging signs appearing of individuals choosing to compose out of school.

New socially-driven models for making music arise within our own society all the time, and the last decades have witnessed much work in community music group improvisation and workshops run by *animateurs* or workshop leaders. It has often been stated that rock music is founded upon group practice, although this is not clearly demonstrated in practice. Most of the music education projects financed by public funds and involving composers and orchestral musicians reinforce the socially interactive model. It may be that this practice will prove to be so artistically fulfilling to both performer and listener that co-operative practice in future becomes the norm, but as yet, the evidence of this happening lies within a small and rather specialist area of post-modern jazz. There are some music educators whose greatest wish now is to see and hear this approach to the creation of music become the norm in our society. One of the hallmarks of jazz is its co-operative approach to artistic behaviour. It may be, however, that the dominance of this collaborative workshop technique is partly founded upon an administrative convenience of the classroom, necessitated by poor resources, inadequate accommodation, and driven by political and philosophical convictions that need constant revision and renewal.

However, arising from present practice in schools, imperfect as it is, is a growing number of young people who like to write and perform their own individually created music in a variety of styles and for diverse occasions.

Research methodology

The main approaches were:

- by observation in the classroom and analysis using key questions;
- by interview with teachers and pupils;
- pupil questionnaires;
- seminar and discussion with teachers;
- follow-up projects.

Objective 1: investigating, observing, and analysing

Pilot project

A pilot project was set up in 1997 with twelve schools in Dorset, identified for me by Kevin Rogers, the Dorset Music Adviser and David Walters of the Music Research Institute. The Institute also provided the venue for our first meeting. Kevin Rogers identified the Dorset teachers as interested teachers who had previously had no formal contact with me through INSET or school supervision.

Through an analysis of lesson plans and comments from these teachers received by email through the Music Research Institute, I was able to determine that as much as two-thirds of the music curriculum time was currently being used for composing activities. All these teachers used keyboards as a primary resource. The most dominant classroom organization was small group-work. A joint seminar with these teachers following up my findings confirmed my figures and gave me the evidence I needed to launch upon a much larger project.

Recruitment of sample teachers

Through the good offices of the Yamaha Educational Supplement magazine, distributed free to all secondary schools in the country, we were able to recruit volunteers for this project. Many teachers volunteered and twenty-six schools were identified as possible participants. The Research Fellow was appointed in August 1998 for two years and the largest part of the investigation took place between September 1998 and July 1999. There were geographical considerations governing our final choice of locations as well as school type, resources and evidence of practice. We worked through music advisers in some areas and were able to involve teachers in all areas of England, one each from Northern Ireland, Wales and Scotland. Inevitably these teachers, being volunteers, single themselves out for investigation and therefore already have an interest both in composing in the classroom and the use of keyboards. All our results must be read in the light of this knowledge and the inevitable 'skew' which results must be taken into account.

1,170 questionnaires have so far been returned to us from the above schools, providing pupils' views and opinions, which we have analysed. We have included both KS3 and KS4 results in the overall figures since it has been impossible in some of the early questionnaires to identify the age and stage of the pupils. In later questionnaires we have been able to look at figures separating out KS3 and KS4; and we have used this information whenever possible. Individual school results have been returned to the teachers concerned for their own use. In some cases this has resulted in teachers reassessing their own practice.

Key questions

We used the following key questions which are the central issues governing the focus of our research to guide our observation work in the classroom and in interviews with teachers. We wanted to find out:

- How do pupils work when they are composing?
- What do they do?
- What skills, attitudes and understanding do we need to develop in pupils to improve their composing?
- What processes and techniques do we need to ensure pupils have experience of?
- How do we plan progression across those skills and processes?
- What is the most appropriate pedagogy to achieve the above?
- What are the best conditions for composing? Physical? Technical?
- What is the relationship between, on the one hand, the building of craft skills and techniques and, on the other, providing the learning environment and ethos to encourage creativity and allow for the possibility of inspirational work?

Each school was visited for a day by the Research Fellow who took every opportunity to talk with all staff and, where possible, with pupils, especially those at KS4 and beyond. Contact was maintained with the teachers by letter, email and telephone and they were all invited to a day seminar held at Bath Spa University College's Michael Tippett Centre in July 1999. Many have also been involved in follow-up studies.

Objective 2: keyboards and other resources

Keyboards are the most commonly found and possibly most under-used resource currently available. Their potential in aiding pupils' work has still to be realized in many schools. Those schools choosing to invest a great deal of time in teaching sophisticated formal piano skills to all pupils do not achieve the same standards in composing as those achieved by schools who do not do so. We have observed some very good practice in which the teacher, to help pupils practise basic keyboard skills, has invented backing-tracks.

Keyboards alone are not an adequate resource and must be complemented by a wide and good quality set of pitched and non-pitched percussion. Where possible, orchestral standard instruments should be used – including pitched percussion. Although there is a place for 'educational' pitched percussion, and we have seen it used well by some teachers, secondary schools need a much more sensitive and wide range of sounds, including a good selection of bass sounds, both electric and acoustic.

Despite the increased security problems, keyboard equipment must be set out, fixed and ready to use if it is to be used efficiently. It is not good practice to manhandle keyboards every lesson and the equipment soon becomes damaged or faulty. An important principle is that the pupils should move to the keyboards.

We have seen some good work using keyboard laboratory set-ups, having at first been rather prejudiced against them. A skilled teacher can be extremely encouraging and monitor work efficiently from a console. Given the right urgency and planning, the experience need not be alienating, and can be very pleasurable for the teacher as well as the pupils. As information and communications technology (ICT) develops in schools there should be more networking of computers and keyboards allowing teachers to set up tasks and projects from the main computer. 'Using them in combination with computers, some pupils compose music which can be compared favourably with the best in visual art' (Salaman 1997: 149).

The development of ICT in the music room is one of the most significant areas. Schools where practice is good in the use of ICT display remarkable results in composing. There is an urgent need for all music teachers to become fully computer-literate. It no longer is acceptable to rely on the pupils knowing more than the teacher does. We would strongly recommend that at least five computers should be available for use by pupils as regular classroom equipment. At present there tends to be one computer kept in the cupboard or office and only used by the teacher or older pupils.

This presupposes a new look at the planning of the delivery of the curriculum using a mixed-economy approach in some lessons. In this approach the teacher plans groups working in a variety of modes and on a variety of tasks including one group on computers. Performing, listening and composing tasks may well be happening at once. Or alternatively, similar tasks in one discipline are experienced by the pupils in working in different media. All groups can then experience these in turn.

Good practice in the use of keyboards for composing requires good support materials specially constructed and designed for the pupils and their equipment. Task sheets need to be laid out in order of process, graded and including extension material for the more able or experienced pupils. Assessment needs to be built into the process and guide-sheets provided for the pupils to enable them to keep track of their work. Pupils need 'idiot guides' to computers and projects. All idiot guides, backing tracks and templates can be pre-loaded.

The resources of most keyboards are rarely maximized by teachers at present. The variety of voices has great potential, but too often the voice is chosen at random by the pupil. Keyboards offer an excellent resource for ensemble performance, but this happens rarely. The manufacturer's attention has already been drawn to the intrusive nature of the demonstration facility. They have taken this matter very seriously and are addressing it. Keyboards provided must have full-sized keys and a memory function. The memory should link into a storage system. Some of the most effective practice observed has used the storage of material by MIDI disc or on to the hard disc of a computer. This enables the encouragement of individual progression through the teacher's analysis of work in progress and provides the same practical method of notating and storing now used by most professional composers.

Technician support is now necessary in all music departments using ICT. Technicians must be appropriately skilled and regularly available and could also function as demonstrators. One school we visited spent over £600 per year on repairs and such a sum would pay for a technician about once every three weeks to do repairs and therefore release teacher time. One school has regular weekly half-day technician support, another had a five-hour per day technician for the performing arts department, but the majority of schools we visited still have none.

Objective 3: managing creative work in the classroom

Music makes a noise. In an art room, a class can work in silence if necessary on their own ideas for the whole lesson. By contrast, in a music room, more than one group or individual working on a composition 'spoils' the canvas of the others by the sounds they make. This has been one of the most significant practical issues which teachers have had to try to solve. They have not all solved it satisfactorily yet. Too many teachers still are struggling against a hostile physical environment and subjecting themselves and their pupils to stress levels that are at best unacceptable. Our advice is to stop trying to adapt completely unsuitable and inadequate accommodation and resources to small group-work and to teach more whole-class lessons, balancing the curriculum as appropriate. The development of ICT may well be a powerful answer to making the best use of space and time in such circumstances.

Some teachers have been able to find practice spaces for small groups of pupils to go to work undisturbed by the noise of others. This is advantageous to the pupils working but teachers then cannot always supervise pupils adequately or be sure that all of them are working equally within their groups. Teachers can become manically active, running from group to group to 'keep the pot boiling'. New schools are being provided with purpose-built group-work areas. Too many teachers, however, are still trying to teach in inadequate environments and becoming frustrated by their pupils' lack of progress. A good deal of what is delivered through group-work at the moment would be better and more efficiently taught through whole-class lessons. As one teacher advised us, 'Working in groups is a highly complex and disciplined skill and should be included in the skills defined as composing skills'. Co-operative learning techniques need to be addressed by teachers as such and pupils need guidance and practice in using them.[6]

From the beginning of KS3, the teacher should determine the construction of groups and should strictly control them. Careful records must be kept of the groups and their working, and an 'on-the-hoof' assessment policy is essential. Teachers should understand that the work that takes place in groups must be predicated upon sound ideas already well understood by the pupils. Too many lessons at present lack a strong modelling process. The best practice is where the teacher works through the task using some pupils as models, but there is still a central place for the teacher as demonstrator. Too few teachers at present show themselves as composers by working with the pupils in a creative way. There is too much 'do as I say and not as I do'. Where the teachers are perceived as working composers the pupils will follow. Teachers who fear that they may influence too heavily or harm their pupils' creativity need have few fears. The problem is most often to keep pupils on task and explore those elements planned by the teacher. Working within a given matrix is one of the most powerful stimulants for creativity.

Teachers must guard against the wily pupils who improvise on the spot when asked to demonstrate or who will argue strongly that they were exploring an avenue of music education more suited to their abilities than that set by the teacher. We have observed several groups who coast during rehearsal time and then improvise their responses – in one case getting praise for it. Pupils who do not feel challenged by an activity tend not to value the experience and lose interest and motivation.

Where small group-work is used, it is important to limit the time and to consider the tasks carefully. Tasks must be planned with a real empathy for those working through them. It is not good enough to place four pupils at a keyboard and expect them to sort out who does what. Tasks should be set that will produce truly musical results and produce compositions on cassette tape that pupils can take home to be admired. Work should rarely be completely open-ended at KS3. Sometimes, work with one class goes so well that the class can be given an open project and the pupils can largely determine the outcome. This, however, is a rare occurrence and can rarely be planned. Paired work aids collaborative work more positively and creativity is less hampered. Keyboard work should never involve more than two pupils at once on one keyboard.

In observing work in the volunteer schools, we were impressed by the array of approaches and techniques these teachers use in engaging pupils in composing. We observed a mixture of whole-class, small group-work, paired work and individual. We have encountered no single method that we could recommend as being the most effective. Observations and teachers' comments have focused clearly on the high level of teaching skill needed. Composing in the classroom presents some very particular problems with which the most experienced teachers sometimes struggle. Many have had to adapt inadequate teaching environments, equipment and training opportunities to accommodate and develop this work. Building in the unexpected becomes more of a problem now that the government demands that all lessons must be planned in detail in advance. Traditionally trained musicians are often more accustomed to order and hierarchical discipline and find the freedom of choice unfamiliar and without a basis in their memory-bank, The multiplicity of skills needed by the teacher in teaching composing are not easily or quickly learnt and are very challenging to many trainees, although newly qualified teachers can be subjected to full inspection scrutiny in their very first weeks in the profession. Many older teachers, and indeed even a fair proportion of those newly qualified, lack composing skill and experience from their degree courses. Teachers who feel themselves at a disadvantage in subject knowledge and skill can often lack essential confidence.

The skills a teacher of composing needs

Structured short observations of good teachers at work in a composing class reveal many ways of working. One teacher in one five-minute observation was seen operating in the following differing modes, demonstrating clearly the complexity of the job. In that short time span she was seen:

- demonstrating by using her own musical and technical skills;
- being a musician composing and improvising on the hoof;
- being a technician mending equipment;
- listening to pupils playing their ideas;
- moving pupils on faster by challenging them;
- responding to pupils' requests, queries and interruptions;
- suggesting refinements to pupils' work;
- making sure of their understanding by getting pupils to show what they meant, not explain it;
- making sure everyone has a turn on equipment;
- making observations and judgements about pupils' work;
- correcting false information;
- structuring pupils' practice;
- giving pupils choices about how to proceed;
- reminding them to save their work.

Analysis of pupils' perceptions from the questionnaires

We had to establish whether composing was a regular activity in the class and the score was 81 per cent, confirming this. A high 72 per cent said that they liked composing in lessons very much and 57 per cent looked forward to their music lessons. Despite this information deriving from selected schools it demonstrated clearly that pupils' antagonism to music is not as in-built as previous research may have suggested. It shows how good teaching through composing has significantly added to the effectiveness and pupils' credit rating of music teaching in secondary schools. We were pleased to find this positive evidence which counteracts some of the largely negative evidence found by previous researchers.

We wanted to find out what pupils experienced in groups and how they felt about their working environment and the resources provided. The evidence gave some conflicting results. A large majority of pupils liked to work with others when they were composing (86 per cent). However, 68 per cent of pupils said that they found it hard to concentrate with a lot of noise in the room as against 32 per cent who said they could do so. The received wisdom has been that teachers should 'learn to develop a thick skin' (Paynter 1982: 78), and that pupils do not notice noise. 57 per cent of pupils agreed that it is hard to hear their own ideas with other people working in the same room. Working in pairs appears to be a more equable mode and 79 per cent of pupils said that they shared in the work in this working mode, whereas 59 per cent admitted to coasting in larger group-work. A significant 28 per cent preferred working on their own. From the fieldwork and interviews we conclude that very few KS3 pupils have the opportunity to work on their own in school composing and therefore lack this experience when they start their KS4 work.

Pupils like using keyboards, which were regularly used (75 per cent) and find they make the composing tasks easier (81 per cent). 60 per cent of pupils use headphones with keyboards but only 27 per cent used memory devices to store their work. This points up a clear matter for development. 79 per cent preferred using keyboards to pitch percussion. As pupils said:

Pupil 1 I do think that some percussion instruments are a bit babyish.
Pupil 2 Percussion instruments aren't very interesting. If you wanted to be interesting you'd need two or three percussion instruments.

Pupils felt that their music wasn't really listened to (56 per cent), and that the music they made in school did not compare in any way with the music they listened to outside (82 per cent). 60 per cent of pupils found it exciting when they heard their music played but 66 per cent felt that their music rarely sounded as they thought it would. One pupil commented:

Pupil 1 Though I like composing, sometimes it seems a bit daunting and also pointless because no one will ever get to play it or hear it.

Most composition exercises take more than one lesson (81 per cent) and teachers often recorded their work (64 per cent). 91 per cent of pupils agreed that you have to think and work very hard when composing, and 81 per cent of pupils felt that they had improved compared with last year. Despite the fact that 49 per cent felt that it was hard to compose if you can't play an instrument well, it was particularly pleasing to find that pupils showed a clear sense of challenge and purpose in composing activities.

Teachers have been surprised by the fact that 63 per cent of pupils said that they could hear the music that they wanted to compose in their head. Following a discussion in the subsequent teachers' seminar, we took this on as a follow-up area and tested the result using a variety of differently worded questions. Pupils in the follow-up enquiry described the audition experience in a variety of ways:

Pupil 1 I sort of listen to them in my head: but sometimes they just sing to me.
Pupil 2 When I hear songs in my head I do remixes of them in my head.

The results have shown very positively that many pupils really do hear what they want to compose in their head before they play or write it and we are delighted to return this information to teachers, since this skill seems more advanced than they would have predicted. It provides more good ground for further building and development. The results also tally significantly with our concern about noisy conditions.

Objective 4: defining progression in composing

One very interesting aspect of the developing composing curriculum has been the accent on free choice of style, especially in the more advanced stages. The 'Creative Dream' was clearly based on a high-art model and the first experiments with children, such as those undertaken by Canadian composer Schafer, arose directly from Cage-influenced music. Paynter did not approach music outside the high-art model with great enthusiasm. 'Indeed a case can be made', he writes, 'for starting afresh with new stimuli in a "neutral" region of sound that does not automatically create associations with the "classical"/"pop" dichotomy' (Paynter 1982: 117). Yet what has happened when young people are encouraged to think freely and make choices is that they do just that. The result has been a strong rejection of the high-art model and a clear aspiration towards popular culture. This, at last, has begun to increase the street credibility of music education and bring it nearer in philosophy and practice to visual art education. There can be little progression without motivation.

Whereas few art teachers would describe themselves as non-practising artists, few of the music teachers in the study describe themselves as composers, though most do occasional arrangements or write class material where appropriate. One teacher was happy to admit that her only purpose in teaching composing was so that pupils would become better listeners. Whilst this is an admirable sentiment it suggests also that there is an area that still needs addressing in higher education both at undergraduate and postgraduate levels. Regular composing practice by the teacher is essential as a basis from which to assess progress in others and to explore and experience their art for themselves.

Observation has confirmed that it is essential that the first composing activities in Year 7 should be practical and searching in order that teachers can construct a baseline from which to work. As Janet Mills put it, 'planning teaching that is diagnostic' (Mills 1996: 13). No progression can be observed without this first step. It is important to seek out, to recognize and to record different levels of experience and ability at the start of the secondary school. In some schools visited there was good evidence of local cross-phase planning. Teachers in primary and secondary schools had come to some basic agreements about content and processes in composing and helpful information had been exchanged.

Progress in composing must be based on the work of individuals and cannot be decided on that of groups or by curriculum content. There must be clear planning for individual work at some point in Year 7. Year 8 needs several individual assessment points and by the end of Year 9 composing assessment should be largely based on individual achievement. There is strong evidence of pupils hiding low levels of technical skills in small group-work right through to Year 9. Many pupils coast (overall, one in five of pupils readily admit to coasting in group-work). About 50 per cent of pupils feel it is hard to compose music if you don't have good instrumental skills but this is an area that the development of the computer can aid considerably.

Many teachers already keep on-going records of individual progress by noting what skills and processes are being understood and applied with knowledge and understanding. Much of this evidence is collected as teachers progress round groups and individuals to review their work. This provides evidence of the absorption and application of curriculum content.

Perhaps it will be helpful also to look for an additional kind of evidence to determine whether pupils are progressing. It is in the process rather than the products that we can best determine movement forward. Pupils who practise their art regularly are most likely to progress, even if individual works are uneven.

There will be clear evidence of progression when:

- individual pupils are motivated to compose on their own initiative;
- individual pupils (or groups) respond eagerly to commissions;
- compositions figure regularly in school performances or other performance opportunities, ensuring that work is completed satisfactorily;
- individuals and groups enter composing competitions at local and national level;
- groups meet regularly to improvise, compose and perform;
- compositions are caringly preserved, displayed and performed.

We can now show that a surprising number of pupils voluntarily compose music outside school. The evidence from our sample of pupils is that 35 per cent at KS3 compose on their own outside school for their own enjoyment and at KS4 this figure rises to 53 per cent. This suggests that the 'Sunday composer' may soon become as much a feature in our society as the 'Sunday painter'. Pupils spoke of composing as a relaxation, a relief from depression and from boredom. One pupil described the experience as 'playing with sounds'.

The research has provided conclusive evidence that pupils often compose music outside school. Once this evidence is fed back into the school assessment system there will be further evidence of progression. Such evidence could help to avoid trying to assess the quality of individual compositions in detail and setting up artificial guidelines for 'more progressive' or 'more complex' compositions equating this with progression.

The following list provides pupils' answers to the question: 'What do you compose for?'

- for practising
- as part of school work
- as part of music
- to test ideas
- for my school choir
- for a school concert
- for competitions/festivals
- just messing about on the keyboard
- to enjoy it
- to express my own feelings
- to have fun with my family
- when I just feel I like it
- for my Mum
- for a birthday/wedding
- for a project on bottle-banks

Objective 5: recommending developments and disseminating ideas of good practice

All participating teachers were invited to a one-day seminar at the Michael Tippett Centre, Bath Spa University College, in July 1999. Fourteen were able to attend and, having been presented with the original research questions and the results of questionnaires in their own schools, were asked to form discussion groups, concentrating on composing skills. The uncertainty we found in school when questioning all the participating teachers was again reflected in the following discussions. This list presents some of their ideas on what composing skills are. Each category is far from exhaustive and can be divided into many sub-categories. Part of our continuing debate about composing skills and processes and part of the unique contribution any individual teacher makes will be found in how these categories are identified, added to and given priority.

What we use	What we do with it	Place it in time	How we use it
Melody	Copy	Binary	Vocalize
Scales	Plan	Ternary	Instrument
Pulse	Hear in the head	Rondo	Record
Rhythm pattern	Compare	Song form	Draw
Concord	Contrast	Blues	Write
Discord	Sequence	Dance forms	Notate
Timbre	Repeat	Stories	Use sequencer

Summary

These final bullet points are a summary of the main issues, which both Anice Paterson and I consider to be the most important learning points we have encountered on our journey of the last two years.

- Planning for individual work is the main area that needs addressing by nearly all teachers. Without this development the composing curriculum will continue to be an uphill struggle. There should be a planned accumulation of individual projects making a tentative start later in Year 7 and rising to a major part of pupils' composing work by the end of Year 9.
- There is a strong need for regular exchange of ideas between teachers. This is especially the case for those in single-teacher departments. Music departments where there is more than one enable a higher level of analysis and understanding about the nature of the job.
- Teachers should work with rather than against their resources. They should plan work that can be achieved without putting themselves or their pupils under unnecessarily heavy stress. Noise stress is very damaging both to

pupils and teachers and should be avoided whenever possible. Valuing sound and being sensitive to its properties is at the centre of the composing experience.

- Music lessons should be practical. Teachers must aim to make every lesson a musical experience at some point.
- Time and energy in setting up composing tasks is time well spent. Teachers must always present their work well and preserve it for future use by themselves and colleagues.
- Develop whole-class strategies for composing where the teacher works with the pupils using the whole class as a resource both for ideas and for performance. Show them how to do it by doing it with them.
- Be prepared to teach as well as facilitate. Don't be afraid to have opinions and ideas. Learning by copying has noble precedents. Pupils tend to gain their own ideas because of you, and most probably in spite of you.
- Develop strategies, spaces and equipment to enable pupils to hear their work undisturbed by the noise of others.
- Develop the use of ICT and master the technology.
- There is a clear and unequivocal need for regular and specialized technical support. This is essential to all well-run and music efficient departments.
- Ensure that all pupils have the opportunity to share their work in class, in the public domain through concerts, events and opportunities inside and outside the school.
- Ensure that taped work is well presented and pupils have the opportunity to take work home. Involve parents' interest in their child's composing work by working in class on take-away projects such as songs, musical Christmas cards or their seasonal equivalent to be sent home.
- Good examples of carefully presented notated work should be displayed on the walls as well as graphic scores. Use both handwritten and computer-generated examples. Sketches and designs for compositions, in words or drawn, should also be seen.
- Hearing in the head results suggests that we may seriously underestimate children's abilities. We must be careful not to assume that because they don't have additional instrumental lessons they are not a 'musician'. Put together with the evidence on noisy classrooms, it suggests even more strongly that we must do everything we can to provide the best conditions for pupils to work.

Conclusion

Composing is firmly established and provides an unique feature in our music curriculum practice in the UK. It is the envy of many other countries that wish that they could establish a similar practice in their own schools. When taught well, pupils look forward to their music lessons in the secondary school and approve of and enjoy composing activities. A growing minority of pupils now compose on their own initiative outside school and view it as an opportunity to improve the quality of their lives and as communication with their families. A majority of pupils experience the ability to imagine their music in their heads before they externalize their ideas.

The development of information and communication technology in the music classroom is essential for the continuing growth and good health of music education in the coming years. Skilled technician support is also both vital and cost-effective. Without both of these the development of the composing curriculum will be severely retarded in the foreseeable future.

Music classrooms must be equipped for the purpose and secure. Pupils should be able to move to equipment that should be fixed and/or easily available. Keyboards with a memory facility are an important resource and must be able to be linked with computers, but both add to and do not replace good acoustic resources in percussion and other instruments. The more we rely on electronically-produced sound, the more important it is to balance this with the best live sound sources of all types to increase and develop pupils' sensitivity to sound which is at the heart of the musical experience.

The voice is a basic composing instrument and tool. All early musical experiences have involved and still involve the voice. This is true of all cultures and histories. Melody is a basic in human communication and the ability to distinguish sound contour develops in all children before birth. Pupils experience composing most often in school by going to an instrument and using their fingers. Singing experience of all kinds in the classroom and in the extended curriculum is an essential part of a composer's music education, helping to guide those composing fingers to the interesting places, following the lead of the 'songs in the head'.

Acquiring the language of music requires immediate experience of it and the chance to use and experiment with it, finding out what it says and how it works by using it. As with language teaching, there is also a need at an early stage to teach grammar and technical matters, but even these can only be experienced fully through using them, as the best teaching in the current primary literacy hour is showing. Writing about things and making up poems and stories go hand in hand with the excitement of acquiring language and being able to express yourself accurately and precisely.

Successful teaching of composing is very dependent, not only on the attitude of the teacher, but also on the physical provision of an appropriate classroom environment where teachers and pupils can work without battling against intrusive and stressful noise throughout the day. This can be achieved in a variety of ways using a variety of teaching methods. Small group-work is highly effective when it is tightly controlled and used as one of the variety of ways to deliver the music education curriculum. It can be the best way to spark off really exciting ideas about music. At present, far too much time is invested in poorly-conceived small-group activities and wasted by the majority of pupils. Small-group activities can be very effective but need to be prepared in detail with a better understanding of the pupils' point of view. Control of such activities needs to be more vital and urgent. At present there is too much off-task and undisciplined work and this prevents lack of progress. Teachers need to be more willing to take a lead in composing activities with their pupils. They must share the composing experience and become confident enough to model, demonstrate and participate in whole-class activities.

> Teachers often play for their classes, sometimes play to them, but rarely play with them.
>
> (Ross 1995: 195)

Whenever possible teachers should strive to involve parents in their children's composing. They should make certain that some work is heard and seen by the parents through homework, take-away projects on tape or in writing, and in concerts. It is very good policy to involve the parents themselves in the experience of composing through special focus parents' meetings.

Composing now occupies a central place in our music curriculum nationally. It can be a powerful medium for delivering listening and performing skills. Composing activities, however, must not overpower the curriculum and should be carefully balanced with performing and listening activities in all planning.

The ultimate aim of the composing curriculum must be to fire individual pupils' imaginations and motivate them to produce work of their own. Composition is a powerful form of self-expression in the individual and this should be at the centre of our work. Much of the creative dream of the last forty years has become a reality even if it has suffered some serious cracks in the process. These faults can be mended through the continuing development of teachers' skills and support of their needs.

Acknowledgements

Although this chapter appears under my name, I wish first of all to acknowledge my indebtedness to my Research Fellow, Anice Paterson, who has so actively involved herself, during the last year, collecting evidence in the field and co-operating in the writing of papers. I am also deeply grateful to Yamaha/Kemble Music (UK) Ltd. for their generous financial support for the Fellowship without which, together with partnership funding from Bath Spa University College, this project could not have been mounted. This funding by Yamaha/Kemble was given freely and was obtained largely through the help and good offices of David Walters of the Music Research Institute, which has strongly supported the project throughout. The funds came without any specified criteria or expectation of commercially determined outcomes. I am also indebted to Gordon Cox of Reading University for his interest and insight.

Notes

1   Jack Dobbs gives an amusing account of visiting the school at Cirencester and finding that the lower school children had very formal exercise books with one semibreve = two minims, etc. He expressed his surprise to Peter Maxwell Davies who readily explained that his assistant taught all the lower years' work and that it was important that this formal work was done. This ties in with his declared views on the importance of teaching formal harmony through primary triads.

2   Bill Colleran worked mainly in the sales department of Universal Edition, London. It was through his personal commitment to and interest in contemporary music that contacts with writers and composers were made.

3   *Two Composers: Two Worlds*. Peter Maxwell Davies and Dudley Moore, Monitor Unit, BBC Television, 26 February 1961.

4   Series directed by Eileen Maloney.

5   Essentially, the responsibility for the content and methodology of a student teacher's practice has been passed from the training institution to the teacher-tutor in the school.

6   Issues such as dominance, reticence, sharing and achievement all need to be discussed with pupils and techniques for dealing with them practised.

References

Coleman, S. (1922) *Creative Music Making for Children*, New York: Putnam.

Cox, G. (1997) 'Changing the face of school music: Walford Davies, the gramophone and the radio', *British Journal of Music Education*, 14(1): 45–55.

Davies, P. M. (1963) 'Music composition by children' in Grant (ed.) *Music in Education* (The Colston Papers), London: Butterworth.

Dennis, B. (1970) *Experimental Music in Schools: Towards a New World of Sound*, Oxford: Oxford University Press.

Department for Education and Employment (1995) *Music in the National Curriculum*, London: HMSO.

Department of Education and Science (1970) *Creative Music in Schools* (Reports on Education No. 63), London: HMSO.

—— *Children and their Primary Schools* (The Plowden Report), London: HMSO.

Mellers, W. (1969) *The Resources of Music,* Cambridge: Cambridge University Press.

Mills, J. (1996) 'Starting at secondary school', *British Journal of Music Education*, 13(1): 5–14.

—— (1997) 'A comparison of the quality of teaching in primary and secondary schools', *Bulletin of the Council for Research in Music Education*, 133: 72–6.

North West Region Development Project (1974) *Creative Music and the Young School Leaver*, London: Blackie.

Paynter, J. (1982) *Music in the Secondary School Curriculum*, Cambridge: Cambridge University Press.

—— (1997) 'The form of finality', *British Journal of Music Education*, 14(3): 5–16.

Paynter, J. and Aston, P. (1970) *Sound and Silence*, Cambridge: Cambridge University Press.

Ross, M. (1995) 'What's wrong with school music?' *British Journal of Music Education*, 12(3): 189–201.

Salaman, W. (1997) 'Keyboards in schools', *British Journal of Music Education,* 14(2): 143–9.

Schools Council (1968) *Music and the Young School Leaver*, London: Evans/Methuen Education.

Self, G. (1967) *New Sounds in Class*, London: Universal Edition.

11 Developing effective practice strategies
Case studies of three young instrumentalists

Stephanie Pitts, Jane Davidson and
Gary McPherson

Introduction

Instrumental teachers have for years been exhorting their pupils to practise, and despairing if they do not, but how many children really understand what 'practice' is? Expecting children to sustain independent learning between lessons is a considerable demand, and one that often becomes a source of friction at home, as practice becomes another chore to add to general homework. Maintaining effective and enjoyable learning between lessons is an important part of playing an instrument, but simply telling children to practise is not sufficient to foster the motivational resources that they will need if they are to make significant progress. Davidson, Howe and Sloboda (1997) point out the high levels of intrinsic motivation – the child's inner drives – needed to sustain the hours and years of investment required to learn an instrument successfully. This paper will use case studies to explore in depth the strategies in evidence when young brass and woodwind players were observed practising their instruments, allowing a consideration of the methods and behaviour that seem to be most effective, and those that seem to generate less successful practice. A case study approach has been taken in order to explore Hallam's (1998) assertion that there is a vast range of practice styles, and strategies that benefit one child may not suit another. Detailed studies allow close comparison of the methods and behaviour in evidence, from which broader discussion can be generated, as the three individuals studied here demonstrate through their varying levels of motivation, parental involvement and musical awareness in their practice.

Hallam (1998) discusses at some length the importance of practice, defining effective practice as 'that which achieves the desired end product, in as short a time as possible, without interfering with long term goals' (Hallam 1998: 142). Children, of course, may not be aware of the long-term goals, or even the short-term end-product, and acquiring this sense of purpose in their practice is an important skill. For novice players, such as those under discussion here, Hallam recommends 'repetitious practice to automatize their developing cognitive, aural and technical skills' (ibid., 145). Repetition, though, is not in itself a sufficient or necessary condition for continuing development, requiring a direction and purpose if it is to address the specific problems that face instrumental learners at different stages. Beginners may not be able to identify particular difficulties in their playing, faced as they are with the immediate challenges of making their instrument sound and remembering fingering and notation. Amongst the children participating in the research from which our case studies are taken, those who are able to identify and imitate the strategies of their teacher in their practice sessions tend to use their time more productively, whilst the majority display few self-correction techniques, and play through their pieces or exercises with little discernible self-evaluation. This supports Hallam's suggestion that teachers should 'model and discuss ways of practising effectively at an early stage in the child's learning' (ibid.,145), although it is clear that many children will take some time to assimilate these strategies for themselves. Practising is a skill to be learned, just as other technical and musical skills require effort and concentration for mastery, and to view practice as simply a means to an end is to overlook its intrinsic complexity.

Reporting earlier research into the practice strategies of novice instrumentalists, Hallam (1997) notes that, whilst 67 per cent of students were observed to use constant repetition in their practice, 69 per cent claimed that they practised in small sections, with only 26 per cent stating that their practice consisted of playing pieces through (Hallam 1997: 99). This suggests that children's awareness of desirable practice strategies is not always carried through into their own work, a point that is supported by our own case studies. As Hallam puts it, musicians must 'learn to learn' (ibid., 103), developing an awareness of the purpose of specific types of practice and employing different strategies as appropriate. McPherson (1993) made similar observations, noting that children who were cognitively engaged in their practice tended to make better progress, drawing on high levels of self-awareness to appraise and develop their own learning.

Ericsson (1997: 38) notes that for many learning activities, particularly academic tasks, teachers are usually present to give feedback on the accuracy or success of a child's performance. 'Self-monitored training' (ibid. 38), including musical practice, demands a model or 'representation', whereby the individual can remember the tasks and comments given by their teacher, and use them as the basis for self-evaluation later. High levels of skill can only be achieved where this internalizing of earlier instructions takes place, so that the teaching of practice skills and strategies is an important part of the instrumental teacher's role, allowing learning to become independent and therefore sustainable beyond the confines of the weekly lesson. Of course, this can take years to develop, and in some cases the avoidance strategies and failure orientation of the children involved will work against any attempt to build up self-reflective skills (cf. McPherson 1993; O'Neill 1996).

Recent psychological research has emphasized the significance of parents, as well as teachers, in ensuring that the home environment supports the learning that takes place within and outside lessons (cf. Sloboda et al. 1996; Davidson et al. 1996; 1997; O'Neill 1997). As our case studies will demonstrate, the involvement of parents in children's practice is a sensitive area, and can become a source of conflict rather than the intended encouragement. Parents, teachers and children need to share similar goals about the child's learning if it is to be effectively supported, but there are many points at which those lines of communication can break down. This is another area of learning and practice which demands deliberate effort and consideration, and cannot be left to chance. It is all too easy to perceive practice as a chore, a view which can be reinforced by well-meaning parental reminders, and yet sustaining musical interest and enjoyment is arguably the most significant factor in the early stages of learning an instrument. In the case studies that follow, the complex interactions and processes that constitute musical practice will be explored, in order to allow discussion of the effective and problematic elements of practice as observed amongst these young instrumentalists.

Methodology

The case studies here are drawn from video-recordings of novice brass and woodwind players' practice sessions, made at regular intervals during the children's first six months of learning. The children were amongst 158 primary school instrumentalists participating in a longitudinal study based at the University of New South Wales, Sydney, for which parents, teachers and pupils were asked to comment on changing perceptions, attitudes and skills during the critical first three years of learning an instrument. In this larger cohort, care was taken to sample for gender, socio-economic status and school background, drawing children from eight different primary schools in Sydney, each with an established instrumental teaching and school band programme. The children are all learning brass or woodwind instruments, as is typical in Australian primary band programmes, and this allowed for comparison of data across the sample. Further research from the study is reported elsewhere (cf. Davidson and McPherson 1998; Davidson 1999; Pitts *et al.* 2000), but the focus for this paper is on the practice strategies employed by three individuals, looking for differences in approach and evaluating which of them seem to be most effective in supporting musical development.

The video recordings were made in the children's homes at 4–6 week intervals, usually by the parents, and the children were encouraged to have as 'normal' a practice session as possible while they were being recorded. Inevitably, some were more easily distracted by the video camera than others, but the practice strategies employed, even when the children were aware they were being observed, reveal much about the way these children work, and have wider implications for instrumental teaching and learning. The video analysis undertaken was based on systematic and repeated viewings of the material, consistent with earlier research (cf. Davidson 1999). Salient themes were then listed and grouped, following the methods of Interpretative Phenomenological Analysis (Smith 1995). The three children under discussion have been selected for the case studies because they each displayed relatively consistent practice behaviour over the time they were being recorded, establishing a personal routine, within which changes in attitude and motivation can be detected. The data generated through the video observations cannot give a complete picture of practising strategies used by this age-group, but important areas for discussion are revealed, which have implications for teachers, parents and pupils.

In the results which follow, different themes form the focus of each report, according to the behaviour observed. For case study one, this meant that a largely chronological account was the clearest way to convey the essence of the child's practice, whilst for case studies two and three, analysis is grouped by thematic content to give the strongest picture of the emerging issues. The difference itself is indicative of the range of behaviours that takes place when children practise, and comparison between the three cases will be made in the discussion section.

Results

Case study one: trumpeter, male, aged 10

This young trumpeter is the most independent of the learners considered here, and the most cheerfully accepting of the new task he has taken on. He begins his first practice session sitting on the floor in his pyjamas, with his music propped up on the floor in front of him. His mother is in the room, and he says, 'So what shall I play?', before starting with technical exercises, in which he plays repeated notes, carefully counting the rests between them. He plays one short piece after another, making no attempt at self-correction, and stopping to chat with his mum occasionally. After about ten minutes, the boy is distracted by a sticky valve on his trumpet, and spends some time oiling the key, explaining the process as he does it. He maintains the concentration and interest in his instrument that has been evident throughout the session, but has lost the stamina for playing; it is, after all, nearly his bedtime. When he has finished oiling the valves, he continues playing for a few more minutes, but the sound is poor, and his first finger often ends up on the second valve as he pauses to think between each note. He stops again to fidget with the mouthpiece, and begins to pack away, chatting all the while. This has been a long first session, in which the boy has demonstrated considerable pleasure in the instrument he has just acquired, succeeding in playing through a number of pieces, if not very fluently.

In his second observed session, a couple of weeks later, the boy is seen sitting more comfortably on a chair, with the music on another chair in front of him. He displays greater confidence, announcing the titles of pieces and playing through them, although without any strategies for self-correction. He still chats to his parents between pieces, but is playing for longer periods, always with immense concentration in his face. He is aware of difficulties to the extent that one piece causes him to struggle, shrug and say, 'That's all I know of number 22'. Having recognized failure at that point, he looks rather dispirited, and begins to oil his trumpet again, very messily. The boy is displaying classic avoidance strategies, renouncing all responsibility for his learning to his teacher, and becoming preoccupied with the maintenance of his instrument in order to demonstrate a skill that he has recently acquired and has confidence in. He begins playing again after a few minutes, returning to an earlier piece, despite saying 'I've got oil all over my hands'. He is now pressing the valves with the wrong hand, wriggling in his chair and making a truly dismal sound, and so the second session disintegrates as he packs up with a disgusted expression.

After what could have been an off-putting start, an observation of the boy three months later shows a cheerful, independent practice session, in which his parents have left him alone in a different room, accompanied only by the video camera and his pet bird. His playing is more fluent and confident; he is still announcing the titles and playing through pieces, only occasionally stopping to re-start or repeat large sections. From the earliest sessions, where his mental strategies limited him to considering each note before he played it, he is now processing longer phrases, counting rests and refusing to be distracted until the end of each piece. The distractions are plentiful, as after around ten minutes the bird begins flying around the room, a fact which the boy ignores except in the intervals between pieces. At these points, he looks around the room to find the bird, and once calls, 'Stay in one place, or I'll ground you for a day'. He clearly likes an audience, saying, 'Did you like that?', and then to the camera, 'My bird *loves* music'.

The boy hums to himself as he changes his music books around, then finds his warm-up tune; 'I should have played this ages ago'. After his self-conscious first practices, he is now in a world of his own, and uses neither the water rattling in his trumpet nor the progress of his bird around the room as excuses to stop work. Even when the bird lands on his head, singing loudly, the boy continues playing, although he is struggling with a more difficult piece and meeting with little success. Shaking the bird off his head at the end of the piece, he returns to an earlier tune, but he is running out of energy after playing for approximately thirty-five minutes, and the session is ended as his father comes in to ask if he has finished.

This boy is remarkable because of his persistence and concentration, which remain even when he is getting negligible results and is coping with considerable distractions. He clearly takes a pleasure and pride in his instrument, despite possessing few helpful practising strategies; he is well motivated and determined. Sharing his practice, even only with his bird, appears to help, as he introduces pieces, apologizes when he needs to start again, and never stops playing before he has completed a 'performance'. This idea of practising to an audience, however, is not encouraging him to develop new approaches, as in his search for fluency he is committed to playing pieces through, rather than working on short sections. This is a problem that can be unwittingly reinforced by parents, who will typically praise recognizable melodies, rather than detailed working, as the former make easier listening. The discernible progress that this boy makes is largely due to his determination, but it is clear that more guidance on effective use of his long practice sessions is needed to sustain his enthusiasm and development.

Case study two: saxophonist, female, aged 10

This young girl is much more aware of the camera's presence, pulling faces into it, and even waving at the end of her first practice session. It seems likely that her concentration would have been poor without the distraction of the recording, and it may even be that the presence of an observer, albeit an inanimate one, keeps her on task for longer than would otherwise have been the case. By her fourth session, the girl is clearly resentful of the camera, muttering, 'I'd rather me do my practice without you in the room'. Clearly, there are methodological difficulties in having any observer present for what is usually a private activity, but this case reveals much about the girl's general attitude: the camera appears to be an authority figure to her, against which she wants to rebel, in the same way she challenges her parents in some of the observed exchanges. Her negative comments about the music she is playing need to be taken in this context, but her frustration with the instrument comes across in her actions as well as her speech.

This girl shows less chronological development, with repeated events and tendencies giving a clearer evaluation of her practising style. Each session begins with her getting her saxophone and music out of their cases, a process which becomes increasingly protracted over the several months of sessions observed. Her practice usually begins with scales, which are played through without correction, despite a struggle with the high notes and generally poor fluency and intonation. The second session introduces what is presumably meant to be a minor scale, which is played inaccurately, and improves very little over the next few weeks. Scales are clearly a focus of the girl's lessons, and something that her mother is aware of when she checks her practice at the end of each session. The exchange between mother and daughter at the end of the second session is revealing:

Mother   Have you done your new scale?
Daughter Yes.
Mother   Have you done it twice?
Daughter Yes.
Mother   And you've done all your pieces?
Daughter Yes – twice.

Throughout this conversation, the daughter has been shuffling uncomfortably with her back to the camera: hardly surprising as her description of her practice bears little resemblance to the reality. She has clearly been taught (as has her mother) some superficial strategies for effective practice – starting with scales and playing things twice. However, she seems to have little understanding of why these strategies could be effective, using them instead to fill in time in a task she obviously sees as a chore. Her practice tends to be disjointed and laborious, and although the length of time spent practising increases over the sessions observed, much of the increase is due to time-wasting behaviour.

The girl's pieces also receive cursory treatment, although there are moments when her concentration is good and her playing fluent. Sometimes she announces the title of the piece, although in the case of *Good King Wenceslas* (in May!) she adds, 'I hate that one'. It is rare for the girl to go back over her pieces to identify and correct any problems: in the fourth session she plays *Yankee Doodle* repeatedly, but its fluency decreases and she makes no attempt to rectify this. Her cognitive strategies for processing the music are limited, although she makes increasing use of singing and fingering a piece before she plays it. Singing is an important feature of her practice sessions; after playing a piece in the second session, she begins to sing far more fluently, moving her saxophone with a jazzy swing and pretending to play. It seems that her image of playing the saxophone is conflicting with the immediate difficulties of making a sound and reading notation, and so adding to her frustration with the task of practising.

As well as singing to herself, the girl talks between pieces, although comments such as, 'Why do I have to do this stupid stuff?' could well be for the benefit of the camera. Her exchanges with her mother support these private comments, however, and at the end of her second session there is a brief conversation about the pieces being 'really boring', and although the mother sounds surprised, she decides not to pursue the subject. The mother's role in the girl's practice is significant, not least because it shows that the disrespectful speech the child shows to the camera is not moderated, or checked, when she speaks to her mother. From the first session, the mother is established as a monitor of practice: she leaves the room, but is within calling distance when the daughter shouts, 'Mum, do I have to keep playing?'. The answer, 'Yes, a bit more', is followed by some repetition of earlier pieces and a good deal of shuffling; quantity of practice is apparently being mistaken for quality. A few minutes later, the following exchange ends the session:

Daughter	Now have I done enough, Mum?
Mother	Well, do you think you've done enough?
Daughter	Yes, I think I'm pretty good at it.
Mother	Okay, that was great.

More effusive praise comes at the end of the third session, when after some dispute about the unsuccessful use of a backing-track tape, the mother says, 'Well it sounded great – I couldn't believe it'. Although both parents play the piano, the daughter has evidently established a position as a musical 'expert' in the family, and uses the paraphernalia of changing reeds, selecting music and packing her instrument away to reinforce the 'superiority' of her knowledge.

Over the sessions observed, the girl's fingering and notation reading skills show some signs of improvement, but her overall playing becomes no more musical or fluent. She is clearly practising under duress, and although her parents are supportive, their exaggerated praise and attempts at monitoring do little to lift the gloomy mood that pervades the practice sessions. Perhaps it is not surprising to learn that the girl stopped playing the saxophone after two years. Whilst she employs a number of potentially helpful strategies in her practice, such as singing and fingering before playing, she does these with such reluctance that the experience of practising becomes increasingly arduous. The girl is apparently following the instructions of her teacher, in starting her practice with scales, for example, and reluctantly accepts the length of session that is controlled by her mother. Intrinsic motivation, however, seems to be entirely lacking, and positive feedback comes from the mother, rather than any self-awareness of successful playing. This girl is indicative of the potentially damaging effect of externally imposed practising strategies, although her attitude is such that much of the responsibility for her dissatisfaction rests with her.

Case study three: flautist, female, aged 9

The third case illustrates even more clearly than the other two that personality and environment are significant factors in children's approaches to practice. This girl is unusual in that she has a music stand rather than propping up her music on the case, and she does her practice first on a small chair, then a larger one, and then the larger one with her feet propped on telephone directories. This is indicative of the importance that practice sessions appear to have for the whole family: the girl herself is unsmiling, and does everything with great deliberation, so that preparing to play can take anything up to ten minutes each time. She is not a 'time filler' in the same way as the saxophonist, but every movement is protracted, and the resulting discontinuity when she plays means that her practice is largely unrewarding. In her early sessions, she is struggling at the most basic level, looking intently at the music, and often removing the flute from her lips to check where her fingers should go. She displays no outward signs of frustration; it is her father who yawns from behind the video camera and says, 'What are you doing now?' as she changes books and prepares to continue.

The girl's parents become increasingly involved in her practice, with the father beginning the second session with a reminder about posture, and the mother intervening in the third session to offer help when the girl is struggling. They have been present from the beginning, however, with the first video including an argument between the parents about what instructions they had been given, and whether the father's videoing technique was adequate. This is clearly a high-pressure household, and the child's incredible passivity in the face of repeated failure adds to the very serious atmosphere. The parents adopt a variety of teaching roles, with the father refusing, or unable, to intervene when the music stand is still a bent-metal sculpture after five minutes of struggling, merely saying, 'Well, it didn't work that way, so fold it up and try another one'. The mother, on the other hand, takes the first opportunity to give assistance:

Daughter   No, that's wrong.
Mother   Well, you still don't know where your notes are, with your fingers. Is that the problem?
Daughter   It's just that D is quite hard.
Mother   Well, look here, you came down like a scale, and then you did the same note three times, and then you just had to go up again.
    [Child shuffles]
Mother   So what page are you up to now?
    [They look for the music together]

Several months later, the child still seems to be getting little pleasure from her practice, and the same slow and serious approach is in evidence. Practising has clearly become a night-time ritual, with the girl sitting in her pyjamas in the lounge, presumably before going to bed. She is still looking at her fingers and peering at the music, obviously relying on visual memory rather than doing any aural evaluation of the sounds she hears. Despite the presence of her father there is no discussion, and even when she announces, 'That's all of my practice', he only says, 'Okay, good girl. You can pack up then', continuing to video the lengthy process as she puts her flute away. Hers is a sad case, in that she seems to be deriving little pleasure from her playing, with it becoming another task to be accomplished rather than an activity with any real enjoyment. Unlike the saxophonist, she is not obviously resentful of her new task, but accepts it passively, submitting to the pressure with which her parents are surrounding her practice sessions. Over the observed sessions, she makes very little progress, as despite the quantities of time she spends with her flute, there is not much actual practice taking place.

Discussion

The many differences between the practice sessions observed illustrate the complexity of the processes involved, and the consequent difficulties of giving general advice on practising effectively. Nonetheless, certain common themes can be discussed here, involving parents, teachers and children, and some of the implications for all parties will be considered in the final section.

The children themselves showed a wide variety of attitudes to practising, and in some cases these changed over time as interest, frustration or enjoyment fluctuated. The saxophonist, in particular, became increasingly reluctant to work, procrastinating over every task and asking repeatedly if she could stop. Even the trumpeter, who began with such eagerness, showed a loss of interest in the months after the video study, saying in a later interview, 'When I first got it I would play until my mouth got sore'. The long summer holiday and subsequent transfer to secondary school changed that, demonstrating that external factors can be damaging to motivation, even where an initial keenness exists. More difficult to understand is the flautist, who displayed no emotion at all, appearing to gain neither satisfaction nor displeasure from her playing. Treating practice as something that is 'good for you' in this way is an attitude unwittingly perpetuated by teachers and parents, and one which fails to connect with children's intrinsic motivation, or to provide them with goals that are attainable and finite. Practising becomes a condition upon which they are permitted to keep their instrument, remain in the band, call themselves a musician; it is not expected to be pleasurable, and as a result it seems it rarely is. Different people will respond in a variety of ways to the challenge, some rejecting it and others seeing it as necessary to their musical development and therefore desirable (cf. Kemp 1996). To expect this level of long-term motivation from children, however, is perhaps unreasonable, and Hallam (1998) cites achievement, reward and social motivation as being powerful forces in supporting a child's interest and developing sustainable intrinsic motivation (ibid. 90). Practice must, at some level, be enjoyable if it is to bring musical development and satisfaction, and our cases demonstrate this, in that the trumpeter is the only one to maintain a level of interest and so make discernible progress.

Parental involvement is another significant factor that emerged from the observed practice sessions, and here the research literature is divided in its evaluations. Sloboda and Davidson (1996: 180) have highlighted the importance of parental involvement, whilst Zdzinski (1992; 1996) has reported mixed results, stating that performance and cognitive outcomes were closely related to parental involvement at the elementary level, with affective outcomes becoming more significant at higher levels of performance and maturity (1996: 43). In other words, parents offer advice and explanations to young children, giving recognition and praise to older and more capable offspring. Our case studies and wider evidence from the longitudinal study (cf. Davidson and McPherson 1998) suggest that this distinction is a simplification, and that quality of parental support is more important than its mere presence. The trumpeter, for example, was clearly comfortable with his parents in the room, and then benefited from their gradual withdrawal from his practice sessions, whereas the saxophonist's and flautist's parents retained such control over their daughters' practice that independent learning was unlikely to flourish. As Johnston (1990) says in his book for children, *Not Until You've Done Your Practice*, 'Sitting at the piano because your parents insist is a silly reason. So is practising just because your teacher told you to do half an hour every day' (Johnston 1990: 80). Practising for other people is not a sustainable motivation, as it encourages performance behaviour rather than the concentrated and disciplined work needed to foster musical development.

In musical and cognitive terms, the children studied displayed few significant changes over time, although those who had begun with very hesitant note-level processing became more fluent and able to think in longer phrases as their familiarity with their instrument and its notation grew. Their practising strategies were negligible, supporting established findings (Hallam 1997; Gruson 1988) that the majority of children will play pieces through without any attempt at self-correction, rather than identifying difficult sections and working on those. The children we observed did not seem to have a real idea of why they were playing through their repertoire, although all had good recollection of what they had been asked to do. They were sometimes aware that a particular piece had not gone very well, but were only conscious of difficulties when they struggled or stopped, rarely picking out small-scale or even global errors such as inaccurate rhythm or pitch, poor tuning or unpleasant tone. In contrast with advanced or expert players (cf. Nielsen 1997; Ericsson 1997), young beginners seem either to ignore the auditory feedback from their playing, persisting despite unrewarding results, or to become discouraged when their efforts appear to be getting them nowhere. Either way, they do not appear to have the strategies to identify and correct problems that arise, making it clear that teachers have an important role to play in fostering skills of self-criticism and evaluation. To quote from Hallam's extensive research again, practice will only become purposeful and self-determined when the pupil has a range of 'task oriented strategies' to draw upon (Hallam 1998: 140).

The case studies given here offer a rare opportunity to witness the activities that children engage in in the name of 'practice'. They highlight the need for systematic teaching of practising strategies, illustrating the sheer tedium and frustration that can result when children have no clear idea of why and how they should be learning. Practising is a significant part of the child's experience of music, and has wider effects than the proficiency on the instrument with which it is ostensibly concerned. If practice becomes a source of family conflict and personal dissatisfaction, the child's whole attitude to music can be damaged, and conversely, practice which is satisfying and enjoyable will in itself be a source of motivation. There is further research to be done in investigating the most effective strategies used by children in different circumstances, and later stages of the current longitudinal study will explore the progress and attitudes of the wider sample of children over their first three years of learning. Effective practice is too important an area to be left to chance, and the final section of this paper will evaluate ways in which parents and teachers can contribute to the development of practising strategies.

Implications

Teachers are in arguably the best position to encourage the development of practice strategies, and need to consider carefully what 'practice that piece this week' actually means to a child. The children we observed had picked up the routine of playing scales first, followed by their pieces, but it seemed unlikely that they knew the reasons for such an approach. Too often, instrumental lessons fall into a similar pattern every week, so that children lose the sense of interest and excitement of the first few weeks, and become acclimatized to a particular teacher's way of doing things. Routine is important, but so is surprise, and encouraging children to improvise by way of a warm-up, to experiment with dynamics and tempi, and to achieve fluency and confidence in their playing by returning to earlier repertoire, are all ways of allowing the child to engage with the music, rather than only with the mechanics of notation and fingering (cf. McPherson 1993). Practice strategies also need to be systematically taught by example and by explanation, with the child given responsibility for identifying problem sections, and the teacher providing a variety of methods for tackling them. A combination of formal and informal practising has been shown to be effective amongst high achieving instrumentalists (Sloboda and Davidson 1996: 183), allowing children to connect with their playing and their instrument through improvisation and exploration, rather than solely by following their teacher's instructions. The music itself is of the utmost importance, and children must be allowed to experience the pleasures of playing familiar pieces, as well as working systematically at current challenges. Amongst the children we observed, practising band parts took up a significant amount of practice time, an activity which gave little scope for increasing personal repertoire or giving immediate musical satisfaction. Making progress on the instrument should not be seen as the only practice goal: musical understanding and cognitive processing must also be allowed to develop, so that learning can be independent and ongoing.

Parents are also of importance in ensuring that a child's musical development takes place in a supportive and stable environment. Unlike teachers, parents have the opportunity to hear their children practising, and are able to offer praise, advice and encouragement immediately, rather than only in lessons. This must be given sensitively, however, as young instrumentalists are at a vulnerable stage of learning, and can easily be put off by undue interference or even by insincere praise. Parents need to have a clear understanding of what practising should involve, so that they are able to tolerate and praise detailed work, rather than expecting performances all the time. They should also be aware that allocating a specific length for practice does not in itself guarantee quality; we witnessed a great deal of time-wasting and avoidance, much of it connected with unnecessary instrument maintenance. Evidence is divided on whether parents should supervise practice (cf. Zdzinski 1992; Sloboda and Davidson 1996), and it seems probable that a variety of approaches is likely to be most effective, in the same way that sustaining surprise in lessons is desirable. Asking children to perform pieces to parents when they are ready, or making it clear that help is available when it is needed, offers support that is not intrusive, but that indicates the parents' commitment to the child's learning. The parents' and teachers' roles are different, and should remain so, with the parent seeking to offer additional, rather than potentially conflicting, encouragement and guidance.

Children are of course at the centre of the learning process, and their individual needs must be recognized and responded to. They also have the most accurate perspective on the complicated business of practising, and encouraging them to share that with other novice instrumentalists can be valuable. Articulating their difficulties, opinions and ideas can be helpful, whether to a parent, a friend or even, as our trumpeter demonstrated, a pet. Ultimately, each child will respond differently to learning a musical instrument, and given the right environment, personality and opportunities, they will be able to enjoy the music, and not just be swamped by the learning. Too often, practising becomes confrontational, and meeting failure in instrumental playing assumes an importance it does not merit. All children have much to gain from the processes and experiences of learning an instrument, and their practice should be concerned with exploring those opportunities and gaining a confidence and familiarity with music that it is hard to achieve in any other way.

This research has been supported by a large Australian Research Council Grant (No. A79700682), awarded for three years in 1996.

References

Davidson, J.W. (1999) 'Self and desire: a preliminary exploration of why students start and continue with music learning', *Research Issues in Music Education* 12: 30–7.

Davidson, J.W. and McPherson, G.E. (1998) 'Self and desire: why students start music lessons', *Music, Mind and Science: Fifth ICMPC Proceedings*, Seoul: Western Music Research Institute, pp. 413–18.

Davidson, J.W., Howe, M.J.A. and Sloboda, J.A. (1997) 'Environmental factors in the development of musical performance skill in the first twenty years of life' in Hargreaves and North (eds), *The Social Psychology of Music*, Oxford: Oxford University Press, pp. 188–206.

Davidson, J.W., Howe, M.J.A., Moore, D.G. and Sloboda, J.A. (1996) 'The role of parental influences in the development of musical performance', *British Journal of Developmental Psychology*, 14: 399–412.

Ericsson, K.A. (1997) 'Deliberate practice and the acquisition of expert performance: An overview' in Jørgensen and Lehmann (eds) *Does practice make perfect? Current Theory and Research on Instrumental Music Practice*, Oslo: Norges Musikkhøgskole, pp. 9–51.

Gruson, M.L. (1988) 'Rehearsal skill and musical competence: does practice make perfect?' in Sloboda (ed.) *Generative Processes in Music: the Psychology of Performance, Improvisation and Composition*, Oxford: Clarendon Press.

Hallam, S. (1997) 'Approaches to instrumental practice of experts and novices: implications for education' in Jørgensen and Lehmann (eds), *Does Practice Make Perfect? Current Theory and Research on Instrumental Music Practice*, Oslo: Norges Musikkhøgskole, pp. 89–107.

Hallam, S. (1998) *Instrumental Teaching: a Practical Guide to Better Teaching and Learning*, Oxford: Heinemann.

Johnston, P. (1990) *Not Until You've Done Your Practice: the Classic Survival Guide for Kids who are Learning a Musical Instrument, but Hate Practising*, Sydney: Kangaroo Press.

Kemp, A. (1996) *The Musical Temperament: the Psychology and Personality of Musicians*, Oxford: Oxford University Press.

McPherson, G.E. (1993) 'Factors and abilities influencing the development of visual, aural and creative performance skills in music and their educational implications', PhD thesis, University of Sydney.

Neilsen, S.G. (1997) 'Self-regulation of learning strategies during practice: A case study of a church organ student preparing a musical work for performance' in Jørgensen and Lehmann (eds), *Does Practice Make Perfect? Current Theory and Research on Instrumental Music Practice*, Oslo: Norges Musikkhøgskole, pp. 109–22.

O'Neill, S.A. (1996) 'Factors influencing children's motivation and achievement during the first year of instrumental music tuition', PhD thesis, University of Keele.

—— (1997) 'The role of practice in children's early musical performance achievement' in Jørgensen and Lehmann (eds) *Does Practice Make Perfect? Current Theory and Research on Instrumental Music Practice,* Oslo: Norges Musikkhøgskole, pp. 53–70.

Pitts, S.E., Davidson, J.W. and McPherson, G.E. (2000) 'Models of success and failure in instrumental learning: case studies of young players in the first twenty months of learning', *Bulletin of the Council for Research in Music Education* 146: 51–69.

Sloboda, J.A. and Davidson, J.W. (1996) 'The young performing musician' in Deliège and Sloboda (eds), *Musical Beginnings: Origins and Development of Musical Competence,* pp. 171–90, Oxford: Oxford University Press.

Sloboda, J.A., Davidson, J.W., Howe, M.J.A. and Moore, D.G. (1996) 'The role of practice in the development of performing musicians', *British Journal of Psychology,* 87: 287–309.

Smith, J.A. (1995) 'Semi-structured interviewing and qualitative analysis' in Smith, Harré and Van Langenhove (eds) *Rethinking Methods in Psychology*, London: Sage Publications.

Zdzinski, S.F. (1992) 'Relationships among parental involvement, music aptitude, and musical achievement of instrumental music students', *Journal of Research in Music Education*, 40(2): 114–25.

Zdzinski, S.F. (1996) 'Parental involvement, selected student attributes, and learning outcomes in instrumental music', *Journal of Research in Music Education*, 44(1): 34–48.

3 Developing the Music curriculum

12 ICT in the secondary Music curriculum
Peter Desmond

Introduction

Over recent years, Information and Communication Technology (ICT) has revolutionized many aspects of life including the way we work and learn. This chapter sets out to discuss the applications of ICT in secondary school music teaching.

The first section outlines common uses of music technology. The second section considers how these resources can enhance the teaching of music as a creative subject, remembering that technology for use in music teaching is not limited to expensive computers and recording equipment but encompasses items such as electronic keyboards and audio-visual aids. In section three, aspects of classroom management and general planning are considered. Finally, appendices include a checklist of ICT skills for music teachers and explanations of some basic music technology concepts.

Contemporary school music curriculums focus on performing, composing, listening and appraising. From time to time the definitions and emphases change but the basic concepts, knowledge and skills required by aspiring young musicians remain broadly similar.

General comments

Lack of funds and initiative have, in many cases, meant that schools are usually far behind the commercial and business communities in quality, quantity and effective use of technology. In this context, it is important to remember that technology should never be the sole focus of study, but rather a tool for enhancing the quality, individuality and accessibility of musical experience.

In a climate where teachers are often required to plan equipment purchase on extremely limited budgets, acquisition of ICT resources needs to be carefully planned. An ill-considered music technology shopping-list often leads to cupboards full of expensive and under-used equipment.

Another important point to make at the outset is the need for teachers to keep several steps ahead of their students, enabling them to troubleshoot the inevitable problems that arise when such versatile equipment is used by a large number of not-so-careful individuals. Some teachers make time before or after school to increase their familiarity with the equipment and software. Others have found it helpful to have similar resources available at home so that meaningful preparation can be achieved away from the day-to-day distractions of school life. This need has to some extent been recognized by recent funding initiatives, but we are a long way from the business model in which all resources needed to do the job well are made available by the company. If teachers are to be comfortable with using and troubleshooting complex software in a pressurized classroom environment, they need to have used it extensively on their own when there is time and a conducive atmosphere for problem-solving, perhaps involving the reading of manuals, etc.

The amount of computer equipment available

The extent to which computers can be integrated into the music curriculum is immediately dependent on the ratio of equipment to students. For a whole class to work on a composition assignment using computer workstations,[1] the minimum effective allocation is one computer for every pair of students. Even in this scenario there is a danger that one partner will be passive, merely watching the other at work. The ideal situation is one workstation per pupil but, at the time of writing, this is a rare luxury. An alternative solution is to split classes and rotate activities. This is not an easy option, especially if only one teacher is available. Even with well-motivated students who are totally at ease with the technology, the amount of meaningful teacher–pupil interaction is bound to be minimal.

If the situation does not allow for a full complement of workstations, the best use of ICT may be for demonstration, individual research/skills development or ensemble accompaniment.

Common uses of ICT in music

Computer-based technology in music

Sequencing   Using computers to control electronic musical instruments (or instruments with an electronic interface). Also covers programs that allow the user to choose from a selection of musical fragments (often 'samples', which are digital recordings), ordering, looping and overlaying them in a musical equivalent of collage in Art.
Scorewriting   Musical desktop publishing.
CAL (Computer Assisted Learning)   Interactive teaching tools.
Digital audio   Digital recording, manipulation and transmission of sound waves.
Soft synthesis   Virtual instruments synthesized on a computer.
Internet   Downloading resources, shared projects with other schools, homework, research, teacher resources.

Sequencing

MIDI allows electronic musical instruments to transmit and receive performance data such as timbre, pitch, duration,[2] touch, volume, pedalling, pitch bend, vibrato and reverberation.

MIDI was initially modelled on the keyboard,[3] particularly the electronic synthesizer. All major manufacturers realized the need for a common means of communication between their products and this started by enabling 'coupling' of instruments so that the performer could play one but both would produce the same music, usually with differing timbres.

The rise of personal computers allowed this to be taken much further as musical equipment was designed to be *multi-timbral*, meaning that it could play back perhaps sixteen different timbres at the same time. The computer is used to play back different music on each of the channels[4] simultaneously, creating an electronic ensemble. This then gave rise to *sequencing* in which music is played in, stored in the MIDI format, edited, repeated, transposed, etc. and sent back to a sound-generating device to create very complex music from simple beginnings.

One advantage of this format is the relatively small amount of data required to store a piece of music electronically. This is because the sound itself is not recorded, just information about what synthesized sounds were used and what notes were played. The process of replaying the music actually involves the computer performing the piece itself from the given information.

A new compositional vocabulary has evolved including words such as *looping*, *quantizing* and *key mapping*. One of the greatest benefits of sequencing is that composers are no longer restricted by the need to notate or play accurately. Musicians who do not read traditional notation or do not have advanced performing skills can create complex pieces. Composition in this context is therefore a totally separate pursuit from performing, notating and understanding traditional music. Synthesized sounds do not have the physical restrictions of real instruments and so can be used in ways that would be technically too demanding of live players, or simply impossible due to restrictions of dynamic and pitch ranges.

Seqeuncing using pre-recorded material

Another type of sequencing allows users to choose from a palette of *samples*, which may then be ordered, looped and overlaid to create new pieces without having to get down to the level of choosing individual notes. The end results are obviously derivative, but this is a good way in for less able students or those with limited performance skills. One major benefit of this software genre is that peripheral equipment, such as MIDI keyboards, sound modules, etc., is not needed because the user is not working at the level of individual notes. All sounds can be stored on a CD-ROM (or in the computer's internal memory) and re-ordered using the normal mouse-based user interface. Current titles in this genre tend to focus on one particular style of music and often allow recording of additional audio samples (live sounds) for incorporating into the finished product. In effect, the user is creating a sound collage, usually within a tightly-defined musical style. This is a valid musical activity, which allows for experimentation with sound, but avoids the need for performing and notation skills. In fact, a complete musical novice can use this sort of product to great effect.

Scorewriting

A musical version of a word processor in which notation is the starting point. These programs often allow MIDI communication for input and output but do not have the more powerful sequencer functions, as their main objective is a neat printout. They are very useful for producing parts from a score and accurate, easy transposition: a very useful tool for a more traditional composer, adept at using notation and writing for live instrumentalists.

Many educational establishments have chosen this type of software for their music technology work. Although such software is very useful for those who are already able to understand notation, it is arguably not the best use of music technology for schools, as the starting point for musical creativity should be the actual sound rather than the notation. This is only one side of the argument, however, as working from notation can impose good discipline and develop an understanding of that notation.

Another advantage of starting from notation is that melodic structure and harmonic relationships are possibly more obvious than when working purely with sounds. Disadvantages include rhythmic restrictions as youngsters often hear and want to use complex rhythms that many of us would find tricky to notate. A disciplined approach to composition that lends itself to this style of software is the *score template* in which an outline structure, with or without some notes, is given and the student must fill in the gaps.

CAL

Interactive learning, often from a CD-ROM, which uses multimedia (i.e. text, sound, graphics and video) to teach some aspect of music. Topics covered include notation, theory, aural training, history, knowledge of instruments and styles. Some of these resources are useful, but this is perhaps not the best use of technology in music. Some of the products available in this category are fairly pedagogically sound and have excellent assessment schemes built in. This sort of package will drill students in notation, theory, historical and stylistic facts and are effectively an individual teacher-substitute. As such they have similar value to CD-ROMs in the school library which may be used by pupils to research facts or practise their typing, reading and spelling.

Digital audio

This software allows audio files – digitized sound waves – to be produced and manipulated. This is newer technology as the amount of data required to store a single note in digital audio form is staggering, in excess of 40,000 numbers per second. The best part about this is that musicians are no longer restricted to the limited sound palette of synthesized MIDI instruments, but can work with any sounds from the natural world, including vocals. This software is very powerful and includes functions such as automatic correction of tuning discrepancies. Very helpful for singers who rely principally on their looks!

Soft synthesis

The faster processing power of the latest generation of PCs allows older physical synthesizers and drum machines to be modelled by software so that, instead of a box with knobs, dials, buttons, etc., you have a picture of it on the computer monitor which can be manipulated via the mouse and produces sound output identical to the original piece of equipment. Advantages include cheaper production costs, easier distribution (including internet downloading) and greater robustness (no moving or heat-generating parts).

Internet

The internet has opened up a world of resources available from the comfort of the home, office or classroom. Teachers and students alike can access articles from many sources; however, there are as many pitfalls are as there are advantages. The availability of information does not guarantee its accuracy and ease of accessibility can sometimes lead to thoughtless plagiarism. The other side of the internet is that teachers and pupils are also able to 'post up' their own work, thus making it available to a wider audience. This opens up exciting possibilities for collaborative projects over small or vast distances.

Summary

Computer-based technology in music

Some pieces of software combine many of the above functions fairly well. Some can produce good quality scores, have advanced sequencing capabilities and integrate them with digital audio. This, for example, allows a singer/songwriter to compose their own song, sequence a backing, print near-publishing-quality sheet music (including lyrics that align to the notes) and make a near-studio-quality demo recording.

Music technology is a powerful tool for the discerning musician. It does not replace live music-making, but has its place in the creative process to a greater or lesser extent. It does not replace human interaction and hopefully never will. It broadens our creative horizons, but does not replace our musicianship. Using a computer to make music no more produces excellent composers than using a computer to type a story produces excellent authors.

Non-computer-based technology in music

Music technology is not limited to the use of computers. Other equipment has its place in music education such as headphones, synthesizers, compact disc players, keyboard workstations, electronic instruments (e.g. digital pianos, drum pads, etc.), microphones, mixers, audio recording equipment (e.g. tape and mini-disc recorders, multi-track recorders – both analogue and digital), amplification equipment, samplers, patchbays, video recording and editing equipment, and special needs equipment (e.g. infra-red beams for MIDI triggering, touch screens, etc.).

Enhancing music teaching through the use of ICT

Many benefits derive from using technology in Music teaching, both in the classroom and for the individual, either at home or in extracurricular work. The use of technology can help overcome the traditional restrictions between innate, creative musicality and acquired performing skills. Technology can enable students to develop at their own pace without the need for constant teacher intervention, waiting for less able peers, or indeed holding up the more able.

This can apply to all areas of study, i.e. performing, composing, listening and appraising. Concepts can be learned and reinforced, knowledge can be gleaned and enhanced, skills can be honed and ideas explored, developed, manipulated and structured.

On a basic level, the use of electronic equipment with headphones allows individual pacing of work, be it listening, composing or performance practice. Perhaps the most useful application of music technology for educational purposes has been MIDI sequencing, which allows the inputting, editing, structuring, storing and retrieving of compositional ideas. Many music teachers have found this particularly useful for students studying GCSE who had limited performing/notation skills. Being able to play small ideas, then alter tempo, pitch, timbre, dynamics and articulation as well as storing them in an easily accessible format proved very useful. In one music department's funding bid to acquire a second set of computers, it was stated clearly that every child entered for GCSE music would be expected to achieve at least one piece of compositional coursework worthy of at least a grade 'D'. This does not sound a high expectation, but in that particular situation, around 70 per cent of those opting for GCSE music in Year 10 had no formal music training outside of the classroom and were not able to express themselves musically either on paper or in live improvisation.

MIDI sequencing in the classroom

One of the immediate benefits of MIDI sequencing is that one person can theoretically produce a note-perfect, rhythmically accurate, seamless performance using several separate instrumental timbres simultaneously, editing mistakes and copying whole sections to produce repetition and/or variations. As discussed earlier, the possibilities for using this technology in the classroom are principally related to availability of resources. Assuming a workable ratio of students to workstations, a wide variety of projects can be tackled including:

- experimenting with timbres to create multi-layered soundscapes;
- utilizing quantization and looping features to create groove-based compositions;
- experimenting with repetitive styles: e.g. minimalism;
- composing from templates: e.g. teacher-prepared fragments for re-ordering;
- experimenting with structure, utilizing copy and paste features;
- composing a soundtrack to a digitized video which is automatically displayed and synchronized by the sequencing software.

What if there is only one computer?

If there is only one workstation, it may be better to use the technology in a different way, perhaps to provide backings for classroom or individual performances. In the case of whole-class accompaniment, the computer can replace the traditional role of the teacher in playing the piano. A carefully prepared, sequenced backing can free up the teacher to move around the class and observe individuals with greater ease, thus enabling more meaningful feedback and assessment. The advantages of a computer-controlled sequence over a tape recording are that tempo, pitch and timbre can all be altered independently and quickly, adapting the backing to suit current requirements. Individual tracks/parts can be muted, boosted or made to play solo depending on the needs of the moment. It has to be said that most of this is achievable in the traditional context through versatile pianistic skills. The principle advantages then are in providing a fuller accompaniment (e.g. including drum, melody and counter-melody tracks) and in giving the teacher freedom to move about and focus on students' activities.

Other types of software in the music classroom

Other types of music software can be used for teaching concepts and knowledge as well as reinforcing performing skills on an individual basis and enhancing teacher or student presentations. Here are a few suggestions:

- musical encyclopaedia CD-ROMs for individual research or possibly team-game learning activities;
- aural/notation drill software for improving individual skills;
- manipulation software for experimenting with raw sounds;
- scorewriting software to produce neat musical notation;
- generic software (e.g. DTP, word-processors, spreadsheets and databases) for improved record-keeping, reporting, presentation, concert programmes, etc.

Relating the use of technology to general music-making

It is not enough to understand the technology. Any use of the resources that is intended to relate to music-making in a wider context also requires the user to understand the limitations of the real instruments being synthesized and any notational conventions used. A common problem is that of students with limited understanding of traditional instruments composing pieces that sound fine when synthesized but, due to problems of range or balance, would be totally impractical if played on those instruments. This does not invalidate the process or the end-product, but a distinction needs to be made between a synthesized sound, which is valid in its own right, and the real instrument that shares the same name. An example of this is music for 'flute' which is perhaps written very low, or beneath the range of the real instrument over a full texture. In reality, the flute would not be heard, but if the synthesized performance is seen as the end-product, this need not be a problem. An electronic synthesizer is as valid a musical instrument as a flute or any other acoustic sound source, so music composed expressly for synthesized performance is perfectly acceptable in its own right.

Stand-alone hardware for music teaching

Various non-computer-based resources also fall into the category of music technology. Here are a few with suggestions for their application:

Individual keyboards with headphones for basic performance and composition tasks – already common in many schools. It is a good idea to set these up permanently, perhaps around the perimeter of smaller classrooms, with one master switch near to the teacher so that power can be cut quickly. This is a safety feature, but also makes class control much easier. The range of facilities available on relatively inexpensive keyboards is ever increasing. Inbuilt floppy disc drives and multi-track sequencing are now commonplace. It is important to weigh up the pros and cons of these against computer-based workstations.

Other electronic instruments including drum pads, digital pianos, MIDI wind controllers, practice mutes, etc. These also enable acoustic isolation for individuals and can avoid the need for keyboard skills at a higher level.

Amplification equipment, including microphones for solo singing. Passing the microphone around, so that each member of the class sings a short phrase, can be a good strategy for encouraging reluctant singers who respond well to the novelty of hearing their own voice amplified. Radio microphones are very useful in the class-room as they give freedom of movement. One application is to take the microphone to individual keyboards and hold it over a speaker so as to quickly amplify that instru-ment above the rest. This is much more crude than wiring into a mixer but avoids trailing wires and gives great flexibility. These are important considerations in the classroom.

Recording equipment, both portable and fixed. Security is an important consideration, but the ability to record small groups in practice rooms with ease is vital. Multi-track recorders still have their place, even though computer-based recording is fast replacing them. Mini-disc facilities are becoming more affordable and are far superior to conventional cassette tape. DAT recorders and CD burners are even more useful, but more expensive. They allow for easy archiving of GCSE coursework for example, as the tape/disc can be indexed for fast retrieval of the desired recording at a later date.

Mixers and multi-core cable links are very useful, allowing the classroom to double as a mini-recording-studio with performers acoustically isolated from recording equipment. The ability to link microphones to a central control room and to 'patch' output to selected speakers in each of the other rooms is a very versatile set-up for teaching across the Key Stages.

Sound processing equipment, such as effects units, can be put to good use with whole classes, small groups or individuals. They also greatly enhance the quality of recording work, although computer-based digital recording is now beginning to replace this equipment as it can often be emulated by software plug-ins.

Special needs equipment, such as light beams for MIDI control, are an impor-tant consideration in certain circumstances but, as mentioned above, a variety of MIDI control devices will increase accessibility for any students who are not compe-tent keyboard players.

Video recorders, cameras and players, ideally with synchronization facilities to link directly to audio recordings or computer sequencers, can be used to great effect in composition and performance work.

Issues of planning and classroom management

Musical focus

As with any teaching, lessons involving technology need to be carefully planned so that the technology is not the primary focus but rather a tool to enhance learning and understanding. It is important that every Music lesson has a musical focus even if there is a need to teach technology-specific skills in order to achieve that end. A specific compositional assignment that enables students to practise their use of technology is perfectly valid but it is important to allow time for 'performance' near the end of the lesson so that musical content can be discussed and evaluated.

Assessment

It can be difficult to assess work based around certain technology applications. For instance, how do you judge the quality of a piece in which students have re-ordered musical samples which were provided by the software and which did not involve them in any decisions relating to tempo, pitch, rhythm or selection of timbres? The answer of course is to focus on the creative and artistic qualities of choices made, which may mostly be considerations of structure and style. These issues need to be thought through before embarking on the use of such resources.

Pupil movement

It is necessary to establish good routines for moving between positions for normal learning and technology-based work. An enthusiastic rush can have disastrous consequences. It is also best to try and have no discernible difference between equipment on workstations as youngsters will often get into needless arguments over cosmetic variations such as the style of headphones.

Maintenance, neatness and safety

A good maintenance plan is essential so that equipment such as headphones, mains adaptors and leads can be put into a repair box and immediately replaced with spares. Neat, well thought-out connections and ergonomic layout of equipment need careful consideration, not only for comfort but also for safety. Never have wires trailing across a classroom or between desks. Try to position work surfaces near to power supplies to avoid these problems. Try to avoid the need to unplug equipment as often as possible.

Permanent installations are much more durable. In this case it is worth hiding wires in plastic trunking. This not only makes the room look neater, but stops inquisitive young hands from messing.

It is sensible to consider headphones as consumables. Even the most robust designs do not stand up to continued use by teenagers. A daily or weekly check on all equipment is a useful discipline to avoid disruption in lesson time.

Technician support is valuable if it can be secured. Certain curriculum subjects enjoy this as a matter of historical precedent, but senior management often require to have the needs of a contemporary music department highlighted before they will consider allocating either budget or support staff time to cover this. Most repairs can be attempted by anyone with basic circuit testing and soldering skills.

Appendix A
Checklist of ICT skills for music teachers

As mentioned earlier, a teacher needs to be several steps ahead of the students in order to troubleshoot difficulties that may arise. This applies in all areas of music technology. The most common skills needed are those directly related to sequencing and scorewriting software. The following list is offered for consideration:

Sequencing Skills

Selecting timbres for individual tracks

It is common to have a choice of 128 timbres available per channel although many sound modules have a much greater choice (see General MIDI opposite).

Recording and playback

Most software has tape-recorder-style buttons on screen, but keyboard shortcuts can be much quicker once learned (e.g. asterisk for record).

Deleting, moving, copying, dividing and combining sequences

These correlate with general editing techniques in word-processing. Most software provides a palette of tool icons for these functions.

Looping, quantizing, transposing

It is worth going beyond knowing *how* to achieve these and thinking through why and when to apply them. These are powerful tools, but coarse usage does not produce the most musical results. The ability to interrupt a looped pattern at regular intervals (e.g. to add drum *fills*) opens up much wider creativity. Similarly it can be more musical to use selective rather than global quantizing or even to use the *humanizing* function (a seemingly bizarre concept in which the mechanical sounds of quantized music are randomly altered by a small degree to simulate human inaccuracy). Useful educational benefit can be derived from exploring the difference between transposition and sequence.

Creating drum patterns and 'grooves'

Again, unless you are a drummer, this is as much an extension to one's musical skills and knowledge as to technological know-how. Researching the rhythmic nuances of popular music styles is very important for teachers who wish to give useful assistance to young composers in those idioms.

Basic editing using score and/or graphical editing windows

For many classically-trained musicians, the ability to edit their music via notation is a great bonus. Other musicians who are not principally notation users can edit using other graphical interfaces, such as piano roll windows. There are also certain types of editing which are better suited to the different windows available. Bar graphs are good for volume and tempo changes, for example.

Fine editing using real-time controllers for enhanced performance

As mentioned above and earlier, MIDI provides control parameters to enhance musical expression and simulate live performance. These include volume, pitch bend, modulation, reverb and pan. They are often recorded or set after the basic music has been recorded.

Mixing down to tape, etc.

Preparing an effective and dynamic mix of the sequenced tracks also requires practice. It is important to be familiar with setting output and input levels for optimum transfer to other media such as tape or mini-disc, perhaps adding in live acoustic sounds or synchronizing to other equipment

Editing tempo for enhanced performance

Live music rarely maintains a precise tempo throughout. Classical styles are often full of expressive rubato, and popular music will often have slight differences in tempo between chorus and verse sections, for example. These can be modelled using sequencing software.

MIDI files, GM, GS and XG formats

General MIDI is a set of rules for data and timbres that allows for portability between different platforms (makes of computer) and applications (software programs). In theory, a piece of music sequenced on one make of computer with a particular sequencing package using a selection of the standard 128 General MIDI (GM) sounds can be saved to disc, loaded onto a different computer running different sequencing software with a different GM sound module and still sound the same. This is not always straightforward and requires familiarity in order, for instance, to make a Standard MIDI File for a student to continue work at home. GS and XG formats are extensions of the GM standard, developed by Roland and Yamaha respectively.

Troubleshooting hardware and software problems

'I can't hear all the sounds'; 'I can hear piano and drums together when I play'; 'all the sounds are wrong'; 'the mouse pointer doesn't move'; 'my headphones only work in one ear'. These are some of the common problems encountered in the classroom and the ability to identify and rectify the precise problem is a must for successful integration of ICT into the Music curriculum. Some problems may be due to misunderstanding on the students' part, some to software faults and others to hardware faults. It is vital that the teacher is able to cope with these interruptions and get the students back on task as soon as possible. Of course, an in-house technician would be a great help, but not a realistic possibility in most cases.

Synchronization with audio and video

This can be achieved in a variety of ways. Newer equipment and software allows such work to be done entirely on the computer, recording and manipulating live audio alongside MIDI sequences or showing a video clip in a floating window. It is also possible to do these things by use of synchronization interfaces but the connections and preparation require practice.

Recording digital audio

This is relatively straightforward once the physical connections and software settings have been established. As this facility becomes increasingly available, the unmusical elements of MIDI sequencing become less of a problem.

Importing samples, digital audio from CD, etc.

Plagiarism is as old as music itself, but the ability to manipulate actual recordings made by others and incorporate them into your own work is more recent and requires technical familiarity as well as artistic (and sometimes legal) discernment.

Manipulating digital audio (plug-ins, etc.)

Using the virtual effects processing offered by advanced sequencing software can, as mentioned earlier, make a big difference to the end-result. Practising time-stretching and pitch correction is good preparation for advanced work with students.

Scorewriting skills

Many of the leading sequencing programs offer comprehensive scorewriting facilities, but these do not always work as automatically as we would like. More sophisticated software incorporates a certain amount of interpretation which compensates for a certain amount of rhythmic imprecision. A simple melody played fairly accurately can be notated immediately, but more complex music requires both an understanding of notation and how to adjust the available parameters to suit a particular piece. Common considerations are detailed below:

Choosing appropriate score styles, transpositions and layouts

It is usually possible to choose what clef will be used and what transposition, if any, according to convention. Beyond this, it is also possible with most software to alter the default layout so that perhaps the number of bars per line is limited or particular staves are grouped together, etc. A common problem is notating piano music, particularly making the division of notes between left and right hands logical in performing terms. Knowing how to alter the way sustained notes are displayed is also a useful trick.

Choosing appropriate score quantize values

There is a difference between performance quantizing, which limits the deviation in rhythm or touch for playback, and score quantizing, which limits the degree of rhythmic accuracy displayed. A common example of this is swing quavers in which the stylistic bounce is maintained for listening but the score is set to display straight quavers, which are easier to read. This is a convention used in jazz music. Beyond this example, understanding how this feature works enables accurate notation of complex rhythms without displaying unnecessary rests.

Adding text/graphics, dynamics, phrasing, lyrics and chords

Of course, there is much more to notation than pitch and rhythm. The ability to draw in other details such as dynamics, phrasing and text takes the user into the realms of music desktop publishing. Some software will automatically insert dynamics, interpreting changes in touch with reference to standard settings that can be altered. Most software offers the facility to do this in reverse, adjusting playback to reflect dynamics and articulation entered manually. Lining up notes with lyrics automatically is a great advantage and usually easy to learn, as is the insertion of (sometimes automatic) chord symbols.

Defining complex score styles such as percussion and multi-stave

Software often comes with preset stave layouts, but being able to tweak these to your specific needs is also very useful. Common examples of this are drum kit/percussion parts and 3-stave organ music.

Extracting individual parts from the score

This is supposed to be automatic with some software, but again requires practice and an understanding of the limitations involved, plus tricks for overcoming them.

Wiring

It is essential to understand the different types of connection made between pieces of equipment and the appropriate connecting leads to be used. Speaker cables should be fairly heavy duty and do not need to be shielded. On the other hand, signal cables for microphones, keyboards, electric guitars and general connections between mixers and effects units should be shielded and ideally balanced to avoid interference from hum-inducing equipment. MIDI cables are different again and become unreliable if not relatively short in length. Different plug conventions can give rise to confusion. Some cheaper public address systems use standard jack plugs for both speaker and signal cables. This can lead to disastrous consequences if, say, an amplifier's speaker output is connected directly to a mixer input. It is very dangerous to trust over-confident youngsters who rarely understand as much as they think. It is essential that the teacher is familiar with the correct methods for setting up and connecting equipment.

Another general rule is to make all connections before switching on the power. This is particularly true of computer systems, which will often fail to function properly if all devices were not detected at start-up.

Appendix B
Some music technology concepts explained

MIDI channels, tracks and sequences

The sixteen available timbres come from the MIDI convention of sixteen separate channels. Each channel reacts independently to the others and can be set to its own timbre and volume (other channel-specific attributes include placement within the stereo field and amount of reverberance). Confusion can often arise between the concepts of *channels, tracks* and *sequences*. A *sequence* is a series of MIDI data pertaining to one aspect of the piece (commonly referred to as the *song*). In normal usage a *sequence* is all the notes for one particular instrument/timbre, perhaps for one verse of the *song*. A *track* is a collection of *sequences* that can be manipulated together. In normal usage a *track* correlates to one instrumental timbre. Tracks and sequences can be freely created and adapted according to the whims of the user. The number of tracks and sequences available is usually only limited by the computer's memory size. *Channels*, on the other hand, are related directly to the physical sound-synthesizing equipment being used. Each of the sixteen *channels* may be assigned to one of the available timbres, which means that only sixteen different sounds may be heard at any given moment. This does not limit a *song* to sixteen timbres however, as the timbre for a *channel* may be changed instantly by sending the appropriate MIDI message (called 'program change'). It is common practice to use MIDI channel number 10 for drum maps; that is, each note triggers a different percussion sound. Thus a set of untuned percussion instruments is treated as a single instrument.

In the example (Figure 12.1), from a popular sequencing application, there are eighteen *tracks* (the last two are named after specific instruments), fifteen *sequences* (boxes of varying length on the right) and sixteen *channels* (see channel numbers next to each track).

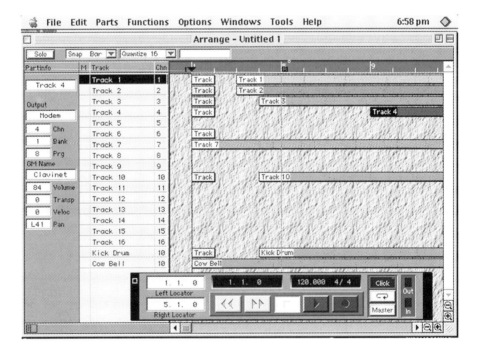

Figure 12.1 A popular sequencing application

Common MIDI set-ups

MIDI data connections are clearly indicated in the diagrams following. AUDIO and LINE OUT indicate analogue audio signals, similar to domestic hi-fi connections.

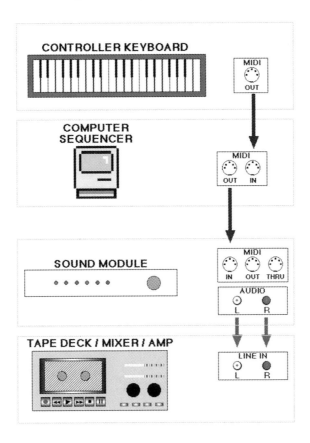

Figure 12.2 *MIDI studio using external interface and sound module*

A controller keyboard may only have a MIDI OUT socket if it is designed solely for this purpose. In this first scenario the keyboard, computer and sound module are three separate units.

If the 'keyboard' is a stand-alone synthesizer with its own internal sounds, it may also have MIDI IN and THRU sockets. In this case, the sound module element is part of the same instrument so that the MIDI OUT from the computer links back to the MIDI IN on the synthesizer. In this scenario it is usually necessary to turn the synthesizer's LOCAL link OFF to avoid the sound module being triggered by the keyboard and the computer at the same time.

Another common set-up is to have the sound module inside the computer (i.e. a *sound card*). In this case, the MIDI connection is made directly from the keyboard into the *sound card* and audio output is from the same panel.

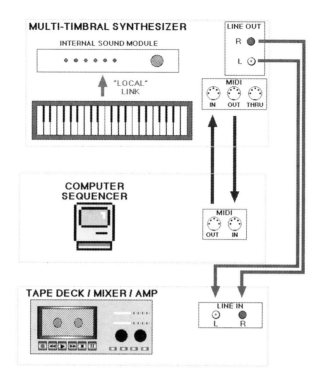

Figure 12.3 MIDI studio using external interface and stand-alone synthesizer

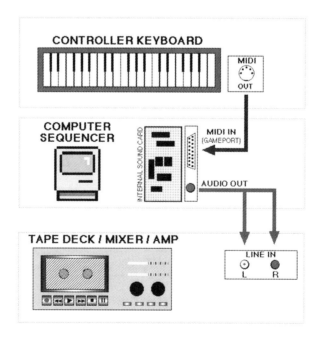

Figure 12.4 MIDI studio using controller keyboard and sound card

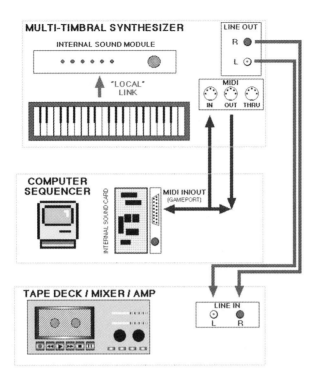

Figure 12.5 *MIDI studio using controller keyboard and stand-alone synthesizer*

The sounds produced by a synthesizer are often superior to those on the computer *sound card*. In this scenario the *sound card* acts as a MIDI interface and its audio output is not used.

A controller keyboard may only have a MIDI OUT socket if it is designed solely for this purpose. If it is also a stand-alone instrument with its own internal sounds it may also have MIDI IN and THRU sockets. In this case, the sound module element can be part of the same instrument so that the second MIDI connection shown links back to the MIDI IN on the keyboard.

Another common set-up is to have the sound module inside the computer (i.e. a *sound card*). In this case, the MIDI connection is made directly from the keyboard into the *sound card* and audio output is from the same panel.

Digital audio and MIDI data signals

Most sequencing packages now offer the ability to record, edit and manipulate *digital audio* in a similar manner to MIDI data. There is sometimes confusion between these two types of signal. *Digital audio* signals are numerically encoded sound waves, such as those stored on a standard CD. On a computer they are usually stored as files with a '.wav' extension. *MIDI data* signals are control codes for musical performance as discussed earlier. It follows that you should not connect a digital (or any other) audio output to a MIDI input or vice versa.

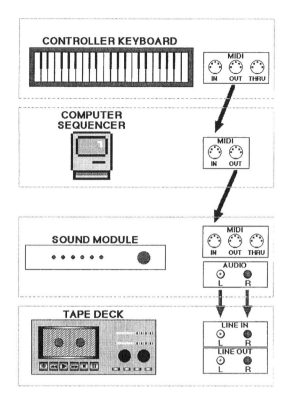

Figure 12.6 *A simple MIDI studio using external interface and sound module*

Notes

1   A music technology *workstation* typically consists of a computer, MIDI controller keyboard and listening/recording facilities (e.g. multiple headphones and a tape recorder).

2   Technically speaking it is impossible to specify a note's duration before it has finished. The MIDI convention is to send a 'note on' message when a note starts and a corresponding 'note off' message when the same note ends. Sequencing software can calculate a note's duration by comparing this data to the computer's internal timer and the tempo selected. This also explains 'MIDI jam' when notes sustain indefinitely because the 'note off' signal has not been detected (perhaps one student changed a setting on the MIDI keyboard before the other stopped playing).

3   Other MIDI instruments and control devices have been developed, but the basic MIDI language is still very much keyboard biased. *Pitch to MIDI converters*, such as MIDI microphones and special guitar pickups, allow singers and guitarists to work in the MIDI domain without resorting to keyboard playing.

4   For a more detailed explanation of channels, tracks and sequences see Appendix B.

13 Designing a teaching model for popular music

Peter Dunbar-Hall

The need for a teaching model for popular music

Popular music, despite its existence on syllabuses in various forms, is still a problem area for many music teachers. This is due to a number of factors: both the study of popular music styles and methods for teaching them are missing from many tertiary courses; the mainly art music backgrounds of many music teachers act against an understanding of popular music; there is a shortage of critical material in this area to which music teachers can refer; and an accepted model for teaching popular music has not yet developed. It is the lack of a teaching model that is the concern of this article.

A teaching model is a framework of ideas about a subject through which that subject can be taught. Such models are often derived from implicit ideas about the subject. In music, these may include beliefs about what music is acceptable for study or is culturally appropriate, ways that music can be analysed, and definitions of music itself. A teaching model usually precedes day-to-day curriculum planning and in this way influences teaching methods and the selection of content. Because it is based on the nature of its subject, a teaching model also expresses values about and attitudes to that subject through the process known as a 'hiddden curriculum'.

The problem of a teaching model for popular music is partly due to the fact that music teachers from art music backgrounds automatically know how music of the western tonal tradition is taught, but lack the same instinctive teaching knowledge for popular music. This is because the study and teaching of western tonal music have been their method of training as teachers and, even before that, a daily activity through the learning of an instrument. In this way an understanding of western art music can be seen as a type of cultural heritage for such teachers. This cultural heritage precludes understanding of the ways popular music might be taught.

These are basic differences between art music and popular music which make the ways of studying the former unsuitable for the latter. Analyses of tonal plans typical of the study of art music are a good example of this. In this type of analysis, key and modulation are related to formal plans, and melodic development is seen as a way of expressing harmony. In such analyses the elements of melody and harmony are usually studied at the expense of rhythm. These analytical assumptions cannot be made for popular music. Popular music does not rely on the establishment, movement away from and return of a key that is the basis of much tonal art music. Popular music can require a greater understanding of rhythm and texture, rather than of melody and harmony. Processes that are not prominent in much art music, for example, improvisation and repetition, become important in popular music and need to be studied. In addition the underlying difference between art music and popular music, which can be seen in their respective philosophical bases, make the methods of studying art music unsuitable for popular music. Art music is created and notated regardless of whether it is ever performed; popular music usually exists in performance and is not primarily a notated music. This short list of simple differences between art and popular music demonstrates that the analytical methods suitable for one are not necessarily applicable to the other and that there is a need for alternative ways to study popular music. Because ways of studying music depend on the prior construction of a teaching model, it is necessary to construct models through which popular music can be taught. One suitable way of designing a teaching model for popular music is through consideration of its etic and emic characteristics.

Etic and emic properties of music

At least since the time of Plato two ways of perceiving music have been discussed by numerous writers in an attempt to define music's meaning. In the first of these, music is studied as a collection of elements (pitch, duration, timbre) and how these have been handled to make pieces of music. In the second, the emotional meaning given to music by its creators and listeners is considered. Even though the terminology of writers differs, there is agreement that music involves both objective fact and subjective response. Mayer explains that 'music … is said to communicate emotional and aesthetic meanings as well as purely intellectual ones … [and is] a puzzling combination of abstractness with concrete emotional experience' (1956: vii). Lippman discusses what he calls the 'familiar referential aspects of musical meaning, and … form or structure' (1981: 184); while Doubravova describes the two sides of music as 'meanings of natural and anthropological nature' (1984: 33). Middleton uses the terms 'etic' ('objective and autonomous') (1990: 175) and 'emic' ('the product of cultural knowledge') (ibid.) to refer to these ways of defining music. What is clear is that to all these writers music can be discussed both as a set of universal elements, and also as a symbolic object that carries meaning dependent on cultural interpretation. The former of these approaches is etic, the latter emic.

The use of the terms 'etic' and 'emic' comes to music from anthropology (for example, Geertz 1973; Lévi-Strauss 1964), and originates in the linguistic concepts of phonetic (the study of sounds) and phonemic (the study of meaning). The idea that music could be taught through consideration of both its etic and emic levels is found in the literature of music education where it is referred to as the study of inherent (etic) and idiomatic (emic) musical concepts. For example:

> if music education began with inherent concepts which pertain to all music … students would not make … value judgements which apply only to some music (*idiomatic concepts*) … but would be able to consider all music without bias.
>
> (Choksy *et al.* 1986: 16f)

The etic approach to music is found in many syllabuses in which music is studied through consideration of its elements. The current importance of this type of study dates from changes in educational thinking that took place in the 1960s. The most important of these changes was the replacement of content-specific syllabuses with ones that focus on processes. In music, this involved the switch from syllabuses which were designed around the study of selected pieces of music to ones that encouraged the study of any music that could teach how music worked. This change in direction led to a broadening of the ways music is studied and taught. It challenges the hold of traditional analysis on music education, replacing music as a collection of historical repertoires with music as examples of how music works. Because this later view of music education studies the question 'How does this piece function?' instead of the former 'Who wrote this, and why is it great?' it represents a paradigm shift in music education for many teachers. Because it focuses on music, and not the people who wrote it, it also allows any music to be used as the basis of study: early music, music of non-western origin, and popular music.

The emic, or interpretative, way of studying music provides a way of understanding what music means to its creators and listeners. This is based on the assumption that different types of music are perceived by their listeners as having national, religious or cultural meanings. This can be broken down into two areas: generally, music as ideology, and specifically, how ideologies are expressed through musical styles. The idea that music can be seen as ideology is expressed by Wolff when she states that:

> works of art … are not closed, self-contained and transcendent entities, but are the product of specific historical practices on the part of identifiable social groups in given conditions, and therefore bear the imprint of the ideas, values and conditions of existence of those groups and their representatives in particular artists.
>
> (Wolff 1981: 49)

An example of this approach is the common academic pursuit of studying popular music as the means of expressing political messages (see Frit 1981; Street 1986; Denselow 1989; Szatmary 1991).

Popular music exists as a set of related musical styles, for example punk rock, ska, heavy metal, thrash, folk rock, jazz rock, reggae and funk (Dunbar-Hall and Hodge 1989; Charlton 1990). To some writers, these styles of popular music are representative of sub-cultural lifestyles and their associated beliefs. Hebdige (1979), for example, analyses the importance of music styles of punk rock and reggae to skinhead culture and Rastafarians respectively. As has been discussed elsewhere (Dunbar-Hall 1992), this can be shown by a diagram in which a style of music represents a lifestyle, and this lifestyle, in its turn, represents a set of beliefs or a philosophy:

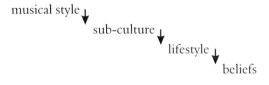

The combination of the etic and emic approaches to music can provide a model for teaching popular music for a number of reasons. First, the etic level provides musicological information, something lacking in the literature on popular music. Frith's comment that 'rock, despite the millions of words devoted to it, is still seldom subject to musical analysis' (1998: 176) is echoed as recently as 1990 by Middleton: 'musicology, "the scientific study of music" ... should study popular music ... With a few exceptions ... it has not done so' (1990: 103).

Second, a combination of etic and emic studies of popular music sets up a disciplined approach that follows a standard procedure of analysis and data collection, followed by interpretation and comment. In this way the teaching of popular music is given an academic framework in which to work. Third, if music is defined as the combination of three factors – creation (composition); works of art (pieces of music); and reception (listening and interpretation) – between them the etic and emic studies of popular music can cover all three areas. The etic level concerns examples of music for their musical construction. The emic levels can show how music's meaning is interpreted by its creators and listeners:

Creation . . . . . the work of art . . . . . reception
(emic)   (etic)   (emic)

Application

An example of the combination of etic and emic studies of popular music can demonstrate how a teaching model based on them can be designed.

Etic

The song 'Exodus', by Bob Marley and the Wailers, is performed by Bob Marley and a vocal backing group. Accompaniment is provided by a line-up of electric guitars, drum-kit, a brass section, electronic organ and extra percussion (including congas and tambourine). The song has a rhythmic profile that includes a bass guitar ostinato,

which also appears on the lead guitar and in the brass instruments. A 'one drop' (a single note on snare and bass drum on the third beat of the bar) noticeable at the beginning of the song,

the repeated tambourine rhythm,

and layers of rhythms on congas, hi-hat and snare drum all add to the song's rhythms.

Melodically, the song uses a hookline,

which is employed to mark the beginnings of the songs three vocal sections. Each of these sections is made up of the hookline followed by four call and response lines between Marley and the backing vocalists. The responses are all versions of the motive,

depending on the amount of syllables that have to be fitted in. Two examples are:

and

while two responses (repeats of the same line) add the note D.

Marley's calls use five melodic shapes:

of which (a), (b) and (c) each occur once, the song becoming alternations of versions of (d) and (c).

Harmonically, the song is static, consisting only of an A minor chord resulting from the ostinato and the build up of layers of melodic material. In this way, 'Exodus' can be analysed to show the use of limited melodic material over a rhythmic accompaniment. Processes of repetition, alternation between soloist and backing group, and voices and instruments, and the use of motivic development, are essential characteristics of the song.

Emic

The emic considerations of this song cover two areas: the creation of style, and the sub-cultural implications of that style.

Style

The musical characteristics of this song are typical of reggae. Reggae is a style of Jamaican popular music that developed from a combination of Caribbean, African and American musics in the 1960s. The prominence of the bass guitar ostinato, its contrasting syncopated and non-syncopated rhythms, the use of a one-drop on the bass drum, the build up of layers of rhythm on both melodic and percussion instruments and the use of a rock style line-up of bass and lead guitar and drum-kit supplemented by a brass section, electronic organ and extra percussion instruments (especially congas) are traits of reggae style (see Bergman 1985; Davis and Simo 1983). The half-speed feel created by the one-drop, which gives the effect of a rhythmically augmented backbeat, is also typical of reggae.

Sub-cultural implications

Reggae assumes meaning for its Jamaican listeners as one of the musical styles associated with the Rastafarian religion. Rastafarianism is a black consciousness religion that deifies the late Ethiopian emperor, Haile Selassie, from whose African title, Ras Tafari, it takes its name. The perception of Africa as the original and ultimate home of black peoples is a fundamental Rastafarian belief. Musical clues to these beliefs are embedded in reggae.

The lyrics of 'Exodus' include the following: 'Exodus, movement of Jah people, we're leaving Babylon, we're going to our father's land (Our Father's Land?)'. The word 'exodus' recalls the use of Biblical reference to the same idea (freedom) in Negro spirituals. In Rastafarian terms, 'Babylon' refers to the poor living conditions of Jamaicans of African descent (slavery, white domination). 'Jah' is the Rastafarian word for God; 'Jah people' are the Rastafarians. The song expresses a wish for movement from present conditions to better ones through the analogy of Africa as a desired home.

References to Africa are echoed in reggae through musical means. In this song this includes the contrasting syncopation and non-syncopation of the bass ostinato, and the use of layers of rhythms to build up a complex texture. The alternation of solo and group in 'call and response'-type patterns and the pentatonic nature of the song (the 'b' of Marley's third motive appearing only once in the vocal parts) could also be interpreted as deriving from African music. To Rastafarians, reggae is a form of religious music that refers to Africa both in its lyrics and through their accompanying music.

After its local Jamaican success, reggae was introduced to world-wide audiences in the mid-1970s. Its subsequent spread was along two separate paths. First, reggae's links to black consciousness led to the style being taken up by other black, but non-Jamaican, musicians in songs that express black/white political ideas. Examples of this are Stevie Wonder ('Happy Birthday', 'Master Blaster'), New Zealand Maori groups (for example Herbs), and some Australian Aboriginal rock groups (for example Coloured Stone, No Fixed Address) (see Breen 1989). This is an emic use of reggae style. Second, the musical style of reggae was initiated by white musicians; reggae copied in this way had become another commercial style of popular music open to use by anyone. Examples of this etic use of the style are Blondie's 'The Tide is High', and Sting's 'Roxanne'.

The etic and emic characteristics of this song can be made into a model for the teaching of popular music in the following way. The etic and emic sides of the song have become two parallel streams running through the model. The places in the model where these two streams coincide and can be linked in teaching are shown by

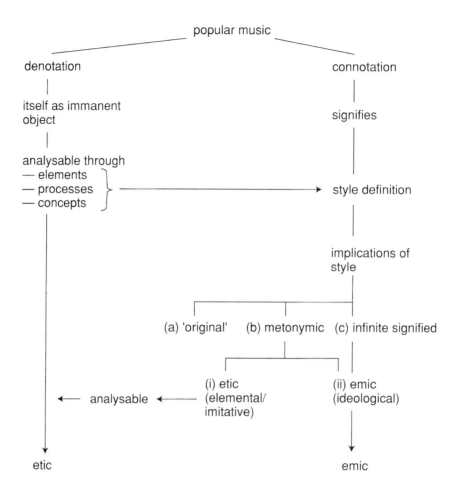

Figure 13.1 An etic/emic teaching model for popular music

horizontal arrows. Notice should be made of the division of 'implications of style' into three areas: (i) original; (ii) imitated; and (iii) unlimited. The 'original' implications of style are those that belong to the originators of the style, its first creators and listeners. The 'imitated' implications are those that follow when the style is copied, both by musicians that agree with the music's original meanings and also by those that use the style commercially (without ideological implications). The 'unlimited' implications consist of any other meanings that a listener cares to give the music. The interaction of the etic and emic levels as a teaching model for popular music can be shown in Figure 13.1.

Conclusion

As long as a lack of developed teaching models for popular music exists, popular music's place in music education, despite popular music's appeal to students and richness as a source of teaching material, will stagnate. Because it is based on the recognition of music's two-sided character as the combination of analysable facts and interpreted meanings, a teaching model based on the etic and emic characteristics of popular music includes consideration of the range of qualities that make up any piece of music. The comprehensiveness of this method could benefit both the teaching of popular music and its standing as an area of research.

References

Bergman, B. (1985) *Reggae and Latin Pop*, Poole, Dorset: Blandford.

Breen, M. (1989) *Our Place: Our Music*, Canberra: Aboriginal Studies Press.

Charlton, K. (1990) *Rock Music Styles: a History*, Dubuque: Brown.

Choksy, L.R., Abramson. R., Gillespie, A. and Woods, D. (1986) *Teaching Music in the Twentieth Century*, Englewood Cliffs NJ: Prentice-Hall.

Davis, S. and Simon, P. (1983) *Reggae International*, London: Thames & Hudson.

Denselow, R. (1989) *When the Music's Over: the Story of Political Pop*, London: Faber & Faber.

Doubravova, J. (1984) 'Musical semiotics in Czechoslovakia and an interpersonal hypothesis of music', *International Review of the Aesthetics and Sociology of Music* 15(1): 31–8.

Dunbar-Hall, P. (1992) 'Semiotics as a method for the study of popular music', *International Review of the Aesthetics and Sociology of Music* 22(2): 119–25.

Dunbar-Hall, P. and Hodge, G. (1989) *A Guide to Rock and Pop*, Sydney: Science Press.

Frith, S. (1978) *The Sociology of Rock*, London: Constable.

Frith, S. (1981) *Sound Effects: Youth, Leisure and the Politics of Rock 'n' Roll*, New York: Pantheon.

Geertz, C. (1973) *The Interpretation of Cultures*, New York: Basic Books.

Hebdige, D. (1979) *Subcultures: the Meaning of Style*, London: Methuen.

Lévi-Strauss, C. (1964) *The Raw and the Cooked*, New York, London: Peregrine.

Lippman, E. (1981) 'The dilemma of musical meaning', *International Review of the Aesthetics and Sociology of Music* 12(2): 181–202.

Meyer, L. (1956) *Emotion and Meaning in Music*, Chicago: University of Chicago Press.

Middleton, R. (1990) *Studying Popular Music*, Milton Keynes: Open University Press.

Street, J. (1986) *Rebel Rock: the politics of popular music*, Oxford: Blackwells.

Szatmary, A. (1991) *Rockin' in Time: a Social History of Rock and Roll*, Englewood Cliffs NJ: Prentice-Hall.

Wolff, J. (1981) *The Social Production of Art*, London: Macmillan.

Discography

Legend: The Best of Bob Marley and the Wailers, (1984), Island Records RML 52042.

14 Concepts of world music and their integration within western secondary music education

Jonathan Stock

Introduction

Other than simply gaining the ability to disseminate a selection of interesting musical facts or combat the growth of one-sided, stereotypical views of different musical cultures, a primary benefit of acquiring familiarity with aspects of non-western musics is that doing so can lead us to see aspects of our own music, whether pop, traditional or classical, with new eyes or, perhaps more appropriately, to listen with new ears. Musical concepts and habits that we have acquired through the enculturation process, through being born and bred within a particular culture, are sometimes overlooked; they become so 'natural' that we may no longer be able to perceive them. Studying a different musical culture brings these issues back to our attention, and thereby encourages a deeper understanding of our own music. Studying musical activity from the perspective of concepts employed, in varying fashions, all over the world assists the western music teacher to teach music, rather than western music alone.

What is music?

The example below is a short transcription of two phrases of Koran recitation from Morocco. I have omitted the text to avoid the necessity of further introduction and contextual explanation. Sing or hum through the transcription, or listen to a recording of this type of material.

Is this music? Certainly, it looks like music because it has been written down in musical notation. But does that mean that it *is* music? Perhaps the answer to this

Figure 14.1 Koran recitation by El Hajj Mohamed al Hakim Bennani (text omitted)

Source: Transcribed, with permission, from 'Musicaphon' BM 30 SL 2027 (n.d.)

question, yes or no, will depend on our definition of music, the couching of which can be problematic. The *Macmillan Encyclopedia* says that music is '[t]he art of organizing sounds, which usually consist of sequences of tones of definite pitch, to produce melody, harmony, and rhythm' (Isaacs 1988: 845).

If so, then Figure 14.1 is not music. There is a sequence of tones of differing rhythmic durations but there is no harmony. Indeed, solo pieces for many instruments or voice from the western classical tradition become non-music when this definition is strictly applied. Looking at an alternative definition, my paperback English dictionary describes music as 'the science or art of ordering tones or sounds in succession and combination to produce a composition having unity and continuity' (Allen 1986: 604). This seems quite a good definition at first, although it is also possible to arrange and combine successive sounds in unified and continuous ways that strike the listener as being not exactly musical.

Divide the class into four groups and perform the exercise below as a round, clapping out the rhythms shown.

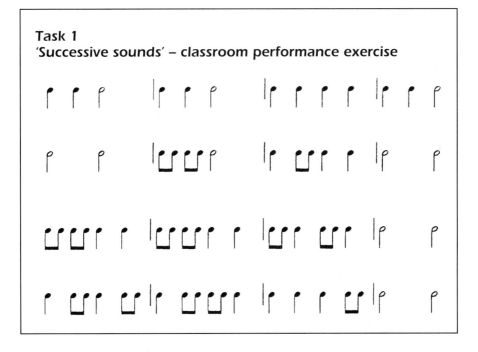

Task 1
'Successive sounds' – classroom performance exercise

Task 1 definitely satisfies the criteria of combined successive sounds ordered into a unified, albeit rather unimaginative, composition. But is it really what we mean by a musical composition? For one thing, there is no melody. At least Figure 14.1 seemed to have a tune. And returning to Figure 14.1, when the same definition is used to decide whether or not this is music, we run into a further problem: when listening to unfamiliar sound structures, how do we know if they are ordered and combined into a unified composition? This is one reason why we need to add the study of history and culture to that of another people's musical sounds.

In the case of Figure 14.1, the sounds are in fact carefully ordered and combined, but the man whose voice is transcribed above might as well be somewhat upset if we said his sounds were music. To the Moslem, the chanting of prayers and religious texts such as that in Figure 14.1 are not music but chant or poetry. *Musiqa*, the Arabic equivalent of the English word 'music', refers only to secular, instrumental pieces. Performing non-religious music has been regarded in Moslem religious theory as dangerous, primarily because instrumental music was often heard in places like brothels and inns. Thus, by association, instrumental music is a potential threat to public morals, something that encourages and accompanies over-indulgence and intoxication. By defining secular instrumental pieces (music) on the one hand and religious vocal chant and sung poems (non-music) on the other as quite separate things, the typical Moslem has a quite different understanding of the concept of 'music' from that of the average European. This pattern is repeated all over the world. For example, people in some African cultures cannot conceive of music without dance. In other societies, there is no general term like our word 'music' at all; people merely talk of songs or poems, pieces or dances, rituals and hymns.

Taking this idea one step further, not only do people all over the world have their own, individual ways of defining and understanding music, but so do people of different times, different social classes and different educational levels, even within the same culture, something which may be overlooked when we study the music of our ancestors. Beethoven provides a good example of this. Today, many consider him a pre-eminent composer. Even those who do not especially care for his music would be unlikely to question whether it is music or not. But in 1857 a well-educated music critic described one section of Beethoven's *Fifth Symphony* with the following words: 'I would say … that it does not belong at all to the art which I am in the habit of considering as music' (Bacharach and Pearce 1977: 19). This critic was not joking, nor was he a philistine; the fact is that he and many of his contemporaries found this part of the piece difficult to accept, even fifty years after it was written. Since he did not understand what he heard, the critic questioned whether it was really 'music' at all. Many of us, when first exposed to something strange or different, may also think like this, and perhaps it is good to question what we hear, but we sometimes need to question our definitions of music as well. An extreme example of this is to notice how we divide up the sounds of the animal kingdom: birds sing, dolphins have language and dogs howl. Do we mean the first sounds like music to us while the second and third do not?

My intention, then, is not to propose a search for a 'better' definition of music. Instead, I have tried to show that our commonly-accepted definitions of music, like those quoted above, have their drawbacks. A definition of music that most westerners accepted might not necessarily be the best, most scientific or only definition of music in the world. It might be very useful for classical musicians in Europe and North America towards the end of the twentieth century, but the further we move away from here, whether geographically or temporally, the less reliable it may become. In other words, to understand the music of a different culture or period, we have first to understand their conception of music. And as a prerequisite to this, we need to know about their social situations and cultural beliefs, their language, their instruments and much, much more.

If, in the end, there is no single, easy and convenient answer to the question, 'What is music?', this is something to celebrate, not bemoan. Music would hold little fascination for us if it was so simply explained. Even questions that cannot be answered may be worth asking for the light that attempting to respond to them sheds on related issues. One such question is whether music is a language or not.

Music and language 1

We often hear the phrase, 'music is a language'. Some might propose this as an answer to the previous question, 'What is music?' There are many similarities between music and language. For example, both are 'performed' through the dimension of time; both seem to have their own rules of structure and grammar; both can (in our culture) be written down using special signs and symbols; and both are essentially 'pan-human' activities that all normal people seem capable of taking part in and appreciating (Sloboda 1985: 11–23).

But there are some important differences between music and language. For example, although music has phrases which are like those found in language, it is difficult to find a specific analogy in music to the lexical word. It would in many instances be impossible to communicate a detailed message musically. To be sure, within our own culture we can recognize music appropriate to a love scene, a dance type or funeral march, but, without any non-musical clues, we don't know who loves whom, where the dance is taking place or what the deceased died of. Any language can efficiently give us specific answers to all these questions, while music cannot. Likewise, although instrumental music can remind us of a conversation, it is hard to envisage a previously unthought-of, tangibly meaningful, two-way dialogue taking part in such a manner.

What music can do in many different cultures is represent, describe or narrate by using sounds which, through habit, we have come to associate with certain events or emotions. The Kaluli people of New Guinea, for example, link different falling melodic patterns with the songs of different kinds of bird. Since they believe that people become birds when they die, the singing of songs based on these falling melodic patterns awakens in their mind all kinds of correlations: sorrow at the loss of dead relatives, loneliness and abandonment. So, although music is not a language, there is no doubt that it can embody certain extra-musical associations or messages. And when we are given a programme, when we are told (in language) what a piece of music is about, then we can often detect quite detailed meanings in the sounds we hear. A short exercise should make this point clearer (see Task 2).

Because music can be meaningful, but isn't exactly the same as a language, it seems probable that we cannot always expect to be able to 'translate' music or musical meaning from one situation to another. This is another reason why we need to understand something about the culture of the people who have created the music we are listening to. If we wish to understand an unfamiliar form of music as one of its creators might, we have to be aware of any extra-musical associations that imbue the sounds with special meaning. Sometimes these can be quite the opposite of our own stereotypes. For example, in many western operas of the last two centuries, younger male roles have been acted by tenor singers, older men by basses. Similarly, lower-pitched instruments are often used to depict male characters in music. Which of us would say a

> **Task 2**
> **Programme music – classroom listening exercise**
>
> *The class listens once or twice to a short instrumental piece or excerpt in several contrasting sections, such as the theme and first few variations from Brahms's 'Variations on a Theme by Haydn', Wagner's Prelude to Act I of 'Die Meistersinger von Nüremberg' or Debussy's Minstrels ('Préludes', Book 1, No. 12). No information concerning the title, programme or composer of the music should be given. Each pupil sketches out a possible programme for the music. During the following lesson, a number of the most varied programmes can be read out and the music listened to again. Without some kind of linguistic clue like a title or programme, or some musical hint such as a theme we already know or an instrument we associate with a particular situation – the organ with Church music, say – even members of the same culture and age-group are likely to produce individual musical interpretations.*

bassoon, trombone or double bass was naturally ladylike? But, in at least one African culture, the higher sounding of a set of drums or horns is believed to represent male characteristics. To us, the pitch of a low sound is similar to that of a grown man's voice; to them, the louder, more assertive sound of a higher instrument is like the stronger, more assertive speech of a man. Lower sounds, they say, are more like women murmuring softly in the background. Whether or not this is an accurate reflection of gender stereotyping in the culture in question, or a more theoretical abstraction used to explain musical practice, would lead beyond the scope of this discussion. The point is that this isn't a case of one analogy being more fitting than the other: both systems have their own logic, and are decoded as such by accustomed listeners.

A second association many of us may share is that, in general, the busiest, more active instrumental parts are the most important. Instruments with slower-moving parts, often those lower in pitch, usually provide the accompaniment. So, in the symphony orchestra, the first violins more often play the tune above a slower-moving double bass accompaniment than the double basses perform with a violin accompaniment. This may seem perfectly obvious to us, but it is not a feature found in music all over the world. A well-known exception is provided by Indonesian gamelan music. Gamelan is the name of many kinds of orchestra or ensemble made up principally of tuned metal chime bars and gongs. Very crudely speaking, the higher the pitch of the instrument, the more notes it plays. But every instrumentalist is deemed to be following the progress of a single underlying melody, and the lowest gong is the most important instrument in the ensemble. The occasional tones of the gong structure underpin the whole performance. Players of the higher instruments decorate the underlying melody by embellishing each step with cleverly thought-out layers of interlocking patterns, and some of them may perform more than two hundred different notes to each note of the lowest gong (Sorrell 1990: 109–19). Listening to gamelan music as to symphonic music, or concentrating on the details of the fast-moving upper instruments, it would be easy to miss the melody at the performance's heart.

So far then, the necessarily inconclusive discussion of what music is, that is, different things to different people at different times, has led to the proposals that we cannot necessarily apply our own, familiar definitions of music to foreign musical sounds, and that basic, fundamental principles which we take for granted in our own music may not be reflected in other kinds of music. Musical communication, it has been suggested, functions unlike linguistic communication. The agent which allows these perhaps uncomfortably negative discoveries to become aids to musical appraisal and understanding is the incorporation of cultural and historical material along with the musical sounds of foreign peoples. If we know what the members of a musical tradition themselves regard as important, what associations their music carries, how they define music, what their instruments are like and what function their music has, we have a better chance of making sense of the sounds we hear.

Does music evolve?

Having temporarily discarded the linguistic analogy, another explanation which is often put forward to account for musical diversity is that folk music and traditional musics from other parts of the world are simple or primitive, and that these kinds of musics are naturally evolving towards a music more like our own: music using twelve equal-tempered semitones, harmony and western instruments. But this view rests upon a number of misconceptions. Noting that another culture's music sounds different from ours, we may be tempted to see ours as somehow more valid, more natural or more fully developed than theirs. By doing so we are again setting up our own definition of music as a kind of universal yardstick against which all others must be measured. But what seems mature and fully developed to us today may just as reasonably be dismissed as childish or preliminary in a few centuries' time or in another part of the globe where the subtleties of our musical styles go unheeded. More importantly, this view suggests that 'music', itself an abstract concept, is somehow alive. Can 'music' develop in the general way which this view requires, and is there evidence of it having done so? Can something so abstract truly be mature or immature, natural or strange, right or wrong?

Music does not live on its own. Although musical ideas can be thought of and written down, they do not become music until, through some kind of physical behaviour, like singing or playing an instrument, they are actually performed to somebody. So, while it is true that styles of music come and go, and some do appear to influence others, what is really occurring is that composers and performers are being influenced by what they hear and by what they think their audiences expect to hear. The music that we perform today may not, therefore, be any 'better' than that performed in other times or places it has just followed the changing preferences of the people who make and listen to music. Because people define music differently and use it for contrasting purposes at different times and in varying cultural contexts, it seems highly unlikely and somewhat ethnocentric to believe that all music in the world is developing from simple, unaccompanied melody along parallel tracks towards complicated, harmonic music. This is not to say that we are wrong to prefer our own kind of music-making; the point is to acknowledge that all humanity organizes its sounds with specific tasks in mind and within particular social systems. Unless we are aware of these tasks and systems, we may not be able to formulate a meaningful evaluation of the sounds in question.

Task 3
'Humanly organized sound' – individual composition exercise

One very simple definition of music is: 'humanly organized sound' (Blacking 1976: 3). Each pupil selects a number of different sounds, whether environmental, recorded or live. Using a graphic score, these sounds are organized into a short composition. The pupil explains what function the music is for (for example entertainment, dance accompaniment, ritual) and then performs the piece.

Music and language 2

Above, I criticized the oft-quoted statement, 'Music is a language'. But it is true that music and language have much in common: they both need to be learnt through imitation, instruction and practice; in their most natural forms, both typically rely upon the human voice and ear; and different cultures have tended to develop their own regional and local forms of both (Sloboda 1985: 11–23). Both music and language involve the interlinked concepts of composition, improvisation, performance and appraisal, which I deal with below and, very often, music and language are combined in songs and chants.

Just as we often have different kinds of language for different occasions, so too we may use different kinds of music for different situations. The entertainment music of any culture may differ from that which supports ritual, although these two categories can also overlap, of course. Groups within a society may 'use' music to represent and present themselves, just as they employ particular styles of speech and clothing.

Task 4
Musical representation – homework sociology of music exercise

Using their peers, families and neighbours as subjects, students create a short multiple-choice questionnaire asking people questions such as their favourite kinds of music, their age-group, their occupations, their normal styles of clothing on the occasions when they hear each kind of music and so on. The results of the questionnaires can then be totalled to see whether it is true that certain kinds of music appeal more to certain types of people than others.

Like speech, musical performances take place through time and are very often built up from 'phrases'. Moments of repose punctuate both speech and music. 'Cadences', 'pauses' or 'breaths' are found in many different styles of music-making. The organization and subdivision of performance time (tempo, rhythm and metre) are significant elements of many cultures' musical styles. We shall now look at these concepts in more detail.

The organization and subdivision of musical time

Tempo, or the speed at which a musical performance takes place, is an important feature in almost all music-making. In some cultures the speeds at which certain pieces can be performed is rigidly fixed, in others there is a certain amount of latitude. Some styles of music may be performed at what seems to us as a freely variable speed, getting faster or slower as the performer desires; other styles are more strictly interpreted. In some cultures musicians have created complex theories and terminology about tempo, in others they just have a feel for what is right and what is wrong.

In western classical music, the term 'rhythm' refers to the relative durations of different musical notes. The use of notes of varied durations is found in the great majority of other musical cultures as well, sometimes appearing in very complicated patterns. The term 'metre' describes how rhythmic patterns are organized into larger musical units. Although some music is not metrical, for instance certain operatic recitatives, a great deal of it is. Dance music, for example, is quite commonly organized into regular units which are repeated over and over. In western music it is the first beat of each unit which is considered the strongest, but in Indonesian gamelan

Figure 14.2 Music for 'nay' (Arabic flute) and 'tabla' (Indian drums). Transcribed part for 'saz' (Turkish long-necked lute) omitted

Source: With permission, from 'Saydisc' CSDL 387 (1991).

music, for instance, the fourth beat of each unit is stronger. In much western music we subdivide each metrical unit into two, three, four or six beats, each of which is of the same duration and can again be divided into notes of half, a third or a quarter of a beat. In some other musical traditions, however, metrical units may have five, seven, ten or twelve beats, perhaps, and these beats need not necessarily be of the same duration each. We must be careful not to think of these as 'irregular' metres, since to their performers they may have very natural, logical patterns of rhythm, movement and stress. Figure 14.2 is an excerpt in 7/8 metre from the Moroccan musician Hassan Erraji's composition entitled *Hiwar* (Dialogue). Note how every bar is regularly divided into two two-quaver beats and one three-quaver beat.

This example also reminds us that influence between different musics is an ongoing process. Hassan Erraj's piece, recorded in Britain, is scored for two Middle Eastern instruments and the Indian drums known as the *tabla*, which, incidentally, are played on this recording by a Belgian musician.

Melody and musical space

One important aspect of music is that although its performance unfolds in time, it also unfolds in what we could call 'musical space'. By musical space I mean two things: first pitch, whether notes are high or low, and second, the musical roles of the performers, whether one group answers another or several people all play at once and so forth.

Many cultures have a concept of pitch, They may not, however, refer to notes as 'high' or 'low' as we do, an idea reinforced by our reliance on a system of notation in which 'high' notes appear graphically 'higher' (nearer the top of the page) than 'low' ones. Quite a number of cultures have names for the pitches they employ. These names may refer either to fixed, 'absolute' pitches (like our C, D, E, etc.) or transposable, 'relative' pitches (like our Sol-fa systems or tonic, supertonic mediant, etc. terminology). Some cultures have both. In ancient China, for instance, each of the twelve semitones in an octave had its own name. A further name was given to each degree of the modes from which Chinese music was composed, and these modes could begin on any of the twelve semitones. Therefore, any note had two names, one which showed its absolute musical pitch and another which showed its relative position within the mode then under use.

The pitch-levels of individual musical notes are the building-blocks of melody, or the successive arrangement of musical notes. A concept of melody is common to many different musical cultures, although the exact definition of what makes a melody sound beautiful or apt may vary quite widely, and, as pointed out above, a melody is not always performed by the highest or fastest instruments in an ensemble.

There are several technical terms by which musicians refer to the way in which a melody is built up into a composition. When a melody is sung or played alone (whether by one performer or many), the music can be described as 'monophonic'. If, on the other hand, more than one melody is performed at the same time, then the term 'polyphony' is used. When all parts in a musical texture move with the same rhythm, the label 'homophony' is usually applied. Another kind of music is that in which the performers all produce the same tune together, but each present it in an individually decorated and adapted form. This kind of music is called 'heterophonic'. Finally, some music is 'antiphonal', which basically means that one part presents a melody and one or more parts then present an answer. Another term for this kind of performance is 'call and response'. Although these are western concepts and terms they are quite useful in helping us to recognize and classify different styles of music-making.

Task 5
The 'phonies' – classroom listening exercise

Pupils listen to a number of short musical extracts, deciding in each case whether the music they hear is monophonic, polyphonic, homophonic, heterophonic or antiphonal.

In most cultures, certain of these ways of organizing musical space are more common than the others. For example, a large amount of African singing is antiphonal, while much oriental ensemble music is heterophonic. Within some kinds of Christian church service, there may be antiphonal (call and response), homophonic (congregational hymns) and polyphonic (specialist choral) musical items.

Modes and scales

Musicians from many parts of the world choose the pitches they use in their music from sets of notes which we call modes. Most of us are familiar with scales; they are simply patterns by which all the notes in any musical 'key' are played or written one after the other, usually in ascending and then descending order. When composing 'in' a particular key, we typically choose our notes from those of its scale, although there are, of course, ways by which additional notes are introduced as well. Commonly, we start and finish with the first note of the scale, or key-note as it is sometimes called. Figure 14.3 shows two scales which are very commonly used in western music, C major and C minor.

'Mode' is often used to translate foreign terms similar in many ways to our words 'scale' and 'key'. However, in many cultures, specific modes may also call for the use of distinctive melodic progressions, patterns of ornamentation, intonation, instrumentation, cadential stress, register and performance techniques. In the Middle East or India, for instance, each mode provides the raw material from which an experienced musician can fashion a musical performance.

Needless to say, different sets of notes ('scales') and different ways of organizing them ('keys') are found all over the world. For example, in some parts of the world people make music from four-note modes (see Sachs 1962: 65, 66, 68, 145–7). These

C major   C minor

Figure 14.3 Major and minor scales

four notes need not be the same as any of our twelve equal-tempered semitones, but even if they are, we should remember that the same rules as in our own scales and keys do not apply to their use.

Task 6
Dialogue – classroom composition exercise

Pupils choose four notes from which to create a short, antiphonal composition entitled 'Dialogue'. Any four pitches may be chosen, not necessarily four consecutive notes like C, D, E and F. The composition should have six phrases (three sets of call and response), and the first and last phrase should end with the same note. The piece may be scored for instruments or voices, and may employ staff notation or simply numbers (for example, '1' for the first pitch, '2' for the second) with a key to explain which pitch each number denotes.

The 'lowest' pitch in a mode need not function the same way as our key-note, for instance. This is one point which can make listening to music from around the world difficult at first. Since the notes and mode used are different from ours, it can be hard to recognize the ends of musical phrases. The expectations with which we have been conditioned through years of listening to tonal music may hinder our appreciation of other kinds of music. But through becoming more conscious of our own conditioning, we acquire the opportunity to overcome its effects, and by, perhaps, transcribing and singing the pitches used in a foreign composition, we can begin to get more of a feel for the music itself.

Musical instruments

The great majority of civilizations have developed their own musical instruments, or adopted and adapted those of their neighbours. Several instruments well known to Europeans are believed to have been transmitted westwards from the Middle East. Others, especially certain types of drum, may have been introduced to Europe from Africa, possibly by way of the United States. Western instruments are now played in many nations all around the world. The use of musical instruments, whether to supplement or replace the human voice, is a feature found in many, many different cultures. The way a musical instrument is built and performed has a strong influence on the patterns of sound it can produce and the music which may be played upon it.

Classically-trained western musicians are familiar with the classification of instruments into the categories of strings, woodwind, brass and percussion. Although this division suits the tradition it was invented by very well, it is not entirely logical. Stringed instruments are named after the section of instrument which is sounded, while woodwind and brass are named after their traditional material of manufacture, and percussion instruments after their most characteristic performance technique. Thus, certain scholars have proposed more scientific ways of dealing with musical instruments. One such method is the Hornbostel–Sachs classification, in which instruments are sorted into the following broad classes:

idiophones, in which the body of the instrument itself provides the sound; membranophones, in which a tightly stretched membrane is sounded; chordophones, where strings are sounded; and aerophones, within which air is the principal substance of musical vibration. Examples of idiophones include such instruments as rattles and wood blocks, typical membranophones are drums, chordophones include fiddles and lutes, and aerophones many types of flute and reed instrument (see Hornbostel and Sachs 1961; Myers 1992: 444–61).

Other societies have their own ways of classifying musical instruments, some of which are quite complicated (see Kartomi 1990). Cultures around the world also have their own ways of explaining, valuing and combining musical instruments. There may be legends of how specific instruments were created by culture heroes. Certain instruments may be reserved for particular classes of people, or for particular occasions. Musical instruments serve as cultural icons, as markers of identity. The study of attitudes toward musical instruments is as important as the study of their construction and performance techniques.

Process of music-making

Music-making worldwide can be divided into a number of activities: composition, improvisation, performance, reception and appraisal. Some of these activities overlap – for example, composition during performance can also be described as improvisation. Appraisal provides feedback to composers and performers, affecting the music they create on subsequent occasions. In some cultures these activities may have different forms from the shape they take in western society. For example, amongst the Blackfoot Indians of North America, the composition of new songs traditionally occurs during an individual's dreams (Nettl 1983: 35). Some cultures do not use musical notations. In these traditions, which are often known as 'oral traditions', musicians have to rely solely upon their memories to remember and recreate music they have previously composed, learned, practised or rehearsed. Although it may be difficult for us to learn to compose in our sleep, we can enrich our own music-making by experimenting with, adapting and adopting many of the other techniques used in foreign processes of music-making. This is possible because even in our own score-centred tradition much of the learning process still takes place in an oral/aural context.

Musicians

There are musicians in every society, but the ways in which they are organized and create their music can differ quite markedly. Who the music-makers are in any culture is often a subject well worth investigating because it can explain much about the function and content of the music itself. Some societies rely on specialist musicians for their most important musical events. These specialists may be professionals, employed through a system of patronage or by payment for each performance. Others are semi-professional, devoting part of their time to musicianship and receiving some money or goods in return for their services. It is interesting to note that although music is often considered an important part of life, specialist musicians are frequently low in social status. In other societies there may be no musical specialists; everyone takes a theoretically equal part in all musical activities.

Within a culture, musical training, and the allocation of the roles of composer, performer or audience member, can differ widely, depending on whether specialist or non-specialist musicians are involved. Some groups do not so much memorize and perform fixed compositions as know how to create a new one together during each fresh performance. Finally, within any one society there are likely to be many kinds of musical activity, from lullabies to hymns and from dance music to war songs. Those who bring the music to life in each case may be quite different groups of people.

Conclusion

Music means many different things to many different people. It is these differences which make music an interesting subject to study. But it does mean that when we listen to someone else's music, we shouldn't expect it to sound the same as ours. When comparing a new style of music with an old favourite it is important to recall that the new musicians may not be trying to do the same things as those we normally listen to. Only through acquiring some familiarity with the way in which a form of music is conceived, produced and received in its original setting can we begin to understand the sound structures themselves. None the less, we can also benefit from asking questions when listening to an unfamiliar musical style.

For instance, are there any rhythmic patterns that keep coming back, does the music often return to the same note, what kind of mode is used, how is the music organized metrically? Although musical sounds differ from one part of the globe to another, there are certain general similarities in the ways in which people think about, organize and create these sounds. Learning about these similarities is a good way to start the study of world music, and an excellent way by which to marry the study of world music to that of the western classical tradition.

Appendix 1 – supplementary class exercises

1   In small groups pupils discuss and prepare their own definitions of music. These definitions can range from idiosyncratic to general, they can discuss what elements constitute music or what music means to its listeners. All the definitions are then read out to the class and compared.
2   As a homework assignment, students list all the similarities between music and language they can think of. They then prepare a list of differences.
3   In groups pupils compose a piece called *Birds of Paradise* in which a few simple melodic patterns, one representing each bird, are freely repeated above an accompaniment of rain forest sounds. These sounds could include the wind rustling in the leaves, rain drops falling to the ground and perhaps the occasional buzz and hum of small insects. One emotion could be attached to the call of each bird. In performance, these simple melodic patterns could become the basis for extemporization. Once the composition has been rehearsed, a programme could be decided upon and the whole piece performed to the remainder of the class.

4   Students compose a short melody for flute which uses a regularly subdivided 11/8 metre. They must decide exactly how to subdivide each beat, and they emphasize this subdivision by adding a simple bass or rhythmic accompaniment.

5   Students listen to at least a dozen pop songs, counting how many beats per minute there are in each and deciding what metrical structure is used. Then they discuss whether or not a certain tempo range and metre seem to be preferred by composers of this kind of music. If composers of pop music do appear to concentrate upon songs of a certain speed and metrical organization, pupils suggest reasons why this might be the case.

6   Pupils look up and write short definitions of the following terms: accompaniment, improvisation, key, melody, metre, pitch and rhythm.

7   Students research the early history of the following musical instruments: guitar, lute, viol, mouth organ, oboe and timpani.

Appendix 2 – cross-references and possibilities for expansion

Possibilities for further expansion in the classroom of some of the ideas discussed above include continuing with more work on the subject of programme music and the introduction of *musique concrète*. The latter would be particularly appropriate if tape-recorded sounds are integrated into Task 3. Definitions of music could lead to a discussion of the innovative work of John Cage. The third class task could lead to the appraisal of western pieces with avian themes, such as Respighi's *The Birds* or various compositions by Messaien. For a more thorough criticism of the idea of musical progress from simple, primitive music to advanced western compositions see Sachs (1962: 210–22).

Mention and discussion of metre could lead to an examination of the varied metrical patterns employed by Stravinsky in the *Rite of Spring* or by Bartók in his 'Six Dances in Bulgarian Rhythm' *(Mikrokosmos* vol. VI, Nos. 148–53). One step further removed, Bernstein's 'America' from *West Side Story* makes interesting use of alternating metrical subdivisions (Bowman 1992: 20–1), while many Baroque compositions include the somewhat similar hemiola effect. Much music theory, particularly that concerned with tonality, could be introduced or reinforced with the very brief mention of scales and keys given above, while advanced groups could become acquainted with the European church modes as well. The subject of musical organization and training is further discussed in Booth and Kuhn (1990). Although their categorization of folk, art and popular musics is rather simplistic, it none the less contains many stimulating points which advanced pupils would be able to comprehend.

Acknowledgement

I am grateful to Joo-Lee Stock for trying out preliminary versions of exercises proposed in this article with classes at Lagan College, Belfast and Grangefield School, Stockton-on-Tees.

References

Allen, R. (1986) *The New Penguin English Dictionary,* Harmondsworth, Middlesex: Penguin.

Bacharach, A.L. and Pearce, J.R. (eds) (1977) *The Musical Companion*, (rev. edn), London: Pan.

Blacking, J. (1976) *How Musical is Man?,* London: Faber & Faber.

Booth, G.D. and Kuhn, T.L. (1990) 'Economic and transmission factors as essential elements in the definition of folk art and pop music', *The Musical Quarterly,* 74(3): 411–38.

Bowman, D. (1992) 'GCSE analysis: songs from West Side Story', *Music Teacher,* 71(7): 20–5.

Feld, S. (1982) *Sound and Sentiment: Birds, Weeping, Poetics, and Song in Kaluli Expression,* Philadelphia: University of Pennsylvania Press.

Hornbostel, E.M. von and Sachs, C. (1961) 'Classification of musical instruments', translated from the original German by A. Baines and K.P. Wachsmann, *Galpin Society Journal,* 14: 3–29.

Isaacs, A. (ed.) (1988) *The Macmillan Encyclopedia,* London: Guild Publishing.

Kartomi, M. (1990) *On Concepts and Classifications of Musical Instruments,* Chicago: University of Chicago Press.

Myers, H. (ed.) (1992) *Ethnomusicology: an Introduction,* New Grove Handbooks of Music, London: Macmillan.

Nettl, B. (1983) *The Study of Ethnomusicology: Twenty-nine Issues and Concepts,* Urbana: University of Illinois Press.

Sachs, C. (1962) *The Wellsprings of Music,* J. Kunst (ed.), The Hague: Martinus Nijhoff.

Sloboda, J. A. (1985) *The Musical Mind: the Cognitive Psychology of Music* (Oxford Psychology Series, No. 5), Oxford: Oxford University Press.

Sorrell, N. (1990) A *Guide to the Gamelan,* London: Faber & Faber.

15 Jazz in schools
A practical approach
Bill Charleson

Introduction

This chapter looks at the way in which jazz can be used in school to develop pupils' musical learning and understanding. It will discuss how jazz in the music curriculum can be used to support music learning and particularly how jazz ensembles might be developed in schools.

The four elements of music education

The four principal elements of music education might be expressed as:

1   rehearsing/performing;
2   composing/arranging;
3   listening/analysing;
4   appraising.

The study of jazz, its history and techniques, can be a valuable contribution to general music learning in schools. Jazz, with its reliance on a strong aural tradition and the emphasis placed on improvisation, underpins each of the elements listed above, particularly that of listening to music (in all its styles) and analysing and appraising what we hear. In the following section we look at each of the four elements in a jazz context.

Rehearsing and performing

Jazz, perhaps more than any other music, is a spontaneous expression of a musician's background, culture, emotions and experience. Jazz performance is essentially a group experience, depending to a considerable extent on the interaction between participants; it is a sharing of collective skills, knowledge and experience realized within an improvisational framework. As in all music performance it imparts and develops team skills.

The typical jazz ensemble consists of a 'front-line' (a group of wind or stringed instruments, or both) which is accompanied by the 'rhythm section' (keyboards, guitar, bass and drums). The front-line will be a combination of varying numbers of trumpets, trombones and saxophones, although other orchestral instruments may be used. The electric guitar can be considered as a front-line instrument or as a member of the rhythm section, capable of carrying a solo line or replacing or enhancing the piano's role as a provider of harmonic accompaniment. The bass can be a double bass or a bass guitar, and the drums can be augmented by other percussion instruments as available.

In performance, the theme (or song) may be played by the front-line instruments in unison, octaves, or voiced (orchestrated) in duet or three or more parts. This statement of the theme is called the 'head' and is almost always played at the beginning and end of the performance. The head frequently provides the harmonic and formal structure for individual improvised solos. The form and structure of the improvised solo will be discussed later on in the section 'Teaching and learning'.

The instruments of the rhythm section have different individual roles. The keyboards and the guitar normally provide a harmonic accompaniment with a rhythmic underpinning, referred to as 'comping'. The bass and drums both provide a continuous rhythmic accompaniment, the bass line employing note patterns drawn from the theme's harmonic progression. All rhythm section instrumentalists are normally capable of playing, and expected to play, improvised solo passages when appropriate.

Composition and arranging

Jazz compositions have often been the product of the performer rather than the 'specialist' composer. Jazz improvisation itself is a form of composition – 'invention on the hoof' – one might say. The extended composition has its place in jazz music but usually it is the small-scale 'theme with variations', often on blues or standard song forms, that constitutes the repertoire of many jazz ensembles. Melodic lines are often communicated aurally, arising as they so often do from improvised phrases, and are later notated when an arrangement is created to facilitate performance. The composer and bandleader Duke Ellington often absorbed composed fragments (riffs) originated by his players into his compositions and arrangements.

The process continues when the performer as arranger takes another composer's theme and arranges it for an ensemble; newly-composed elements are added based on the original composer's harmonic and rhythmic material. In contemporary jazz the leading exponents rely almost entirely on original material originating from within the group or ensemble. The jazz arranger is not merely an orchestrator but frequently co-composer, adding new material to the structure and new levels of creativity to the original theme.

Listening and analysing

Like much of contemporary music, jazz is constantly changing and evolving. The performer must be constantly aware of new ideas, changing styles and forms, while remaining aware of traditional structures and their supporting repertoire. For the beginner as well as the experienced musician it is essential to *listen* to the music and to absorb the influences of its most gifted performers. It is important to understand clearly the form and structure of a performance and to be able to analyse the content, both thematic and improvisational. Many classic solo improvisations have been transcribed, notated and subsequently published; one way of understanding the language of jazz improvisation is by listening to the recorded track while following the solo line as printed. Elements of style and phrasing and the melodic and rhythmic content of the improvised line can all be examined at first hand, thus gaining a valuable insight into the processes surrounding the art of improvisation.

Appraising

The listening experience provides an opportunity for the emerging musician to evaluate the elements and processes that constitute performance. It is important that the appraisal process is at work both when the musician is performing *and* when listening to the performance of others, whether the music is live or recorded. An improvised line may be assessed for its emotional content, technical fluency and, where appropriate, its harmonic accuracy and fidelity to the original theme. The listener must be persuaded that the treatment of the theme in its exposition and development is appropriate in style and provides clear insight into the composer's intellectual and emotional intentions.

Performance, composition, listening and appraisal therefore can be said to be underpinned by:

- knowledge and understanding;
- techniques and skills;
- repertoire.

Teaching and learning

It is proposed that teaching methods should include:

- creative aural techniques in the classroom;
- workshop sessions;
- individual and group listening and analysis.

We will look at each in turn.

Creative aural techniques

Music is an aural medium, but traditional teaching can sometimes create a dependency on written music. Don't let the notes get in the way of the music! The fundamental instrument for the production of music is the voice: encourage pupils in the classroom to sing, and to sing from memory.

Jazz is an aural tradition, communicated by sound, underpinned by use and repetition and committed to memory. Creative teaching of jazz should:

1   emphasize listening, evaluating and analysing;
2   develop pitch recognition, harmonic understanding and memory;
3   lead to a fuller understanding of music of all types and styles.

In the classroom, *all* can sing, clap or stamp rhythms, participating equally with those already possessing instrumental skills. Even experienced instrumentalists should be encouraged to sing before they play so as to establish or improve pitch recognition.

Jazz singers use 'scat': a valuable technique for singing melodies without using words. Single syllables are used to articulate sounds; you can make up your own but some in common use are shown on the next page:

Dat	for a short sound	
Doo or wha	for a long sound	
Doo-be	for a chain of notes	

An example might look like this;

Dat doo-wha …

Call and response

Use call and response techniques to commit common jazz phrases to memory. Sing or play the phrase in time, using a metronome, drum track or off-beat clapping. The class responds in time.

Use the above pitches to sing other common phrases:

The first phrase illustrates how an off-beat crotchet in jazz is traditionally played short.

Question and answer

Encourage the class to improvise a response to a given phrase.

Pitch practice

Music of any style may be used for pitch practice but in jazz it is appropriate to develop pitch and scale recognition by using the blues scale (see example on page 204).

1   introduce flat 3rd by:

2   4th by:

3   flat 5th by:

4   flat 7th by:

Sing the blues

I	I	I	I
IV	IV	I	I
V	IV	I	I

The above diagram represents the root progression of a twelve-bar blues. Copy it to a whiteboard so that it can be seen by all. Then play a rhythm track of the above progression on a keyboard or from a record.

1   sing all the roots of the progression to dat–doo–dah rhythm;
2   add major thirds;
3   add the fifths;
4   and add the flat (minor) seventh.

Combine all the intervals to form a four-part chord sung over the blues progression. This is invaluable in establishing the structural form and harmonic progression of the blues in the memory of the pupil.

Create a walking bass

A jazz bass often walks in crotchets (quarter notes). This can be imitated by the voice and is good fun! Choose singers (probably male) with deep voices, state a key, and sing:

1   the root notes (in crotchets);
2   then: root, 3rd, 5th, root;
3   root, 2nd, 3rd, 5th;
4   improvise a moving line – use ear, prior knowledge or imagination to develop a bass line of chord-compatible notes. It may be useful to double the voices with the piano, bass or similar bass instrument.

Create an original blues

1. choose a blues phrase from the pitch practice motifs shown on page 201 (in the section on 'pitch practice') or make one up;
2. split the class – get one third to sing the chosen motif (riff);
3. get one third to harmonize the harmonic progression as described;
4. the rest sing (or play) the walking bass;
5. all tap foot (stomp) on the 1st and 3rd beats and *clap* on the 2nd and 4th, the off-beats, to provide a rhythm section.

Development of a jazz ensemble in schools

Workshop sessions

It is sometimes useful to use instrumental workshops as a means toward creating jazz ensembles in schools. Pupils bring with them their own individual skills, knowledge and experience, and workshops offer an opportunity to share these with others. An ideal group size for workshop practice is probably four plus a tutor. Exercises and practice patterns can be played together, the stronger player guiding the weaker, melodic lines can be sub-divided into duet, trio or quartet forms and a sense of ensemble created. Groups can be of mixed instruments, or confined to families (such as alto and tenor saxophones), or single instruments, a good example of which might be four trumpets playing in section using big band repertoire.

Solo pieces can be performed for critical evaluation by the performer's peers, and performance ideas and practice shared and discussed. Wherever possible, performances should be recorded for later study and analysis. Discussion might be broadened to include aspects of historical and sociological interest, instrumental style and jazz and popular music forms.

Group practice techniques

This may follow the practice established in schools, colleges and conservatoires of regular (weekly) sessions of instrumental tuition, undertaken by the class teacher, a peripatetic instrumental tutor, a visiting musician or a local professional.

The establishment of a sound instrumental technique in jazz performance is a process not so different from that followed by other musical styles. Scales, arpeggios, broken chords, graded exercises and solo pieces can all be valuable practice material. However, it is possible for the tutor to guide pupils toward specific exercises and practice patterns which are based on authentic jazz phrases (licks) and thereby assist in the assimilation of essential idiomatic harmonic and melodic constructions.

Scale practice

The practice of scales is fundamental to the development of harmonic fluency in jazz improvisation. 'Following the changes' is an expression often used by jazz musicians to describe the process of improvising a melodic line that reflects the harmonic structure and changing tonal centres of a song or theme. The chords that make up the harmonic progression have a direct relationship with the scales from which they evolved. Conversely, changing tonal centres within the piece demand passages based on a correct and accurate evaluation of the scales appropriate to each specific key centre.

A good example of this progression of tonal centres is the bridge of the standard song form based on Gershwin's *I Got Rhythm* – the so-called 'rhythm changes' bridge. This eight-bar bridge consists of a cycle of secondary dominant sevenths, each chord occupying two bars, starting on chord III7 and ending on V7. In the key of B♭ major (see example below) our first chord is D7 (tonality G major); subsequent changes take the player through the tonal centres of C and F major and finally to the 'home' key of B♭ major.

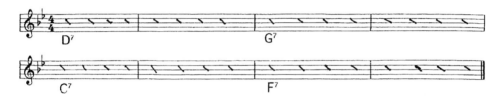

It follows therefore that the player be fluent in the keys of G, C, F and B♭ major to cope adequately with a rhythm changes bridge.

The player will also need to be able to start a passage from any degree of the scale; in bars 1–2 of the bridge, the player may choose to play the G major scale from the root of the dominant seventh chord, that is, D. Thus the scale becomes D Mixolydian (G major from D to D) and might be practised in that form. It is a useful ploy in fact to practise scales ascending on one degree and descending on the next, rather than from root to root.

Already we have identified a scale type appropriate to the dominant seventh chord, namely the Mixolydian (mode) scale based on the root of the chord.

There are several scale types appropriate to the dominant seventh chord, the use of which might be determined by the chord's harmonic colour and these are shown below, in this case using D7.

The scale types so far discussed are not, of course, exclusive to jazz; they form the harmonic basis of much tonal music regardless of genre or style. There is, however, a scale much used in jazz, which can be said to have its origins in not in the European harmonic tradition, but in blues. The blues scale shown below combines the primary degrees of a diatonic scale with the 'blue notes' of the vocal blues idiom.

Many blues phrases are based simply on a running combination of notes of the blues scale and these same phrases (and indeed the scale itself) are harmonically compatible with all the primary chords of the twelve-bar blues.

All the chord types present in the harmonic progressions of jazz and popular music can be said to have related (or appropriate) scales. There are many publications available to assist the teacher and pupil in the understanding and application of jazz scale patterns. It goes without saying that any manual of scales or scale patterns should only serve as a reference. Practice should be from memory!

Chord patterns

It is possible also to apply jazz styles and techniques to the practice of arpeggios and broken chords. This form of practice is common to all musical study but, while it familiarizes mind and fingers with the general shape of chords, it does not render a pattern that is immediately usable to the jazz performer. However, if a chord of the dominant seventh is organized such that the pattern starts on the third and ends on the seventh, it can then be perpetuated in a cyclic fashion as the example below illustrates.

This provides a more useful and essentially 'jazzy' shape that the player can incorporate into the improvised line. Further variants based on extending the chord beyond the seventh – to the ninth and further – provide even more variety.

The saxophonist, John Coltrane, demonstrated that it was possible to evolve chord patterns based on the interval of the fourth (rather than the construction based on thirds found in the triad plus seventh, ninth configuration) and on pentatonic scales. These patterns shown in example below are much used by contemporary performers (particularly saxophonists such as Michael Brecker, David Sanbourn and others) and are particularly appropriate to the rock and fusion styles of jazz-related popular music.

Style and phrasing

Scales, chord patterns and melodic lines as constituents of a practice schedule all have a common need – they must swing! ('It don't mean a thing, if it ain't got that swing,' said Duke Ellington). If there is an essential difference between jazz and classical music performance it is to be found in those elements of interpretation which are concerned with accent, stress and rhythmic syncopation. 'Swing' in its most general sense means a regular, steady pulse – the 'beat'. For the jazz musician the rhythmic impulse is at least as strong an element in performance as is accuracy of pitch and quality of timbre. In jazz the so-called 'weak' beats (2 and 4 in quadruple time) are not underplayed as in 'classical' music but may be emphasized up to, or even beyond, the level of the strong beats (1 and 3). This weak-beat emphasis can be witnessed when jazz musicians clap (or finger-snap) on the 'off-beats' (beats 2 and 4), a skill that often appears to elude the average audience!

In bebop (roughly 1940–60) we encounter a melodic style, found in both themes and improvisation, which has its rhythmic foundation in eighth note patterns (quavers in quadruple time). Gunther Schuller (1968) suggests that the African basic rhythm unit is probably the eighth note, rather than the quarter note division common in European music. This leads to the speculation that the overriding eighth note feel of modern jazz – bebop – may well be related to its African rhythmic origins. There is little doubt that the bebop innovators, Charlie Parker and others, left jazz with the stylistic legacy of continuous running quavers as a major constituent of the improvised solo. In fact, the jazz musician rarely plays even quavers; instead they are rendered as an uneven flow (the term used is 'bounced'), based on triplet groups (shown in example below) often with the reverse, weak-strong accentuation characteristic of the basic rhythmic pulse or beat.

In swing, bebop and indeed most rock fusion styles, what is visualised in 4/4 is usually communicated in 12/8.

Syncopated rhythm patterns common to many musical styles are re-interpreted by the jazz performer: quarter notes (crotchets) positioned an eighth note to one side of the main pulse (or beat) are sounded shorter than the apparent length and the rhythm becomes, phonetically, 'dat-doo-dah'. The jazz musician learns this aurally: notation rarely comes close to an accurate representation. It is folly to try to produce a collective jazz feel by notating pieces in compound time, 12/8 or 6/8, when what is required is 'swing' 4/4 – simple quadruple time. In workshop sessions every opportunity must be taken to communicate this stylistic tradition aurally. This was the way the great jazz performers learned their trade, and it will serve us equally well.

Formal structures

It is in the workshop situation that the task of familiarizing pupils with basic jazz forms is best undertaken. The starting point must be the structure of the blues, both twelve and twenty-four bar forms, major, minor and modal. The essential arrangement of the primary chords (I, IV and V) used in the blues should be understood and, more importantly, *felt* by the student. Chord IV *always* occurs in bar five of the twelve-bar blues; the approach to the dominant (V7), known as the turnaround, always starts at bar nine. These milestones in the blues progression should be felt intuitively by the improviser. Standard song forms of the structure AABA or ABAC should be outlined, and the function and relationship of each section explained. These song forms are the basis of so many themes of the bebop and post-bop periods.

Extended formal structures, particularly those involving modal harmonic progressions should be examined. These are to be found in abundance in jazz recorded in the period 1970–90 and mark the progression of swing and bebop into a period of fusion with rock styles and structures, sometimes reflecting the influence of commercial pop music. Performers whose interests and background are largely in pop music can provide a valuable input into the study of contemporary jazz, particularly in the area of rhythms and rhythmic pulse.

Group improvisation

The term 'jazz' is synonymous with improvisation. The word improvisation is a mis-nomer: a well-constructed solo is not usually an improvised event but a carefully planned and executed construction, albeit delivered (apparently) spontaneously. It is at the point of delivery that the knowledge and understanding of the idiom, its forms and structures, its repertoire of thematic material, are articulated, employing the skills and techniques born only out of hours of personal and group practice. American musicians have a particularly descriptive phrase for the latter activity – 'woodshedding'.

Preparation for the improvised solo can be as much a group activity as an individual exploration. In the performance workshop, group improvisation can be initiated using rhythm section recordings of set-piece progressions or formal structures. These can be used to accompany front-line players if a rhythm section is not available or to demonstrate technique and style to rhythm section members. The best known of these 'music-minus-one' recordings are those produced by the American saxophonist Jamie Abersold: his catalogue contains many recordings featuring hundreds of different titles and are readily available in the UK.

Opportunities exist within the workshop situation for players to input and exchange ideas, but this procedure will benefit from guidance. The music might usefully be broken up into 'bite-size chunks', phrases sub-divided into two- or four-bar periods. Many pieces have harmonic schemes, the building blocks of which are three and four-chord progressions – a common occurrence in standard songs is the sequence based on IIm7–V7–I. A useful practice routine is continuously to loop the sequence over two or four bars repeatedly, and this can be accompanied by a keyboard or guitar. Many such sequences are also to be found on rhythm section recordings, or alternatively the routine may be recorded using a computer and sound module and sequencing software such as *Cubase* or *Band in a Box*.

The exchange of ideas is essential. Many jazz musicians exchange favourite phrases, consciously or subconsciously. This expands a player's repertoire, and there is no sense of something stolen because much of what is played is common currency and players will always interpret and re-invent phrases imparting their particular personality on the music. What is to be avoided is the learning by rote of clichés, phrases that have outlived their usefulness by dint of constant repetition.

Rhythmic complexities within the music can be more easily understood if the performers undertake some form of rhythm training before attempting to play. Rhythms may be sung or clapped until it is felt that the note displacement is correct and the appropriate 'feel' has been imparted to the passage or phrase. The training can then proceed to the playing of a rhythm on a single pitch before attempting the complete phrase.

Solo pieces

There is a wealth of material available for solo performance from many European and American publishers. Jazz themes and standard and popular songs abound, arranged for solo instrument with piano/guitar accompaniment, and they provide an enormous choice of repertoire for the solo performer. There is, however, one further valuable source – the confusingly named 'fake' or 'real' books. These are collections of jazz themes and standard songs notated in a 'top line plus chords' form, that is to say that the melody is on a single stave in concert pitch with chord symbols added to indicate the harmonic scheme. In this form many more titles can be included in one volume than would be possible if the pieces were arranged in full. Players need to transpose for their own particular instrument and – if the intention is to perform – commit them to memory.

Solo pieces can be supplemented by transcriptions of improvised solos by famous artists. These are available from many published sources or can be transcribed by the pupil with assistance from the tutor – a valuable form of aural training. When performed with accompaniment (and here the tutor can play along with the pupil thus adding an extra interpretational dimension) transcribed solos are an invaluable aid to illuminating and understanding jazz style as well as imparting harmonic knowledge and melodic content to the pupil. Many of the leading performers in jazz have developed their own individual styles by close contact with, and study of, the work of an admired soloist. Many trumpet players in jazz will admit to the influence of Louis Armstrong, Clifford Brown or Miles Davis on their own development, as will saxophonists to the influence of Charlie Parker and John Coltrane, and pianists to Art Tatum, Bud Powell or Theolonius Monk.

Arranging the music

Melodic and harmonic ideas can be presented, expanded and developed in group improvisation sessions and the opportunity taken to develop rudimentary 'head arrangements'. The musicians can experiment with melodic lines played in unison, octaves, thirds or sixths, expanding this to three- or four-part voicing as familiarity with the harmonic progression increases. The principles of counter melody and simple counterpoint can be applied as an alternative to voiced sections. It is important that these techniques be applied not only to the theme (or 'head') but to material used as backgrounds to individual solos.

The structure of the performance can be discussed within the context of an arrangement. How many times is the theme played at the head? For a blues it is normally twice, that is, twenty-four bars. How many players will play solo and for how long? Will backgrounds be used behind solos, if so, when, and for how long? Is there to be a composed *tutti* section based on the theme? Will it be improvised or will a member of the ensemble write this? And, crucial this, how will the piece end? Together, one might hope!

Composition

The compositional processes involved in group improvisation and arranging can be readily channelled to create individual or group composition. The raw material for structured compositions, perhaps initially based on familiar forms such as the blues, exists within the material generated during improvisation sessions. If all contribute, then the sense of creative ownership is in itself rewarding and is a positive factor in creating a cohesive jazz performance.

When all the creative ideas for a piece appear to be present, it may be decided to notate, in score form, the developed composition. As an aid to this, a recording by the performers of a head arrangement of the piece, will form the basis of an extended version in which solo improvisation is contrasted with written passages derived from source material generated in group improvisation. The music can be committed to score paper in the traditional way – with pencil and rubber – or advantage can be taken of available information technology. *Sibelius* is a comprehensive and understandable music scoring programme by *Sibelius Software Ltd.* Its playback facility using an internal sound-card or suitable sound module offers valuable aural feedback as the composition progresses.

Whatever method of scoring is used, it is vital to retain the essential spirit and pulse – the feel – of the music. A notated score must strive to capture and hold this elusive property for future performance.

Vocal accompaniment

Much of the material generated during group improvisation, arrangement and composition sessions can be used to provide backgrounds and accompaniment to vocal performance. Instrumentalists can be guided to support and enhance a performance by providing an accompaniment that is sensitive to the needs of the vocal line. The player will learn to interject a melodic phrase only where the song sustains, where the melody is passive; and conversely, sustain when the vocal line is active. Experienced players call this technique playing 'through the window'. The analogy with 'window of opportunity' is obvious and can be experienced if one listens to the muted trumpet of Harry Edison artfully commenting on the vocal line as sung by Frank Sinatra on so many famous recordings of the 1950s.

Of course, singers can also provide a unique 'voice' to the front line of an ensemble, merging their voices with the instruments, singing the lines in unison and even providing improvised solo passages. Vocal improvisation – scat – is a technique employed by many jazz singers, from Billie Holliday to Ella Fitzgerald, Louis Armstrong to George Benson. A valuable input to workshop practice might be made by singers who can encourage instrumentalists to sing phrases accurately before attempting to play them.

Directed rehearsal

In the rehearsal of scored music as distinct from head arrangements, a degree of formal discipline is perhaps appropriate. Neatly-prepared individual parts, and a librarian (one of the group) to distribute them, can ease the way to effective rehearsal. Seat the players where they can see the director (or conductor) and in such a way as to encourage eye contact with one another. It is particularly important that members of the rhythm section learn the value of visual cues; no one should be allowed to bury their heads in a music stand!

Don't tune up immediately! Play the piece to be rehearsed once, then tune up *warm* instruments. Individual players must tune to each other, not to the piano. In many ensembles it is accepted that the (first) trumpet is the leader – the jazz equivalent of the concert master or first violin. Tune to the ensemble leader and trust that the player has checked the pitch against A 440 beforehand. Encourage tuning to chords or triads rather than the solitary A. I have witnessed many student ensembles play a beautiful concert A followed by a desperately out of tune first chord. Adopt the measure used by engineers to balance ensembles in recording studios and organize separate brass, saxophone or woodwind, and string chords in advance. Build the chord from the root, one player at a time until all the players in the section sustain the chord. Check for pitch, intonation and balance of volume. When all appears well, play the piece again and observe the difference.

Attempt a complete performance first time. Don't stop the ensemble after a few bars if all is not well. If the performance can be sustained to the end of the piece, the players will have gained valuable knowledge of the 'geography' of the music.

Establish the performance routines, identifying the sections in which soloists improvise and decide on the order of solos. Earmark those passages needing attention and establish with the players visual cues to start and stop repeated sections and to cue backgrounds to solos if needed.

If the ensemble is of a traditional type, for example a big band, it may be necessary to subdivide the rehearsal schedule to allow for instrumental sections to rehearse separately. In this way each instrumental group may deal with its problems and issues without encroaching on the rehearsal time of others. Similarly, key improvisers may choose to rehearse solo sections with the rhythm section only.

Balance the rehearsal schedule as one would a concert programme. Contrast the exciting blockbuster with a slower calmer piece. Insist on observation of playing dynamics. In fact, arrive at an ensemble dynamic that suits the size and composition of the ensemble and scale all other dynamics to this. Urge the maintenance of tonal quality in even the quietest passages. Don't allow wind players to overblow to the detriment of tonal quality and good intonation. Most of all – enjoy the music!

Individual and group listening and analysis

It is important that the process of listening to and analysing musical performance be guided and structured. A good starting point might be the analysis of pre-recorded music by the pupils themselves (as suggested previously) and a critique of individual and group contribution.

The tutor can provide a valuable listening experience by demonstrating style and technique using an instrument or voice. An extract of music recorded by a well-known artiste could be evaluated establishing the style and period of the music, comparing the track with other recordings of the same theme or with earlier or later work by the same player.

In group sessions, guitarists might be encouraged to listen to saxophonists, trumpeters to pianists and so on. Front-line instrumentalists could be required to listen carefully to keyboard, bass and drums, analyse their differing roles in the ensemble and evaluate the interaction present in an effective rhythm section. In the classroom, all pupils could be encouraged to analyse the differing roles of players in the jazz ensemble and the function of the different instrumental sections to the style and structure of the music being played.

The analysis of an improvised solo has been briefly discussed previously. There will be, in any classroom group, a range of instrumental ability and level of experience. The more advanced performer will be in a position to input information and constructive criticism on the content of the solo being analysed. The harmonic and formal structure may be familiar ground and the pupil, with guidance, may be able to offer an analysis that illuminates areas of chromatic substitution or re-harmonization. The contour of the improvised line may yield information on the scale tones employed, and this information can be measured against the sequence of chords. The less experienced performer on the other hand may make a useful contribution to the debate by assessing the apparent style and period influencing the exposition of the theme and its subsequent variations, and evaluating the emotional range and content of the solo.

The teacher or group leader, encouraging and facilitating critical awareness, can summarize by evaluating the critical information and placing it in context with regard to style and period. Everybody interested in jazz should be aware of the principal stylistic periods of the music and their development and progression through the twentieth century. From the turn of the century, the music progressed from blues to ragtime, through New Orleans (Dixieland) and the Kansas City styles, to swing and the dance-band years. From about 1940, bebop developed, then a period of experimentation and apparent freedom from the shackles of form and harmony labelled the 'free jazz', and finally, a move towards rock which resulted in an eventual fusion of the different forms. In the closing years of the last century and into this century, we are enjoying a rich diet of all these styles and genres and an association with popular music and world musics that has enriched the jazz repertoire enormously for both player and listener.

Resources

Human resources

The teacher as a communicator

The teacher has a key role in inculcating an appreciation and understanding of the nature of the music and its relationship with other musics. Jazz performance is the art of the unexpected, its history and development full of twists and turns. Sociological and economic factors exerted their influences on an art form that grew largely out of the entertainment media. An inspired teacher can do much to illuminate the cultural and economic forces that moulded the music. There is a wealth of historical data available from sound and video recordings and the many texts published on the subject and its key performers.

The teacher as a facilitator

Jazz needs a fertile environment if it is to flourish. It is the music of the street, the pub and the nightclub; it is closely bound up with the entertainment industry. Our Year 7 and 8 pupils are unlikely to experience at first hand the influence of such an environment, but the teaching space – the classroom – can be made to take on the ambience of the world from which the music evolved. Posters and photographs are graphic evidence of the success and popularity of the music and might be used to decorate the learning space. Listening and viewing facilities should be accessible, and the apprentice must be immersed in the sights and sounds of jazz.

Practice and rehearsal schedules need to be initiated and every opportunity taken to encourage musicians to meet, discuss and debate and play together. Performers must perform. Look for space in the school timetable, perhaps break and lunch periods, to set up impromptu performances in which performers can experiment and demonstrate to their peers.

Find gigs! Think about arranging concerts for other schools, and for local authority establishments such as hospitals, nursing homes and leisure services.

Encourage public performances several times each term and provide an informative programme of information about the music and its performers. Enlist other interested staff to act as roadies (see glossary!), sound engineers and to help with publicity and promotion. In my experience there are jazz enthusiasts on every academic staff. Try not to say no! Make things happen.

Teaching teams

Many of the basic requirements of music performance transcend stylistic barriers. The peripatetic instrumental tutor, whose work perhaps services a school orchestra or choir, wind or brass band, can be a valuable resource for the training of jazz musicians. If you are fortunate enough to have more than one such visiting professional, a team can be established to undertake section rehearsals appropriate to particular instrumental groups. Stylistic advice may be the responsibility of one such team member, and while a brass band professional, for example, may not feel equipped to advise on jazz phrasing, they can provide invaluable information on practice techniques.

A visiting teacher or professional musician will almost certainly have some arranging or composing skills. Others will have directing or conducting experience to add to the mix. The key skills of team members will soon become apparent and established within the teaching team structure.

The team leader, be it the classroom teacher or an instrumental tutor, must set aims and objectives against a timescale. The latter may be dictated by a termly performance programme in which events must be planned, programmed and resourced. Schemes of work for both individual and group tuition should be directed toward individual performances within the programme as well as toward the individual progress of the student musician. The team must meet regularly to formulate policy, evolve a strategy and – perhaps most important of all – keep each other informed. As we said earlier, jazz performance depends to a considerable extent on the interaction between participants, and so does its organization.

Physical resources

Instruments and associated equipment

- Piano: acoustic or electronic, preferably one of each in each teaching space
- Synthesizer or electronic keyboard: with a range of orchestral voices and internal sequencer for multitrack recording
- Guitar: acoustic and electric if possible
- Bass or Bass Guitar: double bass is more appropriate in some respects for swing and bebop, and bass guitar more appropriate for rock
- Drums: kit drums are essential and a range of tuned percussion instruments is an advantage
- Backline amplification: backline means amplifiers and speakers for keyboards, guitar and bass
- PA (public address): a number of microphones, a PA amplifier and speakers – to amplify solo instrumentalists and singers

Suggestions of useful recordings

The following list contains the details of particular tracks that you may find useful in the classroom.

Artist	Album, date and label details	Track and duration
King Oliver	The King and Mr. Jelly Lord (1923)	Canal St. Blues
	Parade PAR 2303	2:24 mins.
Louis Armstrong	Louis Armstrong Hot Five (1928)	West End Blues
	Giants of Jazz CD 53001	3:15 mins.
Duke Ellington	Swing 1930–1938 (1930)	Rockin' in Rhythm
	BBC CD 686	3:13 mins.
Fletcher Henderson	Under the Harlem Moon (1933)	King Porter Stomp
	CD AJA 5067	1:48 mins
Benny Goodman	Compact Jazz (1970)	King Porter Stomp
	Verve 820 543–2	4:11 mins.
Count Basie	Count Basie and the Kansas City 8	Basie's Bag
	(1986) Pablo CD 2310–924	3:06 mins
Charlie Parker	The Savoy Recordings (1945)	Billie's Bounce
	Vogue VG 655 650107	3:08 mins.
Miles Davis	The Birth of the Cool (1949)	Godchild
	Capitol Jazz CDP7 92862 2	3:07 mins
Gerry Mulligan	Gerry Mulligan Concert Jazz Band	Come Rain, Come Shine
	Verve 2683 057	2:37 mins
Ornette Coleman	Ornette Coleman Trio at the Golden Circle, Stockholm (1965)	Dee Dee
	Blue Note CDP7 82224–2	1:56 mins
Chick Corea	Elektric Band	Inside Out
	GRD 9601	5:08 mins.

Glossary

Bebop A largely quaver-based, linear style of improvisation in response to a stated or implied chord progression.

Bridge The B section or middle-eight of an AABA structure.

Busking Playing by 'ear'.

Changes Chord progression.

Chord Symbol of a system of shorthand harmonic notation.

Chorus A complete cycle of a chord progression, used in connection with jazz themes or standard songs.

Feel The style and essential pulse of a performance.

Front-line The instruments of an ensemble excluding rhythm section.

Gig A performance or engagement.

Hard bop The 1950s development of 1940s bebop, a more thrusting, driving approach.

Head The theme of a composition.

Improvisation Spontaneous composition.

Jam session A musical gathering with the specific purpose of improvising.

Lick A jazz phrase, usually personal to the player.

Line A melodic phrase or section of a solo.

Mainstream Small band swing based on repertoire of the 1930s and 40s.

Middle-eight Bridge.

Modern jazz Post-1940 jazz.

Quotation Material from other compositions used within an improvisation.

Release Another term for bridge or middle-eight.

Roadie(!) One who assists in the transportation and installation of equipment needed for a performance.

Rhythm changes A chord progression based on *I Got Rhythm* by George Gershwin.

Rhythm section That part of the ensemble providing the harmonic and rhythmic accompaniment, usually piano, guitar, bass and drums.

Riff A short melodic and rhythmic phrase, often used in repetition.

Scat Improvising with the voice.

Sitting in Joining in a jazz performance.

Standard A popular song which has become an accepted part of the jazz repertoire.

Swing If you have to ask, you ain't got it!

Theme The principal melody of a jazz composition.

Top line The notation of the basic melody of a theme or song.

Transcription The notation of a live or recorded jazz solo.

Turnaround The progression of chords resulting in a perfect cadence, normally occurring at the end of a theme.

Voicing The vertical arrangement of notes to form a chord.

Walking bass A bass line which moves in crotchets, 'walking' from chord to chord through a harmonic progression.

References

Owens, T. (1995) *Bebop,* Oxford: Oxford University Press.

Sadie, S. (ed.) (1981) *The New Grove Dictionary of Music and Musicians,* London: Macmillan.

Schuller, G. (1969) *Early Jazz*, Oxford: Oxford University Press.

16 Music education and GCSE Music
Paul Atkinson with Gary Spruce

A historical perspective

Prior to the introduction of the GCSE examination in 1985, external examinations in music at the age of sixteen were available at two levels: GCE (General Certificate of Education), O Level and CSE (Certificate of Secondary Education). Originally, the CSE examination had been developed exclusively for secondary modern pupils with O level taken only by those at grammar schools. However the comprehensivization of British schools during the sixties and seventies resulted in the both exams running in parallel with each other, often within the same school. However, the association of CSE with secondary modern schools inevitably resulted in it having lower status than O level .

One of the main functions of the O level examination was preparing students for A Level and possibly university entrance. The O level examination focused on a prescribed body of knowledge to be learned, understood and then assessed through formal timed examinations. The examination tested knowledge of a relatively narrow range of western classical music through the study of a number of set works, generally with no examples earlier than Bach and few insights into twentieth-century styles. Composition was restricted to formal four-part harmony exercises, two-part exercises and simple melody writing, all in accordance with the 'rules' of classical music.

There was an optional practical element where a student could demonstrate instrumental skills through the performance of set pieces of a standard approximate to grade 5 of the Associated Board of the Royal Schools of Music (ABRSM). Alternatively, a grade 5 pass in one of the ABRSM examinations could be accepted as a substitute. Instruments deemed to be acceptable for assessment were exclusively those of the western classical tradition. There was little or no provision for pop, rock, electronic or non-western instruments. O level music was appropriate only for pupils educated through the heritage of western art music.

The CSE examination recognized more diverse musical skills and styles, including, most significantly, popular musical. However, for many, the inclusion of popular music confirmed the lower status of the CSE examination. As Lucy Green says:

> The very fact of its inclusion both ensured its relative inferiority and legitimated the system of musical stratification by giving the appearance that a wide variety of music had been carefully hierarchised according to its value. The music in such a curriculum was in question, because [it was] … not really *studied*, not in comparable detail and quality with the serious curriculum. As such, this music did not

delineate high value – if it did, we would study it properly of course. Most importantly, its lack of such value did not present itself as a result of the music's low position in a hierarchy of value, but rather as a natural property of the music itself: the music, having been justly relegated, appeared to communicate the message: 'I am not inherently valuable', 'I am not susceptible to serious study'.

(Green 1988: 54)

Although the CSE examination did offer some opportunities for students to compose, generally speaking it continued to treat the acquisition of information *about* music as being of equal importance to engaging *with* it. Many CSE syllabuses, especially those devised and examined by the schools themselves (modes 2 and 3), encouraged activities such as making musical instruments and writing 'projects' about the lives of composers or the lifestyles of current pop stars, in a misguided attempt to be 'relevant'. These projects often resulted in highly attractive coursework folders but provided little opportunity for the candidate to engage with music or to demonstrate real musical attainment. However, a few schools did take the opportunity to devise syllabuses that focused upon performance and composition.

The transition to GCSE

Some music teachers and others outside of the profession had serious misgivings about the way in which the new GCSE examination challenged the orthodox, establishment view of what music and music education were about and how musical ability should be defined and assessed. The new GCSE examination formally articulated the so-called 'progressive' ideal of music and music education as being about the *experiential* activities of performing, composing and listening. Inasmuch as the GCSE examination represented acceptance of this principle by the wider educational and public world, it helped to reshape the nature of music education in this country.

The effect that the new GCSE examination would have on the actual *teaching* that took place in the music classroom was acknowledged in the guidance for teachers:

For most subjects the impact of the GCSE criteria will be principally upon how the subject is assessed rather than on the content of the curriculum for that subject. For music, however, the National Criteria have clear implications not only for how music is assessed but also *what* is taught, especially in the later years of secondary schooling.

(Secondary Examinations Council/Open University 1986: 8)

Paynter makes a similar point, arguing that fundamental change in the public examination system inevitably has implications for the curriculum in the earlier years of schooling:

When the GCSE was introduced it was the subject criteria that promoted new educational ideals and helped to give credibility to ideas which were still to some extent regarded as experimental ... both the National Curriculum and the GCSE have become important influences for change in the design of the secondary curriculum.

(Paynter 1992: 9)

The GCSE examination therefore provided the opportunity for music educators to reassess the key aims and objectives of music in the classroom and the means by which these aims and objectives could be achieved and effectively assessed.

However, for some time, there was an option for those teachers who regretted the passing of the 'academic' O level. Some examining boards initially published two music syllabuses: one that reflected the spirit of the O level (Syllabus A) and another that more fully embraced the ideals of the new approach to music education (Syllabus B). The reason for the existence of the Syllabus A option was described by the Midland Examining Group in its 1992 syllabus as a recognition that: 'For some candidates, certain aspects of the traditional approach may be essential as well as enjoyable' (MEG 1990: 3).

Although somewhat disingenuous, the main purpose of this was to placate or reassure those departments and music teachers who perceived GCSE as introducing in the examination system lower standards and music unworthy of serious attention. Perhaps, more importantly, it was also arguably a less challenging option for those teachers who were unable to adapt readily to the new challenges and demands of the practical, experiential approach to music education. Syllabus A was especially popular with the selective and independent sectors, whereas the vast majority of maintained schools followed the more practically-based alternative. By 1993, however, all examining boards had conflated the two syllabuses into a single one that more closely resembled Syllabus B and mirrored the aims of the recently introduced music National Curriculum.

During 1994, the Schools Curriculum and Assessment Authority (SCAA) developed new GCSE regulations that 'were settled in the light of recent practical experience of GCSE examining' (SCAA 1995a: 1) and that took account of the Dearing review of the National Curriculum. The *GCSE Regulations and Criteria* were published in final form in March 1995 in time to be adopted for the syllabuses for examination in 1998.

The government took this opportunity to reduce the amount of assessed coursework for many subjects to as little as 30 per cent. However, because of the accepted practical nature of the assessment criteria, music was allowed to devote up to 60 per cent of its marks to coursework.

The GCSE Music criteria

From 2003, schools will be entering candidates for the GCSE newly prescribed syllabuses. The syllabuses for these examinations must all comply with the *GCSE Subject Criteria for Music* published by the Qualifications and Curriculum Authority (QCA). As with all subject criteria, the subject criteria for music have to:

- conform to the general requirements for GCSE;
- provide opportunities for the development of key skills and the teaching of the Key Stage 4 Citizenship programme;
- 'build on the knowledge, understanding and skills established by the National Curriculum' (QCA 2000).

The last stipulation is very important as its aim is to aid continuity and progression in music education and ensure that GCSE music remains rooted in the taught music curriculum. This is emphasized further on in the music criteria where examination boards are required to 'ensure that the highest grades are accessible by those candidates who may not be receiving additional specialist musical lessons' (QCA 2000:6.9). This avoids the situation created by the O level examination, where there was often an assumption that those continuing with curriculum music beyond fourteen would have specialist music lessons and quite often have ambitions of a career in music. Curriculum music was not something you did simply because you enjoyed and had ability in it in the same way that one might enjoy and have ability in, say, geography.

The aims

Following on from the introduction, the music criteria go on to define the aims, specification content, key skills, assessment objectives and schemes of assessment and assessment techniques to which all music syllabuses must adhere.

Significantly, the aims of the music criteria (see below) are not about the acquiring of musical skills as an end in themselves. Rather, the aims are concerned with how the acquisition of musical skills can lead, through participation in the widest possible sense of the term, to an increased understanding of the nature of music and a consequent enhancement of a person's emotional, creative and cultural life.

Aims

1 All specifications must give students opportunities to develop their understanding and appreciation of a range of different kinds of music, extending their own interests and increasing their ability to make judgements about musical quality;
2 all specifications must give students opportunities to acquire the knowledge, skills and understanding needed to:
   a make music, both individually and in groups;
   b develop a life-long interest in music, e.g. through community music making;
   c progress to further study, e.g A/AS level and other equivalent qualifications, and/or to follow a music-related career, where appropriate;
3 all specifications must give students opportunities to develop broader life-skills and attributes, including critical and creative thinking, aesthetic sensitivity and emotional and cultural development.

(QCA 2000)

The specification content

The first aspect of the specification content below acknowledges the existence of two layers of musical meaning. Firstly, inherent musical meaning – meaning that is articulated through the relationship and organization of musical materials within an autonomous musical object, and secondly, musical meaning that derives from the context in which the music is created, performed and experienced – fundamentally the social context. The acknowledgement of these two levels of musical meaning, and the symbiotic relationship that exists between them in most musical styles and cultures, has implications for the repertoire which students are required to study. Prescribing 'set works' would be at odds with this dual view of musical meaning for 'set works' – or at least the way in which they have been traditionally studied – acknowledge only inherent and autonomous meaning. Consequently, the music criteria emphasize the importance of studying music of a wide range of styles and cultures. However, the criteria still maintain what is arguably a false distinction between inherent and socially-constructed musical meaning by suggesting that they can be separated from each other: 'For each area of study the specification should identify clearly the particular aspects of musical knowledge and understanding from 1 (in box below) that are to be studied' (QCA 2000: 3.2). Such an approach also contradicts the intent of 4 (overleaf) which requires specifications to 'make connections between the three aspects of musical knowledge and understanding described in 1'.

Specification content

1   A specification must require candidates, through performing, composing and appraising, to develop aural perception and musical knowledge and understanding of:

   a   the use of musical elements, devices, tonalities and structures;

   b   the use of resources, conventions, processes and relevant notations including staff notation;

   c   the contextual influences that affect the way music is created, performed and heard, for example the effect of different intentions, uses, venues, occasions, available resources and the cultural environment.

2   The aural perception, musical knowledge and understanding described in 1 must be determined through a contrasted range of three to six areas of study (two or three areas of study for the short course) selected across time, culture and musical tradition. An area of study could be based on a specific genre, e.g. music theatre; a specific style, e.g. jazz; a musical device, e.g. call and response; a musical process, e.g. improvisation; a contextual influence, e.g music for celebration. This list is neither exhaustive nor prescriptive. For each area of study, the specification should identify clearly the particular aspects of musical knowledge and understanding from 1 that are to be studied. The range of areas should include music from the past and present, from western and other world cultures.

3 In the full course, at least two areas of study, and in the short course one area of study, must be based on the western classical tradition. At least one area must draw together at least two different cultures. In the full course, at least one area must require candidates to develop and demonstrate understanding of the impact of ICT on music.

4 A specification must require candidates to make connections between the three aspects of musical knowledge and understanding described in 1.

The assessment objectives

Although not described as such, the three assessment objectives (see below) are, broadly speaking, performing (AO1), composing (AO2) and listening/appraising (AO3), but defined sufficiently widely to accommodate the range of activities that these terms might encompass across a range of musical styles and genres. The criteria also emphasize that the assessment objectives 'are interrelated and connections should be made wherever possible in the assessment components' (QCA 2000: 5.2).

Assessment objectives

1 A specification must require candidates to demonstrate aural perception, musical knowledge and understanding and communication through:

a AO1 singing and/or playing an individual part (i.e. one which is not doubled. This could be a solo, accompanied or unaccompanied or an individual part in an ensemble) with technical control, expression, interpretation and, where appropriate, a sense of ensemble (this could include realization of own composition in the short course) – performing skills. In the full course, at least one performance must include a significant part in an ensemble.

b AO2 creating and developing musical ideas in relation to a given or chosen brief (in the short course this could include improvisation) – composing skills;

The brief must describe the stimulus for the composition, provide a clear indication of the candidate's intentions and, for at least one composition, make connections with an area of study.

c AO3 analysing and evaluating music using a musical terminology – appraising skills.

2 The three assessment objectives are interrelated and connections should be made wherever possible in the assessment components.

This reflects the move in Curriculum 2000 to one Attainment Target in music and acknowledges that in many musical styles and cultures there is no clear distinction between composer, performer and listener.

The schemes of assessment and assessment techniques

These give clear guidance as to the weighting of the assessment objectives. The main requirements are that:

- the assessment objectives must, broadly speaking, be equally weighted;
- there must be a terminal examination of at least 40 per cent.

One way of realizing this is illustrated in the draft proposals drawn up by OCR for its GCSE music examination. The relationship between the components and the assessment objectives is shown in the following table:

Table 16.1 Weighting of assessment objective

	AO1 (performing)	AO2 (composing)	AO3 (appraising)	Total
Coursework	30 or 20%	20 or 30%	10%	60%
Terminal task	10%	10%		20%
Examination			20%	20%
Overall	40 or 30%	30 or 40%	30%	100%

Source: OCR (2000) p. 5

Though each assessment objective will be clearly identifiable in each piece of work produced by the candidate, some pieces may be prepared using more than one assessment objective. This is being termed 'synoptic assessment' and can be detailed as follows:

Table 16.2 Synoptic assessment

Component	Piece of work	Assessment objectives	Weighting
1	Appraised performance	AO1 and AO3	15%
1	Appraised composition	AO2 and AO3	15%
2	Realized response	AO1 and AO2	20%

Source: OCR (2000) p. 13

It is possible, therefore, for 50 per cent of the assessment objectives within the specification to be assessed through coursework that links the assessment objectives. This is realized in the following way: candidates are expected to present five pieces of coursework, two of which must be performance and two of which must be composition. The fifth piece may be either performance or composition. One piece of performance and one piece of composition will then be appraised by the candidate.

Finally, the music criteria make two further requirements of assessment schemes. First, they must provide appropriate assessment information when 'music technology forms part of a candidate's performing composing and listening activities' (QCA 2000: 6.7). Second, 'Assessment information *specific to the type of instrument or voice being offered* must be included' (QCA 6.6). This latter stipulation is particularly welcome. It acknowledges that criteria appropriate for the assessing the skills exemplified through a performance of a Beethoven sonata are not equally appropriate to a rock guitarist playing Bob Marley. Consequently generic criteria along the lines of 'The piece is played with some breakdowns but the pitch and rhythm are recognisable' (OCR 1998: 32) have been replaced by instrument-specific criteria such as, in the case of untuned percussion, for example, 'rhythmically more difficult, use of rolls, use of flams' (OCR 2000: 41).

Implications for teaching GCSE Music

In this final section we will look at the implications of all of this for the classroom teacher including:

- the place of music within the Key Stage 4 curriculum;
- building upon good practice established at Key Stage 3;
- providing for the needs of all pupils;
- other issues that impact upon the teaching of GCSE.

Music in the Key Stage 4 curriculum

The place and status of music within the KS4 curriculum can vary enormously between schools. The increase in the number of subjects at KS4 often results in music having to fight for its place on the timetable. Some schools insist upon a minimum number of students choosing to study the music before allowing it to go ahead. Other schools, however, are able to maintain a broad and balanced curriculum at KS4 which recognizes the importance of expressive and performance arts. They typically achieve this in one of the following ways:

- through option blocks that are entirely arts based (music, drama, dance, art, etc);
- by the provision of short courses in arts subjects;
- by abandoning discrete arts subjects in favour of an expressive or performing arts GCSE which contains elements from a range of performance arts subjects;
- by introducing for all students a compulsory core curriculum which includes the arts.

However, the most important factor influencing whether or not children choose to continue with music in KS4 is the quality of musical experience they receive in KS3. Unless children feel that their experiences of music lessons during the early years of secondary schooling have been valuable, enjoyable and worthwhile, they are unlikely to decide to continue with the subject in KS4. Failure in KS3 to develop creative musical skills through composing or to provide opportunities for performing in a wide range of musical styles will almost inevitably result in:

- children whose musical attainment is best reflected through composition, feeling that music is not for them;
- those who have well-developed skills on 'traditional' instruments coming to the conclusion that their development as performers can continue away from the classroom through extracurricular activities and external instrumental exams such as those provided by the ABRSM.

It is crucial that children enjoy music within the Key Stage 3 curriculum. It must provide them with stimulating opportunities and exciting experiences that cannot be obtained elsewhere.

Prior learning and differentiation

The GCSE music criteria are clear that music examinations are intended to provide for the entire range of attainment, skills and interests and that teachers should encourage children from the whole ability range to study music at GCSE. In KS3, it is perhaps all too easy to concentrate upon a few children with high formal musical attainment (often those receiving instrumental lessons) in the hope that they will opt to study music and thus provide the teacher with a pleasant and fulfilling two years. This does a disservice to the subject, and has a detrimental effect on children's perception of music in KS3 if they perceive that the only children who are 'good enough' to carry on into post-14 education are those with the more formal musical skills. For although providing for the whole attainment range brings enormous challenges in terms of planning and, especially, differentiation, the benefits to many who would otherwise not choose this 'specialist' subject can be enormous.

Furthermore, it is only by demonstrating that the subject has something to offer for the entire attainment range that the music department can articulate its case for inclusion in the KS4 curriculum. This is particularly important at a time when increasing pressure is being placed upon the KS4 curriculum, and where one solution to this pressure may well be to reduce the creative arts element, thereby narrowing children's entitlement to a broad and balanced curriculum. For restricted curriculum time and parental pressure can lead to children of higher attainment being guided towards a narrow, highly 'academic' curriculum while 'lower attainers' are encouraged to 'concentrate on the basics'. In *both* scenarios, the role and value of the creative arts can be overlooked.

Teaching strategies

Where recruitment to GCSE music has been successful, and assuming that the class reflects a wide range of attainment and skills, a number of issues arise concerning the organization of the teaching. Two pitfalls should be avoided:

- concentrating entirely upon the higher attainers while justifying the lack of attention to the lower attainers through a philosophy that assumes they would get a low grade anyway;
- paying less attention to the higher attainers (particularly those who have instrumental lessons) because they are sure to 'pass' (that is, get a grade C or above).

The argument against both of these approaches is that although the final grade achieved is of great importance, the musical experiences that children encounter *during* the course are of equal value. If due attention is paid to all children in the GCSE music group, not only will they achieve the grade that reflects their ability, but they will also perceive the course as personally valuable and fulfilling.

With high attainers, it is tempting to allow them to spend music lessons simply developing their instrumental and composing skills in relative isolation, safe in the knowledge that they will certainly gain a C grade or higher. Much more difficult, yet much more musically and educationally demanding, is to encourage them to develop other musical skills. For example, a grade 5 violinist who has strong musical literacy skills but who only ever plays music of the western classical tradition might be encouraged to play by ear or to improvise, perhaps performing some jazz. Similarly a student who only composes in a 'pop' idiom might be encouraged to try and compose in a different style, perhaps drawing on non-western music or aleatoric techniques. In both cases, the result is to further develop the student's understanding of the many ways in which music makes its meaning.

Of course, providing such opportunities requires careful planning and organization by the teacher. Essentially, it means using the GCSE syllabus as a framework for devising an individual learning programme for each student in order that they can be carefully directed and encouraged whilst taking increasing responsibility for their own learning.

It is very important that teachers are constantly aware of the progress that students are making towards fulfilling the requirements of the course. Simple proformas which monitor students' progress can be useful. Other teachers prefer a more public 'chart on the wall', which they feel is an effective way of bringing pressures to bear upon the more dilatory members of the group. Alternatively, some schools have a GCSE 'Performance Day' or concert in which compositions and performances are given, thus providing an imperative for work to be completed. In any event one should seek to avoid a last-minute panic, with performances and compositions being recorded on the final day for submission.

Integrating musical activities

Although the Assessment Objectives of the GCSE criteria treat performing, composing and listening as somewhat discrete activities, this does not mean that they need to be taught in this way – indeed, the music criteria specifically warn against this. For, although the teacher needs to have due regard to student progress in each of these key areas, the teaching of them as separate activities is arguably a somewhat unmusical and unreal approach. Music learning will have greater meaning for the student if it is part of a real musical experience in which many aspects of music and musicianship are brought together. So, the ideal KS4 music curriculum will account for the requirements of the GCSE music syllabus through interrelated activities which result in performances and compositions that satisfy the examination requirements. The organization of the KS4 curriculum should continue to reflect the National Curriculum requirement that musical activities 'are developed through the interrelated activities of performing, composing and appraising' (DfEE/QCA 1999).

As the end-of-course (summative) assessment of appraising is usually achieved by means of a formal examination, this will necessitate *practising* listening skills, through activities similar to those that will be encountered in the examination. However, this does not mean that appraising cannot or should not be an integral part of performing and composing activities. To this extent, *nothing* is being asked of the teacher that isn't already required at KS3. The demands of the examination syllabus must not allow us to lose sight of the good practice established in earlier Key Stages.

Fulfilling students' potential

As the date for the submission of coursework approaches, teachers will need to focus clearly upon those aspects of music with which the students feel most comfortable and those with which they need more help. Teachers will particularly identify those pupils who are on a grade borderline – particularly between grades C and D – and devise strategies for fulfilling their potential. This will not simply mean giving them extra attention, but also re-reading the examination syllabus and marking criteria to ensure that the work presented for assessment fulfils the criteria as closely as possible and provides pupils with maximum opportunity for gaining marks. It is, for example, important to select for performance, pieces that preserve the often delicate balance between quality of performance and difficulty level. Most teachers know their pupils well enough to be able to anticipate the kind of mark they are likely to achieve with any particular piece. By applying the appropriate difficulty level, a reasonable idea can be gained of the optimum mark that might be achieved from a performance of this music and whether the choice of piece is a good one for that particular candidate. Even though there is not always an absolute requirement that compositions be recorded, it is much better that they are recorded wherever possible. An examiner moderating or marking a school's work will be much more positive about something that is presented as a musical event.

In order to assist teachers in the marking process, most boards provide exemplar material, often accompanied by tapes of candidates performing in previous examinations. This material contains examples of work from the entire grade range and is a rich source of information for the teacher. It provides examples for the pupils of pitfalls to avoid and also, most importantly, of the standards towards which they should be striving.

Preparing for studying music beyond GCSE

Much has been made in this document of the importance of providing students with worthwhile musical experiences *during* the GCSE course rather than simply using it as a preparation for study at a higher level. However, teachers also need to identify those who may wish to continue to study music at post-16. The choice of options within the particular GCSE syllabus itself may then be governed by this knowledge. For a student anticipating studying music at A and AS level, a certain amount of propositional knowledge and developed literacy skills will almost inevitably be required, and the best course of action is to develop these within the musical environment of a GCSE course. This is far better than trying to 'top up' the missing skills in the abstract context of a grade 5 theory exam during the early months of A level.

Conclusion

In a music department whose priority is providing for the needs and aspirations of all the children, the GCSE music classes can exemplify the ideal of music as an experiential subject whose aim is to develop all children's abilities as composers, performers, critical listeners and appraisers. The groundwork that has been laid at KS3 can now be further developed and honed to suit the specific needs of each student in a way that, due to constraints of time and numbers, is not possible in those earlier years. The opportunity to work with smaller groups of highly motivated pupils is both a pleasure and, at the same time, a heavy responsibility. This responsibility can only be fulfilled through careful and detailed planning which, firstly, ensures that the pupil will gain the grade that their attainment and work-rate merit and, secondly, results in them looking back on the course as a worthwhile and musically fulfilling experience.

References

DfEE/QCA (1999) *Music in the National Curriculum*, London: HMSO.
Green, L. (1988) *Music on Deaf Ears*, Manchester: Manchester University Press.
MEG (1996) *GCSE Music Syllabus 1998*, Cambridge: MEG.
Oxford, Cambridge and RSA Examinations (OCR) (1998) *Music Syllabus 1998*, OCR.
—— (2000) *Specification for Music 2003*, OCR.
Paynter, J. (1992) *Sound and Structure*, Cambridge: Cambridge University Press.
Secondary Examinations Council/Open University (1986) *Music GCSE, a Guide for Teachers*, Milton Keynes: Open University Press.

17 Music education and research
Alexandra Lamont

Context

In the closing years of the twentieth century, assessment of the quality of education in the UK is all-embracing, extending from pre-school nurseries to the university sector. Coupled with this drive to assess is the increasing growth of 'consumerism' in education, as in other areas of public policy such as health care and public transport. Parents want to know they are getting 'value for money' for their children and that they are guaranteed to experience a minimum standard of education, wherever they live and whichever kind of educational institution they attend.

Alongside the pledge from the Labour Government in 1997 of 'education, education, education', educational research has come under considerable attack from, amongst others, the former Chief Inspector of Schools, Chris Woodhead, and a professor of education (Tooley 1998). A similar state of affairs has developed in the USA, as evidenced by numerous articles in the American Educational Research Association's journal, *Educational Researcher*. As noted by Pring (2000), some of this criticism may be justified, as there are as many examples of good research as there are of bad. The pressure of the Research Assessment Exercise in England and Wales for all higher education teachers to publish research, regardless of their training, is at least partly responsible for the growth of lower quality research being published in academic journals. The dictum of 'publish or perish' is certainly very pressing for anyone engaged in teaching in higher education.

Is it, as David H. Hargreaves writes, that much educational research 'does not make a serious contribution to fundamental theory or knowledge; is irrelevant to practice … is uncoordinated with any preceding or follow-up research' (1996: 7). Or does educational research have something to offer the practising teacher? This chapter deals first with some issues relating to educational research in general, and then considers some examples of the kind of research that can be carried out in music education.

What is educational research?

There are almost as many types of research carried out within education as there are different research questions waiting to be answered. However, all of these have certain features in common. Research is seen by researchers as systematic, controlled, empirical and critical investigation of a given area. It involves judicious choice of a research topic, formulation of a research question, methodology and methods for carrying out the research, techniques of analysis, and above all a firm connection to existing research and to relevant theories. Some research does break boundaries to create new paradigms, but most research is carried out within well-established frameworks. Research is a professional arena: beginning research students undergo rigorous training in a range of methods and theories before embarking on a guided research project.

Research is often seen as something which can deliver objective facts about the world. This is most applicable in the natural sciences, where a degree of objective reality can be assumed. The object of study, whether it be formal algebra, chemical combinations, cells, or suspension bridges, behaves in a logical way and logical questions can be posed and answered. The kinds of research that fall within positivist traditions often adopt a *quantitative* or *experimental* approach, involving tightly-controlled and sometimes artificial situations. When considering the social sciences, this positivist approach to research has been strongly challenged. People do not behave in consistent ways, and findings can be reduced to the point of view of the person drawing the interpretation: 'one person's terrorist is another person's freedom fighter'. This has led to a second equally important tradition of *qualitative* research, involving a different range of methods for studying real-life situations in all their complexity. Let us explore the different kinds of educational research that fall into these two broad camps.

Positivist educational research

The kind of research that would be categorized as positivist, adopting the 'scientific approach', is likely to begin from some kind of *hypothesis* and work through some kind of *empirical* (experimental) enquiry to prove or disprove the hypothesis. It is based on the assumption that the world behaves in a regular way and that causes and effects can be uncovered, and aims to explain these causes and effects in the most economical way possible. Results of an empirical study of a particular setting are then generalized to apply more broadly.

In education, positivist research can take many forms. Surveys, statistical analyses of large-scale trends over time, experimental investigations of teaching and learning situations, or historical enquiries may be based on firm and clearly stable hypotheses and involve the analysis of numbers through the use of statistics to look for patterns of significance. Statistics serve to inform the researcher that particular trends, commonalities or differences are real and not simply a product of chance. These statistics can be applied to existing data, such as published tables of GCSE examination passes, or to data collected by the researcher, such as the results of an experiment. They only act to confirm or reject a hypothesis and do not provide answers in themselves, but they do allow the researcher to go beyond a description of a given situation in order to tease out the important features underlying it.

The experimental method is particularly common amongst researchers working from a psychological framework. It involves the researcher manipulating a particular setting in order to test the effects of a carefully isolated variable. An example of this interventionist approach is the work of Frances Rauscher *et al.*, where some children receive formal music tuition and other children receive tuition in a different activity; after a given period of time, their scores on particular cognitive skills are examined for differences that result from the intervention (Rauscher *et al.* 1997). The questions answerable by this approach can be important for policy and practice, although it is important to be certain of the generalizability of the results: what works well in the US, for instance, may not apply in the UK.

One of the strengths of positivist research is the degree of control it affords. If the only difference between one group of children and another is the extra tuition they receive, for instance, then the outcome is very clear. However, the research by Rauscher and colleagues provides an example of one of the drawbacks of this type of study. In a recent review, Caroline Sharp collected together the results of a number of different studies attempting to show that music training improved children's thinking skills (Sharp 1998). Her own analysis of the various results indicated that it is hard to be sure about the reliability of these findings, as some researchers show robust data that support the hypothesis whilst others seem to follow the same procedures yet find different and negative results. In real-life situations there are always plenty of other factors that may influence the outcomes of experimental studies.

Qualitative educational research

In contrast to the rigour of the experimental approach, qualitative research methods typically involve real-life situations which are studied in all their complexity. These kinds of research allow space for the views of all those involved in the research, including the 'objects of study' as well as the 'subject' of the researcher. The kinds of research methods that fall within this approach include participant observation, focus groups, interviews, ethnography, and the most popular form of educational research, action research. Necessarily, this is a 'messy' approach, yet it is one which can yield important answers to real-world problems.

A good deal of educational research tends to be qualitative in nature, and this aspect formed part of the critique of educational research discussed above. However, qualitative researchers argue passionately that this approach is vital for getting to grips with the complexities of education, whether it be focusing on interactions in the classroom or policy documents (e.g. Hammersley 2000). It is important to see that qualitative approaches require the same degree of rigour as more quantitative methods, and that they also have clearly elaborated and agreed procedures. Qualitative discourse (analysis of the talk in classrooms, for example) can be as systematic as statistical analysis of a large dataset.[1] Whilst the questions this kind of research poses can appear less rigorous, the answers may be more important in the context of education.

Case study research is one example of qualitative research which seems to directly contradict the idea of generalizability mentioned above. By studying a single example of a highly particular situation, case study research works towards a 'science of the singular'. The particularities become the important and interesting outcome, rather than attempting to uncover broader trends. Qualitative researchers can sometimes find it difficult to question or challenge their own assumptions when researching a context they know well. In ethnographic studies, the researcher participates in a different setting, observing, noting, and recording and later analysing how the setting operates (Hammersley and Atkinson 1983). This kind of research often generates thick descriptions, but can be thin on explanation. The reader is required to adapt relevant findings as metaphors which may shed light on their own situation or context.

These different examples show how the particular view of research adopted by the researcher and the questions being asked will determine the way in which the research is carried out, and ultimately the relevance of its findings. Let us explore these two approaches in relation to some questions which are more useful to music education.

The research process in music education

Scenario A: positivist research

> In a large secondary school, a new music teacher has joined the staff from another school where they had a radical way of teaching composing. He is surprised to find his new school using what he thinks is a very old-fashioned approach to practical music-making. He tries to convince the head of music of the merits of the teaching scheme used at his old school. She thinks the scheme sounds interesting, but she wants to know whether it works before suggesting that it should be implemented by all the music staff. She gives him a term to evaluate its effectiveness with the pupils he teaches in Years 7–9. At the end of the term, the new teacher's classes have better marks in their composition assessments than the other classes in the school. The teacher reports back to the head of music that the new scheme is working and that everyone should adopt it immediately.

Would you be convinced by this research? Several issues may have come to mind. The new teacher may have been lucky and been allocated classes that were better at composing to start with, so the improvement might not have been due to the new scheme. However, he teaches classes in Years 7 – 9, so improvements across all of these classes would be less likely to happen by chance. A more plausible explanation is that he could be more charismatic or motivating than the other music teachers, so the pupils were more motivated to learn and hence their scores improved. However, we would want to know more about the assessments before being wholly convinced. Were these marked by the teacher himself? In this case, he might be a more generous marker than the other teachers. One tricky aspect of this scenario is that the teacher himself is acting as a researcher. This is not necessarily a drawback in itself, as much educational research is best carried out by people who are closest to the situation. But in this case, the teacher has his own agenda. He wants to impress the head of music, and he is more committed to making his scheme work. For these reasons he may have perhaps unwittingly influenced the outcome of the evaluation.

This scenario can be used to highlight some of the central features (and difficulties) of quantitative research in education. The most important issue is the question that the research is attempting to answer. The underlying research question in the above evaluation might be expressed as follows:

> Is Scheme X a good way of teaching musical composition in secondary schools?

Stating the question in this way, it becomes apparent that we need to know whether Scheme X works better *than* something else, for example the old-fashioned Scheme Y which is already in operation at the school. It would be hoped that any teaching scheme would result in some kind of learning, and so it would be hard to argue for the merits of Scheme X versus no teaching at all. But we can compare the outcome of pupils in Scheme X against those in Scheme Y in order to produce more convincing evidence. The question now becomes more specific:

> Is Scheme X a better way of teaching musical composition in secondary schools than Scheme Y?

A carefully-formulated research question is the first step of any research project, however small-scale. With a clear research question, one can then begin to move on to think about how the research itself might be done. This involves the issues of methodology discussed above. The focus in this question on 'doing better' means the researcher would want to measure an outcome (or outcomes) and compare it against some other standard. This implies a quantitative approach, involving some kind of measurement of 'doing better' which can be statistically compared.

To compare the results of two different groups of pupils, one would need to make a careful selection of 'matched' groups, so that the classes who receive Scheme X are balanced in ability, motivation, readiness to learn and so on to the classes who receive Scheme Y. If Scheme X was given to the highest ability groups, and Scheme Y to the lowest, for example, it would be much harder to compare the different effects of the two schemes. To be even more certain that the improvements were due to the new scheme, one could also test the abilities of pupils in both schemes twice: before they begin the programme and again afterwards. In this way the *relative* improvement of both groups can be measured, rather than just comparing scores between the two groups at the end of term.

Having established a suitable design, the researcher needs to address the question of appropriate measures. In this case the question focuses on the outcome of successful teaching of composing, and so we would want to look at the pupils' compositions. If pupils' compositions are to be assessed by the teachers who taught them, there is a risk of different teachers' assessment styles affecting the research. This also allows the new teacher to have a biasing effect on the results of the study, as shown above: he has a vested interest in the scheme, so his assessments may reflect his desire to show how well it works. A more *reliable* measure would be to have a third teacher, who is not involved in teaching any of the pupils, make assessments of compositions from the pupils in Scheme X and Y. This third person can make more objective judgements about the compositions without being biased by knowledge of the teachers and their pupils as well as what has been happening in the composing lessons. It would be important for this person to be 'blind' to the particular conditions of the study, assessing the compositions without knowing whether the pupils had been taught under Scheme X or Scheme Y. It might be useful to have two different independent judges making assessments, and their judgements can then be compared for inter-rater reliability: if they consistently give similar assessments to the same compositions, their assessments will be more reliable.

This issue of 'blindness' to the study is also important when thinking about the pupils themselves. Although it is ethical to inform participants as far as possible about the nature of any research study, it is important that this knowledge does not bias the outcome of the study. The pupils should know that their compositions will be assessed but not be aware of what the expected results are. It is also vital in an educational setting to ensure that the process of research does not affect the normal course of events. It would be considered unethical to subject a group of pupils to a teaching scheme which is known to be poor, for example, or to exclude them from receiving any teaching at all.

Following through this kind of research study, with careful control of as many as possible of the factors that might bias the outcome, should lead to a rigorous research study that would be able to go some way to evaluating the new scheme and convincing the head of music that it is a better way of teaching composing. This is an example of the *experimental approach* in operation in a classroom setting. The situation is not as controlled as could be achieved in a laboratory, but the research makes every effort to counteract anything that might influence the outcomes. There is a clear *intervention* – the new Scheme X, compared against a *control* – the old Scheme Y. And the results should be clear-cut: a higher degree of improvements in pupils' compositions in Scheme X compared with pupils' compositions in Scheme Y tells us unequivocally that Scheme X is a better way of teaching composing.

Scenario B: anti-positivist research

> In the same secondary school, the new music teacher is concerned about the low uptake of GCSE music in Year 10. Whilst there is a vibrant extracurricular musical culture in the school, with visiting peripatetic teachers and thriving orchestras and bands, very few pupils choose to study music beyond Key Stage 3. The head of music is resigned to the fact that GCSE music is unpopular amongst pupils nationally and concentrates her efforts on the extracurricular programme. The new teacher wants to explore this issue, and asks the pupils why they do not choose GCSE music. They tell him it is because they think it is pointless and that they will not improve their chances of getting a job with a music qualification. He tries to convince them of the value of music as a curriculum subject.

Is this research likely to succeed in making all the interested parties feel better about the situation surrounding GCSE music? Would the teacher's enquiry convince you of the situation that is currently in place at the school? Again this example can be used to follow through some of the principles of a more subjective anti-positivist approach to research.

Rather than beginning from a clear research question, this kind of study would begin from a statement of a perceived problem. The new teacher feels that music is important, and from the above description senses that the head of music, perhaps through lack of energy or through a degree of disillusionment resulting from bitter experience, has resigned herself to teaching very small groups of pupils in Years 10 and 11. In order to study this perceived problem in a research-based enquiry, the teacher needs to do more than describe the situation. However, a broad research question can still be posed:

> What are the reasons for the low uptake in GCSE music in Year 10?

It is clear that this kind of question is not as amenable to a straightforward answer as the question formulated earlier, which had clear outcomes that could be measured (effective teaching leading to improvements in composition). A simple question-naire that asks this question directly of the pupils will not shed much light on the situation. From an anti-positivist perspective, one would need to take into account the positions of the respondents to this kind of questionnaire: will the pupils give honest answers to a new music teacher? Will they feel that the teacher has his own agenda, or worry that their responses will be transmitted to the head of music? Are they able, indeed, to express the reasons for their subject choices? Who else might be involved in this process?

At this stage, some background knowledge is needed before going any further with a research enquiry. How do pupils make choices about GCSE subjects in general? Are their decisions based only on 'usefulness' or career prospects, or do other factors play a role? Armed with some appropriate evidence, the teacher/researcher could add some related sub-questions which attempt to delve deeper into the situation, for example:

> What are the attitudes towards music GCSE amongst pupils at the school?
> What other subjects are more popular than music in Year 9?
> Are pupils who engage in extracurricular music more likely to choose GCSE music?

With some firmer ideas in mind, a range of techniques could be applied to explore the issue in more detail. The teacher might enlist the help of colleagues in other schools where a similar situation occurs, or try to find more fortunate colleagues in schools with a high uptake at GCSE. Attitudes towards the music lesson and music as a subject will be an important part of this enquiry, both from the pupils and the teachers – and perhaps also the other teachers in the school, who may fight more vigorously to 'win' students at GCSE level or act unconsciously in ways which lower the status of music. The teacher might set up focus groups with pupils, led by an independent third party to whom the pupils will be more likely to 'spill the beans'. He might invite parents to become involved in the research, carrying out semi-struc-tured interviews asking them about how they are involved in their children's choices of subject and seeking their views on music. There is a place in this research for some numbers too – a first step might be to compare the numbers of pupils taking GCSE music at the school with national figures.

As well as these methods that could be applied to the 'problem', a truly reflexive and subjective approach to this kind of question would also raise the issue of whether it is a 'problem', and who is concerned about it. The teacher himself plays a central role in this part of the research process. He needs to examine his own assumption that poor uptake at GCSE is a problem, and integrate this into the analysis of the views of a range of other people involved. The messiness of this kind of research is doubtless becoming apparent. In the short term, no clear answers will be provided, and the list of research questions will grow as the research progresses. Yet there is scope for a small-scale study of this nature to get under the skin of some deep issues that cannot be addressed by numbers alone.

This brief (and polarized) illustration of different types of educational research may have given you a taste for it, but may also have led you to wonder whether educational research is at all important for your work in practice. If research cannot offer clear answers to simple questions, why bother? If each piece of research needs to be interpreted in the light of the situation in which it was carried out, is this helpful for you in your classroom? Can a teacher be a researcher and still teach effectively?

Why should teachers be bothered about research?

In a recent survey, Everton *et al.* (2000) found that 96 per cent of a sample of over 300 (mostly senior-level) teachers reported that they had seriously considered educational research findings since first qualifying as teachers. The main ways that the teachers obtained research information were through accredited and other INSET courses and official publications. Dissemination of research in the media, journals and books were the next most popular sources of information, with other teachers and television scoring lowest on the list. Everton and his colleagues found that teachers did not agree with the perceived uselessness of educational research suggested at the start of this chapter. Teachers saw research as being useful for informing classroom practice and for their own personal involvement in research (as readers or researchers themselves). Interestingly, teachers with more years of experience placed a greater weight on the relevance of research for informing practice than less experienced teachers.

Christine Counsell and colleagues (2000) put forward three arguments for the necessity of educational research for beginning teachers' learning (their article focuses on initial teacher education but the points have equal relevance for practising teachers):

1   The quality of teachers' professional craft knowledge depends on individual practitioners having and using opportunities for learning about high quality new ideas – through educational research – which they can use in developing their practice;
2   Teachers, individually and collectively, can justify their practice as being appropriate and effective if it is consistent with the accumulated findings of high quality research;
3   Understanding and engaging with research issues enables teachers to question their own practice and evaluate whether ideas from research might be suitable to adopt in their own particular specialized contexts.

These proposals do not simplify the nature of education, and they recognize the differences between the fields of research and teaching. In many ways, every teacher is an implicit researcher. As a teacher, you try out new ideas in the classroom and are often evaluating these as you go. But researchers are often detached from the situation they study and often do not have extensive experience of the particular specialized contexts of teaching and learning. Counsell and colleagues' arguments show that research can be extremely important for the teacher. Although research is not about telling teachers how to do their jobs more effectively, it can provide the benefit of reflection, theory and established practices to shed more light on the nature of education.

Next steps

This chapter has provided an illustration of some different types of research, but is necessarily an over-simplification of some important and hotly debated issues. There are plenty of textbooks aimed at the classroom researcher or researchers in education, such as those by Cohen and Manion (2000), Loughran (1999) or Walford (1991). Journals like the *Oxford Review of Education* or the *Cambridge Journal of Education* provide plenty of original source material as well as debates around the nature of educational research. In music education, the *British Journal of Music Education*, *International Journal of Music Education*, and a new journal, *Music Education Research,* provide excellent source material for teachers. There are numerous courses open to teachers wanting to become involved in education, and the Open University's Masters Programme in Education is based around taught modules involving a research component.

Note

1   (See Mercer, 1995 for an excellent example of this kind of educational research)

References

Cohen, L. and Manion, L. (2000) *Research Methods in Education*, London: Routledge.

Counsell, C., Evans, M., McIntyre, D. and Raffan, J. (2000) 'The usefulness of educational research for trainee teachers' learning', *Oxford Review of Education*, 26(3 and 4): 467–82.

Everton, T., Galton, M. and Pell, T. (2000) 'Teachers' perspectives on educational research: knowledge and context', *Journal of Education for Teaching*, 26(2): 167–82.

Hammersley, M. (2000) 'The relevance of qualitative research', *Oxford Review of Education*, 26(3 and 4): 393–405.

Hammersley, M. and Atkinson, P. (1983) *Ethnography: Principles in Practice*, London: Routledge.

Hargreaves, D.H. (1996) *Teaching as a Research-based Profession: Possibilities and Prospects*, The Teacher Training Agency Annual Lecture 1996, mimeo.

Loughran, J. (ed.) (1999) *Researching Teaching: Methodologies and Practices for Understanding Pedagogy*, London: Falmer Press.

Mercer, N. (1995) *The Guided Construction of Knowledge*, Clevedon: Multilingual Matters.

McIntyre, D. (1997) 'The profession of educational research', *British Educational Research Journal*, 23(2): 127–40.

Pring, R. (2000) 'Editorial conclusion: a philosophical perspective', *Oxford Review of Education*, 26(3 and 4): 495–501.

Rauscher, F.H., Shaw, G.L., Levine, L.J., Wright, E.L., Dennis, W.R. and Newcomb, R.L. (1997) 'Music training causes long-term enhancement of preschool children's spatial-temporal reasoning', *Neurological Research*, 19: 2–8

Sharp, C. (1998) *The Effects of Teaching and Learning in the Arts*, London: QCA/NFER.

Tooley, J. (1998) *Educational Research: a Critique*, London: Office for Standards in Education.

Walford, G. (ed.) (1991) *Doing Educational Research*, London: Routledge.

Index

Hill, D. 108
Hirst, Paul 5
Hodge, G. 175
Hodges, Richard 8
Holden, John 40
Hornbostel, E.M. von 193
Howe, M.J.A. 140
Hullah, John 4

improvisation 130, 198, 207
information and communications
    technology (ICT) 155–72; amount of
    equipment available 156; composition
    and 128, 137; computer assisted learning
    (CAL) 158; digital audio 158, 171;
    enhancing music teaching and 159–62;
    explanation of concepts 167–72; general
    comments 155–6; Internet 159; MIDI
    165, 167–72; planning and classroom
    management 162–3; samples 157;
    scorewriting 157–8, 166–7; sequencing
    156–7, 160–1, 164–6; singing and 118;
    skills checklist for teachers 164–7; soft
    synthesis 158; technical support 129, 163;
    uses in music 156–9; wiring 167
instrumental performance 192–3;
    developing effective practice strategies
    140–51; developing a jazz ensemble
    202–10; flute 146–7, 148; gender and 55,
    57; Islam and 184; jazz 197–8; saxophone
    144–6, 148; trumpet 143–4, 148
intelligence: general intelligence and musical
    ability 69; multiple 69–72, 77
intelligence, musical 41–3; ability tests and
    66–77; development of 72–3
Intelligence Quotient (IQ) 68, 74–5
Internet 159
Islamic music 182–3, 184
isolation: professional 32, 34

Japan 101
Jaques-Dalcroze, Emile 121
jazz 197–214; appraising 199; composition
    and arranging 198, 208–9; creative
    teaching 199–202; developing a jazz
    ensemble 202–10; glossary 214; listening
    and analysing 198, 210–11; recordings
    213; rehearsing and performing 197–8;
    resources 211–12
Jeanneret, Neryl 39
Johnston, P. 148
Jordan, J. 108

Kaluli people 185
Kartomi, M. 193
Kayes, G. 108

Kemp, A. 102, 103, 104, 148
keyboards 128–9, 132, 137, 161–2
kinaesthesia 102–4
knowledge: assessment of 88–9;
    intelligence and 69
Kodály, Zoltán 6
Kuhn, T.L. 195
Kwami, Robert 7

Lacey, C. 35
Langer, S. 20, 69, 75
language 44; music and 185–7, 188–94
Laurence, F. 108
Lawrence, I. 99
Lawton, Denis 5
learning: music learning and learning in
    other subjects 43–4; planning for
    learning outcomes 88–90; prior learning
    224; theories of 74
Leibniz, Gottfried 43
lessons: planning 16–17
Levi-Strauss, C. 174
Lippman, E. 174
listening 97–104
literacy: aural skills and 97–101
Loane, Brian 97
Loughran, J. 236
Lundin, R.W. 68, 73

McPhee, Cohn 101–2
McPherson, G.E. 141, 142, 148, 150
Mainwaring, J. 102
Manion, L. 236
Marland, Michael 37
Marley, Bob 176
mathematics 43
meaning in music 53–4; gender and 54–8
Mellers, Wilfrid 121
melody 190–1
Meyer, L. 72, 75, 174
Middleton, R. 174, 176
MIDI 165, 167–72; sequencing 156–7,
    160–1, 164–6
Miller, R. 108
Mills, J. 118, 119, 124, 133
mixers 162
models: devising curriculum model for
    music 19–21; for teaching popular
    music 173–81
modes 191–2
modules of work 16
Moore, Jillian 12
Motegi, K. 101
motivation 67, 73, 74
multi-core cable links 162
multiple intelligence 69–72, 77